Lessons
From A Loving
Father

Adeoye Oyewo
Foreword By Reverend Aderemi Fakorede, PhD

Halo
PUBLISHING
INTERNATIONAL

ISBN: 978-1-61244-857-2
Library of Congress Control Number: 2020909819

Printed in the United States of America

Halo
PUBLISHING
INTERNATIONAL

Halo Publishing International
8000 W Interstate 10
Suite 600
San Antonio, Texas 78230
www.halopublishing.com
contact@halopublishing.com

To the Memory of My Loving Parents

Adebayo & Omowunmi Oyewo

Acknowledgements

I first and foremost wish to appreciate God for His Grace upon my life. Looking back at how my life has progressed, all I can say is that God has been gracious to me. The Bible says to us in Lamentations 3: 22 – 23; The faithful love of the LORD never ends! His mercies never cease. Great is his faithfulness; his mercies begin afresh each morning. This verse is the testimony of my life. I appreciate my parents Deacon John Adebayo Oyewo & Mrs Maria Omowunmi Oyewo both of blessed memory for the seeds of righteousness they had sown into my life. To God be the Glory for their lives and everything concerning my life.

I also wish to appreciate my evangelical partners for their role in the kingdom business that God has found for me to do over the last few years. They have been my pillars of strength all the way. I thank God for Reverend Dr Aderemi Fakorede, who, I regard as my chief sponsor and encourager. It is to him also that most credit must go for being used to actualise God's plan to rescue my life from spiritual death and destruction. Thank you, sir, for finding time to write the foreword to this book. It is indeed a great honour to which I am very grateful!

I cannot fail to acknowledge the role of my aunt, the Reverend Mrs Beatrice Bolanle Oyewo, who took her time to go through the manuscript of this book. Her investment in this book, if measured, can qualify her as a co-author. She has been a strong supporter and a close confidant. To my friend, silent contributor and supporter Mr Nsasak Ekah my prayer is that God will reward all your labour in Jesus' name.

I will also like to acknowledge other persons who have impacted my life and ministry. The Revd Dr Samuel Adeleye and his wife Abigail, Revd Segun Owolabi, and Pastor(Dr) Vincent Anyanti, to name just a few.

To my brothers and their spouses Oluwafunmisho & Aderonke, Ayotunde & Pukande, and not forgetting my nephews and niece - OlaOluwa, Oluwaseun, Oluwakoni-dojutimi, and Oluwatitofunmi; I need to say this from the bottom of my heart - You are the very best!

To my older uncle, Chief Bisi Oyewo, for the seeds of kindness bearing fruits that God has allowed you to sow in many lives, including mine, I will like to say that you are very much loved and valued.

To my younger uncle Mr Abraham Oyewo for the excellent counsel and being an example of practical Christian living in many ways and not forgetting his ever-youthful wife, Aunty Julia, the Lord will continue to be mighty in your lives.

To my indefatigable cousins – Adenike, Oluwasegun, Oluwaseun, Olorunleke, Adeyemi, Iyabo, and Adedoyin; you are worth more than diamonds to me.

I cannot conclude without giving a special mention to my darling wife. Christine has been one of the manifestations of God's favour upon my life. In her, I have found a good thing. To my two exceptional and wonderful daughters, EbunOluwa & Oluwamiwunmi, I thank God always for both of you and do want to say that you are indeed God's treasures in our lives.

Finally, I must not fail to acknowledge my darling cousin, Mrs Olanike Adekunle – Abraham and my friend, Mr Oluwaseun Addie, who always found time to provide insights. God will enlarge your coasts in Jesus' name, Amen!

Adeoye Oyewo
Lagos, Nigeria.
April 2020

Contents

Foreword

God is loving, caring, compassionate and gracious to all human beings. In His fatherly role, He cares, provides, guides and leads His children tenderly in the right direction He had destined for their lives. God has created diverse ways of imparting lessons He so desires such that His targeted audience do not miss out on the last day.

The book, "Lessons from a Loving Father" is a product of the author's encounter with God. I came to know him when I took over the pastorate of Bethel Baptist Church, Idimu, Lagos, Nigeria, about two decades ago. He used to be a man who was only passionate about his professional career. He pursued his career development with zeal leaving little time for the work of God. He gave generously to the course of the church's ministry, particularly mission work, but offered little attention to know the will of the owner of his life. Although he was a member of the Church Council, he still harboured some struggle with God on his spiritual life.

I recall an incident that remains indelible in my memory about the author, which defines his personality. In 2009, our church decided to elect the first set of deacons. After several teachings and discussions, the church members were asked to nominate candidates for the office of the deacon. The author was the third person with the highest nomination. The committee saddled with the responsibility invited all nominated candidates for interaction. When it was the author's turn, he declined taking office. Consequent to this, I called him to my office to know the reason why he refused the nomination. He told me bluntly that he was not qualified to hold the office. When I probed further, he said there were some areas he needed to address in his life to be able to qualify for the highly respected office. He, however, promised to address those areas because they were a challenge to his spiritual life. I believe that was the turning point in the life of the author, which produced what has manifested today. Since then, his spiritual growth has been progressive.

The concern of this book is Salvation and holy living. It is a product of a series of write-ups by the author for the Hour of Divine Mercy, a non-denominational programme sponsored by him. He came up with these worthwhile write-ups at a time when there was a need for God to speak to a large number of people that usually gather for the quarterly programme. God used him as an instrument to convey these important messages to His people. He is, in my opinion, well equipped to disseminate them.

The author in the book shares his personal experiences on the issues of sin, ungodly living, struggle with hidden sin and worldliness. The book gives practical teachings on God's love, care for humanity and most importantly, His Salvation plan to save man from eternal damnation and provision of life everlasting through the sacrifice of Jesus

Christ, His Son on the Cross of Calvary. He presented good theological explanations on the sonship, birth, death and resurrection of Christ. The book takes a look into many questions that may be agitating believers' minds on how to make their Christian journey on earth less encumbered in accordance with biblical guidance.

The author also displays a good sense of hymn interpretation. In this book, he has used appropriate hymns as reference sources for issues raised, to buttress them to the understanding of his readers. Songs chosen were interpreted in such a way that helps strengthen each of the topics discussed. Also, biblical passages were quoted to help readers have them handy for easy referencing. The book is a compendium of sermons to sinners, lost souls, backsliders, and those who are being challenged by the demanding situations of life. It inspiringly speaks to many situations of life. It tells about the love of a Father to His beloved children, His plan for their Salvation, earthly and eternal blessings if they live according to His will and laws. It is a road map to Holiness, Christian living and a reminder to them that, living here is not forever, but that they are sojourners and before they die here, they will need to ask the question: where will I end up in eternity?

This book is a great asset and a useful resource for evangelism. It could be given as gifts to friends, loved ones and those who have not known or accepted the love of Christ through Salvation.

I recommend it for all categories of people. It is a must-read book.

Reverend Aderemi Fakorede PhD
Senior Pastor,
Bethel Baptist Church, Idimu, Lagos
May 2020

Preface

The seeds for the writing of this book were sowed in my heart sometime in the year 2013. At that time, I was experiencing a repeated challenge to my health, which necessitated my having to go for a monthly follow up visit to my doctor. I was fed up with the hospital visits but had no choice, and my consultant had not settled me into a treatment regime that allowed for quarterly appointments. My clinic visits were made difficult by the constant queue of haulage trucks, which meant that I had to set out at least 4 hours in advance of my 10 am appointment. On a particular morning, as I dressed up, a very distinct question dropped into my mind, and this was: WHAT IF YOU DIE TODAY? This question reflected the situation concerning my health, and God wanted to bring me the practical reality of these medical challenges ending in my passing on to the great beyond. I held on to the question and reflected on it for a long while; I also noted that the matter was not a personal one as all who come into the world must go back to the Creator one day and so will be wise to ask this question daily. I, therefore, resolved within myself to share the message in this question with everyone. At that time, too, I was facing a funding difficulty concerning a decision I had made to provide Christian literature for the Hour of Divine Mercy programme. God then laid it upon my heart to follow the example of the servants who used their talents well for God. I began to write as directed by God. God gave me lessons in Salvation, Holiness and Christian living that He inspired me to share under unique topics, each with a clear message to both the writer and the reader.

The lessons that God shared with me were for only one single objective; to guide man on the path, he must go to gain eternal life. These lessons are to put to rest the common misconception that Salvation through Jesus Christ requires no other building blocks. God reminded me and, by extension, all my readers that the walk after Salvation is so important that it can make or mar the saved, and except we embrace a life of holiness, we cannot see God (Hebrews 12:14). The lessons are to help us pass the ultimate test, which all must undertake at His judgement throne to gain eternal life in His heavenly home. Jesus spent three years teaching these lessons to all His disciples so that they will understand how to "come after Him." It was so important to Him for us to know His mind that He devised innovative ways to simplify the lessons so that no one will misunderstand His message and thus miss out on the last day. Jesus chose to tell short stories referred to as parables and never shied away from giving meanings to them, so all who heard went away with clarity. After He completed His assignment, Jesus sent the Holy Spirit as promised, and He too taught many the mind of God concerning His expectations from us. Many of Jesus' disciples and later Apostles also found Grace to teach these lessons as led by the Holy Spirit. They showed the people under them that undiluted and unadulterated teachings about Holiness and Christian living are a practical possibility.

You have no choice but to take these lessons very seriously. It is in your interest to do so as failure is not an option under any circumstance. God's desire is for all to be saved and to understand the truth (1 Timothy 2:4). However, God is a God of Justice! He will also not overlook sin, and He rewards all persons according to the work of their hands. God hates sin though He loves the sinner and has decided that no sin will find its way into His abode in heaven. You must, therefore, take all His lessons at heart and be doers of all His words (James 1:22). He has made it clear that under no circumstance will he wave His no sin rule as entry criteria to heaven.

> *"Nothing evil will be allowed to enter, nor anyone who practices shameful idolatry and dishonesty—but only those whose names are written in the Lamb's Book of Life."*
>
> *(Revelation 21:27 NLT)*

I recently had the privilege of sitting down to talk with a senior citizen. He being an Octogenarian, had one or two severe health challenges. He had shared the below encounter with me, which he had during one of his stays in the hospital. During this particular admission, he had been in feeble health and was under rigorous medical supervision. His encounter was of note as it was at a time when he felt the end had come, and the doctors were battling to save his life. His minders had reported afterwards that they thought they had lost him when all of a sudden, he came back to life. His after recovery account goes thus:

I suddenly found myself in a room. In front of me was a door few yards from where I was sitting down. I wanted to go through the door and so sang the song: "The door will open for me because of the sacrifice of the Lamb of God crucified for me a sinner." I sang the song three times, believing that the door will certainly open, but to my dismay, the door refused to open. Then I asked myself, was the Lamb of God not crucified for me a sinner? Since I truly believed He was, why then did the door not open? I did not receive an answer at that time.

A few hours later, I pondered on why the door was not open. Then the answer came to me: did you not preach on many occasions that no sin or shady thing, no matter how small, will enter into the heavenly home so as not to defile the glory of the place? Then I asked my conscience: what is that filthy thing in my life? I then got a reply, and it was in respect of funds held in my custody on behalf of a third party. Although I did not intend to misappropriate the money in any way, I had kept it for too long, and this delay was not acceptable to God as the Bible warns against it. It, therefore, dawned on me that if the door had opened, then God would not have kept to His words – which is that no single sin will enter into His presence. God was not ready to bend His standard for anyone.

I posited that considering my past service to God, to throw me into hell for breaking this "little" of God's injunction will look to be contradictory since God does not owe anyone for services rendered. However, to over-look any shady thing and take me to heaven will amount to God breaking His law. No matter His reason, it is clear that God wanted to give me another opportunity for redress, and that is why the door did not open.

After this encounter, I miraculously recovered and came back to life. All I noticed were doctors around me, asking me to confirm that I was now alert.

Many people choose to take God's anti-sin posture lightly. They do so under different assumptions, even at the risk of their eternal damnation. The rich fool in the Bible also took the same gamble and paid dearly for it. God is reminding you today that under no circumstance would He compromise His standard. The encounter above is a message God is sending to all of us. Take heed and mend your ways. I pray that no unconfessed sin will be found on you when you meet with your Creator, Amen.

The lessons from this loving Father also made an impact on my life and ultimately bore fruits. I have had many brushes with death that made me believe that God wanted me to have a long rope opportunity to retrace my steps. Although my parents took the pains to show me the way to go very early in life, I was never serious with God in the real sense of it. I knew all I needed to know about God so I could learn to follow after Him. All was, however, to no avail as there was no change to my nature; I was just a religious young boy who put up a show for people to see, growing up to be a man without being born again. Life progressed for me and with no space for God in my life; the devil had a field day, ensuring that everything sinful was always easy for me to do. Of critical note later in my life was the fact that God's word to which I was exposed early on took a recessive position in my heart, waiting for an opportunity to take control. From adolescence to adulthood, nothing changed, as I continued in the way of the world. All of wine, women, and money were my close and inseparable companions throughout my dark years. Sadly my mother went to be with the Lord in 1995 with "hunger in her belly" that I had not given my life to Christ. In 2005 at age 40, an audit of my life revealed to my dismay that my spiritual achievements were nothing compared to my secular life; I retained only a profoundly religious toga without any substance. During this period, I often took one step forward and two steps backwards making the friends I had at that time to boast that I was only on sabbatical leave when I finally became saved. I recall my pastor challenging and praying for me to take the bold step of righting the wrongs in my life upon reading a tract I had written entitled "How old are you?" Looking back now, maybe this was the reason God continued to give my pastor sermon topics that hit hard at the deficiencies in my life. The good news was that every time he sent out the "double-edged sword," I never shut my ears to it.

The Word always did convict me, but it never took root. Just like in Jesus' parable of the sower, hindrances abound around me for why I did not let go to turn over my life to Jesus entirely. Simply put, I still enjoyed the indisciplined life laden with sin that I lived and so was not prepared to do away with it. Sometimes I did find my way back into the Good shepherd's pen, but many a time, I sneaked back into the world to join with those who unfortunately were my kith and kin. Earlier on in the year 2002, precisely on Thursday the fifteenth day of August, tragedy struck when I lost my mother inlaw. She was the pillar of the family as her husband had been a wheelchair user after a life-threatening accident many years before then. God had blessed her with good health, which she used to the good of her family. Suddenly from nowhere, her health was challenged with a terminal illness, and within ten months or probably less, the once towering and influential matriarch was no more. The lesson of her sudden passing to me was obvious – "life is but a fleeting moment." The losing of someone close to me brought me back to my spiritual senses. The foundation of God's words built in my life over the years began to speak through my loss. It made me appreciate the practical reality of the Bible verse, which says: For God says, "At just the right time, I heard you. On the day of Salvation, I helped you." Indeed, the "right time" is now. Today is the day of Salvation (2 Corinthians 6:2 NLT).

This sad and sudden experience made me begin to see the wisdom in undertaking a new resolve to turn from my wayward and sinful lifestyle and rededicate my life to God. I saw from this occurrence that life without Christ was the biggest gamble a man can take with his eternity. Unfortunately, my resolve did not last at all. I was battered from the left, right, and centre, and it was a big struggle to hold on to my new decision. All I could do was blow hot and cold with an inconsistent walk with God as my testimony. Sadly this was how I continued with my life for close to ten years. Jesus kept knocking on the door of my heart, which is what led to self-appraisal three years down the line on my 40th birthday, yet I did not seize the opportunity with both hands. God just left me to do as I pleased though He made His Grace available and the door of divine mercy open to me. During this period, I was constantly under the barrage of God's words. I could almost say that every single sermon I listened to in my church was targetted at me as God virtually pulled all stops to make sure that I was not lost. Unfortunately, I still wobbled and fumbled along with my life. The problem I had was an unwillingness to crucify the flesh; I "enjoyed" this dangerous life making the devil celebrate my capture every day. Holiness stank to me, and the idea of following the footsteps of Jesus looked like an impossibility.

Then came the year of my miracle, when God finally answered the prayers of a dying mother. It was my mother's desire as she went to meet with her God that none of her three sons will know peace until they gave their lives to Jesus. In January 2010, I again faced another misfortune as a friend and confidant of over twelve years went to be with the Lord. He was someone whom I felt was more committed to Christian living than myself. I was to learn later that on his sickbed, he had prayed for divine intervention to his situation with a solemn pledge to dedicate his life further to God's purpose. Unfortunately, he did not get another chance. It was the hearing of this that finally turned my life around for good. I knew at that time that if God had called me, I would not have anything good to tell Him about my life. It would have been a disaster for me at His judgement throne. The fact was that holiness, which meant so much to God, did not matter to me, and neither could I lay claim to having used my life purposefully for God's kingdom. My first resolve was to lead a purposeful life. I determined that nothing will make me come to the end of my life with any regret. I also knew that God could only accept my work if I make myself acceptable to Him. I cannot put the cart before the horse. The "horse" in this case is my regenerated life, while the cart is the work I will find for myself to do in His vineyard. I knew that if I come to Him with just my offering without making myself acceptable to Him, He will have nothing to do with my gifts; certainly, He also won't accept my work if I did not turn from my evil ways.

It was at this point that I took "another decision" to go back and commit myself "again" to God. It is now close to a decade, and to the glory of God, I have not looked back. Although I have stumbled on many occasions, the difference now is that I always get "help" not to stay down. I have a new resolve to please God and be in His good books. I no longer enjoy sin, and in all instances, I lose my peace anytime I step out of His line. I have lost the capacity to go on sinning, and the Spirit of God assures me that a life modelled after Christ is a possibility. My goal remains to focus daily on "living with eternity in view." The story of my life is that of a man who had all it takes to begin his life's journey early with God, having long packed all that he requires for the trip but who instead decided not to set forth at dawn. I can only thank God today for the Grace to finally pick up my luggage and set out. God's divine mercy may not be available to you for so long. You must take advantage of it right now! Today as God continues to help me grow, I have found for myself good work to do in His vineyard; this has helped me in no small measure to keep going on as God strengthens me every day.

Although it is the pervasion of sin and man's impending doom that made God send His only begotten Son to the world, the same sin, when unconfessed and unforsaken, will bring condemnation to a person at the judgment throne of God. What an irony for Jesus to have died for you, and you will still not make it to heaven. God is a consuming fire, and He will reward everyone according to the work of his hands. My prayer is that you and I will meet at the marriage supper of the Lamb.

"For I am not ashamed of this Good News about Christ. It is the power of God at work, saving everyone who believes — the Jew first and also the Gentile."

(Romans 1:16 NLT)

Adeoye Oyewo
Lagos, Nigeria
April 2020

Room at the Cross

"When Jesus had tasted it, he said, "It is finished!" Then he bowed his head and gave up his spirit."

(John 19:30 NLT)

The Hymn entitled "Room at the Cross for you" was written by Ira Forest Stanphill in 1946; It was one of his earlier songs. At the age of 17, Ira Stanphill (1914 -1993) wrote his first gospel song. He travelled with evangelists, playing the piano, organ, ukulele, and accordion. At one of these meetings, the sermon was entitled, "Room at the Cross." Stanphill wrote the words down on a scrap of paper. Later, after finding the words again, he wrote the tune and lyrics for the hymn, "Room at the Cross for you."[1]

Although I do not have a recollection of any particular encounter with his song, on a quiet May morning just before noon, I sat with my Aunt, who was visiting from the USA and as we discussed many subjects, the song just popped up into our conversation. At that time, we were preparing for one of our evangelical meetings for which I usually found Grace to write a relevant message for our guests, so it was very apt that this message about a room at the Cross was coming to me. Although we had material ready for that particular meeting, I immediately felt that the reason this song dropped into our conversation was that God wanted me to say something about the room He made available through His Son at the Cross. As I reflected on the song, it became clear to me that God wanted me to talk about the adequacy of what Jesus did on the Cross to save man from eternal damnation.

> *"For this is how God loved the world: He gave his one and only Son so that everyone who believes in him will not perish but have eternal life. God sent his Son into the world not to judge the world but to save the world through him. "There is no judgment against anyone who believes in him. But anyone who does not believe in him has already been judged for not believing in God's one and only Son."*
>
> (John 3:16 – 18 NLT)

The Salvation plan of God could not have been complete without the Cross. It was at the Cross that the exchange took place between Jesus and the sinner; the sinner deserving to die for his sins while Jesus who was without sin was supposed to be set free by Pilate. Jesus was crucified at the place of the Skull because the people chose to set Barabbas free. The Cross was the climax of the Salvation journey, which began when Jesus accepted the responsibility of reconciling man back to God. The Cross provided for man, access to God's perfection to right all that was wrong in our lives. Jesus said: "it is finished" (John 19:30) just before He gave up His life, confirming the sufficiency of what took place at Cross. It is the Cross that made Calvary and not Calvary that made the Cross. Convicted criminals are put to death at Calvary, but the

Saviour died on a Cross that provided room for all and sundry. Though not a criminal, Jesus accepted this kind of death in humility because He wanted to gain redemption for man who had become a "criminal" in the sight of God. There were three Crosses when Jesus was at Golgotha, but only one of them had the room to take all manner of human beings. This Cross was distinct because the Son of God was nailed to it, and His blood was all over it.

> *"Look! The Lamb of God who takes away the sin of the world!"*
>
> *(John 1:29b NLT)*

Jesus won for us a final victory at the Cross. It is a victory that we can access through faith in Him and in what He has accomplished. You must believe not only in the existence of this Cross but that there is a room for you in it. The room space is sufficient, and it provides succour for all manner of persons who come into it in faith. Jesus laid down His life and committed His Spirit into His father's hands because of the absolute assurance He had that He will rise again on the third day. You also must demonstrate similar faith if you want to have a room for yourself at the Cross. To come to the Cross is not a physical action to take as there is no Cross for you to go to right now. Though you may visit the Jewish homeland, and take a trip to Calvary, this does not translate into getting into the room at the Cross. All you need to do is to make room for Jesus in your life if you want to have the Cross experience.

"Look! I stand at the door and knock. If you hear my voice and open the door, I will come in, and we will share a meal together as friends."

(Revelation 3:20 NLT)

The room at the Cross, according to Stanphill, provides excellent shelter for those who choose to hide in it. This is the reason King Solomon bore testimony to the name of the Lord being a strong tower – for the righteous to gain safety (Proverbs 18:10). The Cross came about as a result of God's matchless grace, and it is up to you to exercise your faith in its direction. Apostle Paul confirmed this truth when he reminded the people of Ephesus about their Salvation, which comes to them by faith in God's only begotten Son. He posited that it has nothing to do with our good works – so we cannot boast about it (Ephesians 2: 8 – 9). The Cross has many rooms too. It can accommodate millions provided they come in repentance. Jesus sits patiently at the door, waiting to open it immediately, the sinner knocks. His longsuffering patience is driven by love for the sinner whom He has shed His blood to save.

"Who wants everyone to be saved and to understand the truth."

(1 Timothy 2:4 NLT)

Man cannot fold his hands and claim that he is unaware that there is the Supreme Being; that He has supernatural power and is divine. God, in His wisdom, made man know Him, so there is no hiding place for us. The fact that man chooses to live in the way pleasing to himself cannot be said to be because he has not realised the existence of the Almighty. Man can only blame himself for his confusion, which has made him turn his back to God. He has found solace in the emptiness of idols, and this leads to being abandoned by God. Life has, therefore, become worse for man, and with God leaving him to his machinations, he has moved from the frying pan to fire. Man has veered into all forms of perversion, breaking all sin records as his life becomes all about how to please himself – a clear departure from God's plan and purpose, which is distasteful to the Creator.

> *"For everyone has sinned; we all fall short of God's glorious standard."*
>
> *(Romans 3:23 NLT)*

One of God's most significant investments in the life of a man was that which He made to rescue Saul from eternal damnation. Saul was one of the chief persecutors of the early church, and because of his education, training, and commitment, he did an excellent job of it. He took no prisoners as nothing was too much for him to do provided; it will help his cause. Saul was not only a Jew but a Roman citizen, so this gave him the required impetus to accomplish a lot for himself and his pet project. He is arguably one of the biggest recipients of divine mercy as Jesus personally decided to meet with him on his church persecution journey to Damascus. Saul did not have to wait for a second chance. He took the offer of Salvation and opportunity of evangelism with both hands and never looked back again. He became in God's hands a vessel of honour to the non-Jewish populations of the world. He was a committed and unwavering messenger of the Gospel good enough to emulate and with a testimony of finishing his race very well. Saul, later to be called Apostle Paul travelled far and wide in his campaign for the message of the Cross and gave us many teachings fit for our consumption today and helpful for our daily living. He taught that the message of Salvation is for all, and is received by Grace through faith in God's only begotten Son.

Although God made man into a perfect creature, nevertheless he made the worst possible decision and went downhill with his life. From the day he lost his position as God's friend, man embraced all kinds of sin, love of wickedness and hatred for the truth. Man cannot deny that his origin is from God. He knew God to be Almighty in every sense of the word, but with the entry of sin into his life, man lost the capacity to relate to God the way that will be beneficial to him. He chose to rely on himself and in doing so continued to fumble and wobble along with his life. He then lost the power to lead a godly life, and he began to see sin as second nature resulting in his breaking all sin records there is in the world. Many unthinkable occurrences started to find a place in his life, blocking away God completely. God being a lover of holy living, decided to walk away, leaving man to continue the way he has chosen to go - down the drain!

"But God shows his anger from heaven against all sinful, wicked people who suppress the truth by their wickedness. They know the truth about God because he has made it obvious to them. Forever since the world was created, people have seen the earth and sky. Through everything God made,

they can clearly see his invisible qualities — his eternal power and divine nature. So they have no excuse for not knowing God."

(Romans 1: 18 – 20 NLT)

God had walked away indeed, but He was not too far. He had stayed within reach because His desire is that man will realize his folly and come to repentance. He knows that due punishment must come from Him upon all who have done wrong and because He desires that all should be saved to avoid this punishment, He is waiting and watching for anyone who will say; COME INTO MY HEART LORD. Many have walked past Him, ignoring His plea and thinking they have made a better choice; yet some have realised their mistakes and have retraced their steps back to the Cross to receive mercy. God's judgement is firm and fair, so all must reap what they sow and not one will be held unaccountable; no, not one. For those who are overtaken by the desires of the flesh, they will reap eternal condemnation, but for those who give in to the Spirit of God, they have eternal life awaiting them.

"But because you are stubborn and refuse to turn from your sin, you are storing up terrible punishment for yourself. For a day of anger is coming, when God's righteous judgment will be revealed. He will judge everyone according to what they have done. He will give eternal life to those who keep on doing good, seeking after the glory and honour and immortality that God offers. But he will pour out his anger and wrath on those who live for themselves, who refuse to obey the truth and instead live lives of wickedness. There will be

trouble and calamity for everyone who keeps on doing what is evil—for the Jew first and also for the Gentile. But there will be glory and honour and peace from God for all who do good—for the Jew first and also for the Gentile. For God does not show favouritism."

(Romans 2: 5 – 11 NLT)

The room at the Cross was built to save man from eternal calamity. It is for all humanity. Anyone who takes up the offer of Jesus to get a place for himself is free indeed. God's Word is unambiguous and has been made available to all. We must be doers of these Words all the time. The offer to give the room at the Cross is made only to those who have faith in God and are prepared to obey His commandments. In reality, what it means is that you come into the room as a sinner who is ready to repent of his sins and then you proceed to forsake those sins and sin no more! These are the ground rules of the room at the Cross. A lifestyle of religiosity as against that of spirituality is a misnomer in the room at the Cross. Some see the observance of religious laws as a requirement for occupancy in the room at the cross; this is not the case at all. Some believe that a life of holiness is not achievable and so they hope to be allowed to stay in the room at the Cross with a halfhearted commitment to God; this room is not for you. The room at the cross is for those who are more intent on pleasing God than man.

"For merely listening to the law doesn't make us right with God. It is obeying the law that makes us right in his sight."

(Romans 2: 13 NLT)

The room at the Cross is for all who have sinned and come short of the glory of God (Romans 3:23) and because the wages of sin is death (Romans 6:23), Jesus went to the Cross to pay for your Salvation. God knew that no one could meet the expectations of the law; hence this new and unique Salvation package birthed by Jesus. All that we need to do is to put our faith in Christ. We do this by believing that God's only begotten Son Jesus Christ died on the Cross of Calvary, and through the shedding of His blood, we are made righteous. This miraculous and straightforward sacrifice inspired the hymn "Nothing but the Blood of Jesus" by Robert Lowry.

> *"As the Scriptures say, "No one is righteous— not even one. No one is truly wise; no one is seeking God. All have turned away; all have become useless. No one does good, not a single one." "Their talk is foul, like the stench from an open grave. Their tongues are filled with lies." "Snake venom drips from their lips." "Their mouths are full of cursing and bitterness." "They rush to commit murder. Destruction and misery always follow them. They don't know where to find peace." "They have no fear of God at all."'*

> *(Romans 3: 10 – 18 NLT)*

The faith that we speak of does not relegate the importance of the law. This is because the Holy Spirit is given to those who have put their trust in God and it is this Spirit that now makes it possible for us to obey the law; we cannot follow the law by ourselves. This is why, without faith, it is impossible to please God. Since we gain our Salvation by faith and not by obeying the law, then we cannot boast about it. For those who seek to obey the law as a means of obtaining their righteousness; this is impossible because then you do not have access to the Holy Spirit which comes when you have faith in Jesus Christ. The reality is that you must always go through Christ except you desire to fail; no wonder the Bible says the righteousness we obtain by ourselves is like filthy rags (Isaiah 64:6).

"We are made right with God by placing our faith in Jesus Christ. And this is true for everyone who believes, no matter who we are."
(Romans 3: 22 NLT)

"Can we boast, then, that we have done anything to be accepted by God? No, because our acquittal is not based on obeying the law. It is based on faith."
(Romans 3: 27 NLT)

"Well then, if we emphasize faith, does this mean that we can forget about the law? Of course not! In fact, only when we have faith, do we truly fulfil the law."
(Romans 3: 31 NLT)

The life of Abraham also teaches faith above the law. He trusted God to take the leap of faith, and it was for this reason that he was counted as righteous. The availability of a room at the Cross is predicated on the death and resurrection of Jesus Christ. If you believe this, then you have faith in Him who was hung on the Cross, and it will be counted for you as righteousness. The promise that Abraham ultimately received is akin to the eternal life that Jesus also promised to you and me. You can only receive it by faith when you believe. Abraham never wavered; you too, must not waver. God kept His promise to Abraham, and Jesus will keep His promise to you. He has gone to prepare a place, and He is coming back to take you home. It is in your interest to believe Him for He honours His words. Paul too believed, and that is why he was sure that a crown of righteousness was awaiting him at the end of his race here on earth. You also will receive your just reward when the Master comes back again. Many will tell you He is too long in coming and so laugh at your steadfastness. Never waver as Abraham also looked stupid waiting for the promised son after Sarah had reached menopause. Instead, his faith increased because he was sure that God could do whatever He promises (Romans 4:21). Jesus agreed to die because of our sins to make us righteous because He had faith in His Father to put His life in God's hands. You too can have such confidence in the risen Son of God.

> *"Clearly, God's promise to give the whole earth to Abraham and his descendants was based not on his obedience to God's law, but on a right relationship with God that comes by faith. If God's promise is only for those who obey the law, then faith is not necessary, and the promise is pointless. For the law always brings punishment on those who try to obey it. (The only way to avoid breaking the law is to have no law to break!)"*
>
> *(Romans 4: 13 – 15 NLT)*

The room at the Cross brings you peace with God and confers on you the privileged position of sonship. It presents to you the opportunity of sharing in God's glory if you hold on to the end. Many years ago, my life was filled with so much fear as I knew that God was not happy with the way I was handling His temple – my body. I was afraid of the consequences of my actions and inactions for I knew that God was a consuming fire who would not spare the rod of justice on all sinners. Today I can say with all sense of humility that God is working wonders in my life, and I am at peace with myself following daily after His footsteps. The entry to the room at the Cross is not free from challenges. The challenges will come, but you will overcome when you walk faithfully with God. You must be encouraged by the fact that Christ who sought for you when you were a sinner loves you and so will not leave you alone in the room. He has set for you a perfect example of genuine love so you can sleep with your two eyes closed when you are with Him.

"So now we can rejoice in our wonderful new relationship with God because our Lord Jesus Christ has made us friends of God."

(Romans 5: 11 NLT)

The room at the Cross is not an architectural masterpiece. It refers to the opportunity you have as a man to change your destiny by reversing the curse of death brought from the womb through your connection with Adam. The consequence of the first sin committed by Adam did not terminate with him. This sin brought death to Adam and also to all of humanity. By implication, all who are born of a woman automatically inherit this Adamic sin and the death it brought along with it. No one can get rid of it by himself; this is where Jesus comes into the equation. The fact that this inherited sin which brings death is in you and cannot be erased if you act alone means that you must receive help from somewhere to escape from the deadly sting of sin. The room at the Cross offers you an opportunity to gain this help. Jesus alone provides the remedy for your sins which God has graciously made available free to you. The truth is that if you fail to gain access to what Jesus has done for you at the Cross, you are condemned already but if by faith you come willingly to Him for Salvation, he will not cast you away (John 6:37). You are assured of being made right with God in this small room because He has promised that "though your sins are like scarlet, they shall be as white as snow; though they are red as crimson, they shall be like wool."(Isaiah 1:18)

> *"Yes, Adam's one sin brings condemnation for everyone, but Christ's one act of righteousness brings a right relationship with God and new life for everyone. Because one person disobeyed God, many became sinners. But because one other person obeyed God, many will be made righteous."*
>
> *(Romans 5: 18 – 19 NLT)*

You cannot help yourself. The law will always break you if you do not come to Jesus to obtain His righteousness freely given. It is for the reason of our continued failings that God brought Grace to the table. God's Grace is the vehicle that bridges the gap between our best efforts and God's standard. It is by this Grace that we are saved through faith in God's only begotten Son Jesus Christ. The fact that man is under Grace is no excuse for continued sinning. God expects us to hate sin and live a life that mirrors that of Christ in every way and every day. The life we are supposed to live must be one where sin has been completely buried never to raise its ugly head again. This life translates into one where we have received power over sin, and it no longer controls our lives. It is a life that is joined with Christ's life so that just like He overcame death, we too will overcome and be raised to a new life. It is a life of complete dominion over sin where sinful living is under subjugation, and a new life birthed not under the requirements of the Law of Moses but one ruled by the Grace of God. It is a life that embraces holiness and sees righteous living as second nature. It's a life that now hates sin and loves godliness. A life that seeks to avoid the second death and looks forward to eternal life in the bosom of the Lord Jesus Christ.

> *"Do not let sin control the way you live; do not give in to sinful desires. Do not let any part of your body become an instrument of evil to serve sin. Instead, give yourselves completely to God, for you were dead, but now you have new life. So use your whole body as an instrument to do what is right for the glory of God. Sin is no longer your master, for you no longer live under the requirements of the law. Instead, you live under the freedom of God's grace."*
>
> *(Romans 6:12 - 14 NLT)*

The room at the Cross justifies that complete compliance with the law as a means of meeting God's expectation is an impossibility. This is why God gave the best route to meeting His righteousness criteria through His Son at the Cross. God knew that all our righteous acts cannot fulfil His expectations and that by nature, the flesh is weak and always pursues that which is wrong and unacceptable to God. The law of God on its own is perfect, but due to the rebellious nature of man, he finds it challenging to live in conformity to it. This then tends to generate a harvest of sinful acts which is not the original intention of the law. The room at the Cross releases you from the "shackles" of the law, giving those who live in Christ freedom from the law, but this freedom does not preclude that one continues to live in sin. For those who hold on to the way of life that is based on the law, their desire to please God is impossible; they must, therefore, access the Cross if they want to meet God's expectation. Failing to accept Jesus, they find themselves on an endless journey in futility, trying to attain God's prescribed righteousness level without success.

> *"So the trouble is not with the law, for it is spiritual and good. The trouble is with me, for I am all too human, a slave to sin. I don't really understand myself, for I want to do what is right, but I don't do it. Instead, I do what I hate. But if I know that what I am doing is wrong, this shows that I agree that the law is good. So I am not the one doing wrong; it is sin living in me that does it. And I know that nothing good lives in me, that is, in my sinful nature. I want to do what is right, but I can't. I want to do what is good, but I don't. I don't want to do what is wrong, but I do it anyway. But if I do what I don't want to*

do, I am not really the one doing wrong; it is sin living in me that does it. I have discovered this principle of life—that when I want to do what is right, I inevitably do what is wrong. I love God's law with all my heart. But there is another power within me that is at war with my mind. This power makes me a slave to the sin that is still within me. Oh, what a miserable person I am! Who will free me from this life that is dominated by sin and death? Thank God! The answer is in Jesus Christ, our Lord. So you see how it is: In my mind, I really want to obey God's law, but because of my sinful nature, I am a slave to sin."

(Romans 7: 14 – 25 NLT)

The room at the Cross tells you that there is no alternative to Jesus Christ. The Cross is about Him, and Jesus is all about the Cross! The Cross belongs to Jesus, and it is Him who has made that room available to you free of charge! He is the only one who can free you from the sin power that will ultimately kill you if you don't get help from Him. The purpose of the Cross is to save us from the sinful nature we have inherited from birth. Jesus demonstrated the possibility of human power over sin as he came in the flesh to live among us, thereby teaching us how He wants us to live our lives. The room at the Cross is uncompromising in its expectation that we must meet the standard of God every single day. Those who live in this room must submit to the dictates of God's Spirit by turning their backs totally to the nature of sin driven by the flesh. They must choose the peace that the Spirit gives over death which is the ultimate result of the sinful nature. The Spirit of God when you submit to Him will make you right with God. The same Spirit will give life to your mortal bodies when you die, just like it did raise Jesus Christ from the dead. The choice is yours to make – the life-giving Spirit of God or Death which arises from submission to the flesh.

> *"So fear the LORD and serve him wholeheartedly. Put away forever the idols your ancestors worshipped when they lived beyond the Euphrates River and in Egypt. Serve the LORD alone. But if you refuse to serve the LORD, then choose today whom you will serve. Would you prefer the gods your ancestors served beyond the Euphrates? Or will it be the gods of the Amorites in whose land you now live? But as for me and my family, we will serve the LORD."*
>
> (Joshua 24: 14 – 15 NLT)

The Spirit of God when you submit to Him confers on you the title of sonship. God will no longer regard you as a slave. You can through His spirit confidently approach your Father, who is God Himself. The same Spirit, by implication, makes us heirs of God's glory to come. This Glory of God is, however, not freely given. It is for those who have partaken in suffering with Christ. The good news is that the suffering we must accept is negligible when compared to His Glory that we will share upon the return of Christ, the only begotten Son of God. It is indeed an excellent investment to make. This Spirit is the one who empowers you, so you must allow Him to have His way in your life. You cannot even pray properly without His help so you will do well to enable Him to take control of your life. His role is to help align your life with God's purpose for you so that all will be well with you and all that concerns you too.

"And we know that God causes everything to work together for the good of those who love God and are called according to his purpose for them."

(Romans 8: 28 NLT)

The occupancy of the room at the Cross is to be a permanent one. You must come wholeheartedly and be prepared to stay put. This is the desire of Jesus, who has made the room available for you. He is never going to cast anyone away except they choose to take after the "son of perdition" by refusing to follow after Him or His ways. God's commitment to those in this room is unwavering. Nothing can make Him turn His back at them. You too must show reciprocal commitment. Be warned that those who are looking at you from outside will do all they can to drag you out. They will come to you with all manner of problems; you will face persecutions and all kinds of danger as you stand firm within the confines of the room. Sometimes it will be hunger and poverty, calamities of varying proportions and even bereavement, but you must remember that it is only those who persevere to the end that will be saved (Matthew 24:13). The assurance that you have is that provided you stay inside the room at the Cross; these things cannot overwhelm you. The troubling experiences you are having do not in any way signify the absence of God in the room that you occupy. God's presence and love are ever sure and are with you always. Jesus has already won your victory on the Cross! All you need to do is to stand your ground. Do not move out of the room under any circumstance whatsoever. All power on earth, beneath the surface and in heaven is with Him who is staying with you (Matthew 28:18). You can never lose!

> *"Can anything ever separate us from Christ's love? Does it mean he no longer loves us if we have trouble or calamity, or are persecuted, or hungry, or destitute, or in danger, or threatened with death? (As the Scriptures say, "For your sake we are killed every day; we are being slaughtered like sheep.") No, despite all these things, overwhelming victory is ours through Christ, who loved us."*
>
> *(Romans 8: 35 – 37 NLT)*

The occupancy of the room at the Cross is made available out of the mercy of God. You get your room key not because you deserve it but because the Almighty has withheld His anger and has not dealt with you the way He should; He has exercised so much patience so that you may come in and enjoy all the benefits therein reserved for all His children. Though this mercy is unmerited, yet He makes it freely available to whosoever will come to Him in repentance. God's purpose is to save you, but this will only happen if you go to Him in faith and with the willingness to put away your sins and embrace a new life in Christ Jesus. You must, therefore, take advantage of the opportunity of Grace that you have and seize it with both hands. God will then turn you into a new person, and your life will never remain the same. After that, He then begins to shower you with His love and proceed to teach you the best pathway for your life. The life you now live is one where you put all trust in the One who has saved you from your old life of sin. You no longer see the keeping of the law as the way to meeting the mark set by God; instead, you now put your absolute faith in Him to gain His approval.

> *"In the same way, even though God has the right to show his anger and his power, he is very patient with those on whom his anger falls, who are destined for destruction. He does this to make the riches of his glory shine even brighter on those to whom he shows mercy, who were prepared in advance for glory."*
>
> *(Romans 9: 22 – 23 NLT)*

Some still cling to their way instead of God's way. They do so out of an uncommon zeal which though is to be admired, gets them nowhere near the heart of God. The reason they cannot find a way to God's heart is that they are trying with human strength and wisdom. Their righteousness is never able to measure up to God's standard as they keep sinking into sin just because they fail to meet the expectation that they must obey all His commandments. They reject the adequate option of faith, which only requires genuine acceptance and confession of the Lordship of Jesus – and also that He died and was raised from the dead. This is the only way available in which man can become right with God. Those who are wise take it in both hands while those who are not continue to struggle. God is, however, no respecter of man; He deals with all as they deserve and to those who honour Him, in

His glory they shall share, but those who turn their backs to His commands find no peace at all – for this our God is a God of justice. He wants all to value the Salvation He has provided through His Son and to grab it with both hands and in humility because it has not been earned; only freely given to all who come to Jesus.

> *"Notice how God is both kind and severe. He is severe toward those who disobeyed, but kind to you if you continue to trust in his kindness. But if you stop trusting, you also will be cut off."*
>
> *(Romans 11: 22 NLT)*

The room at the Cross has its ground rules. It is not acceptable that you come into the house that Jesus has provided free for you without being ready to surrender your life. God expects you to set a holiness example that is unparalleled so that others will be motivated to do likewise and glorify God, who has made it possible for you to attain that level. This is non-negotiable. You must have it at the back of your mind that though you live in the world, you must not to be like every other person around you. Your life must always show a distinct difference from others such that everyone will see that it is God who has transformed you. Your mind and what fills it must be pure as it now reflects the new way God wants you to think; having values that are of a heavenly origin that aligns with God's good, pleasing and perfect will for you. God expects you to remain humble at all times, never regarding yourself as being more important than other occupants of this room. You must see all others as your equal; members of the same family of God living under the same roof. You must show love to all who are in your new family as it is God's command to all His children. God expects you to set an example in godly living in all its ramifications so that you will shine as stars in this dark and evil world. All that look normal and acceptable in the world becomes repulsive to you as you love God and hate the world. In most instances, you will act "stupidly" if you must please God; please remember this is the path you have chosen and cannot surrender from it. Your life will, as a result, be a pleasing aroma to God while the world will hate you the way it hated your master – Jesus.

> *"Don't just pretend to love others. Really love them. Hate what is wrong. Hold tightly to what is good. Love each other with genuine affection, and take delight in honouring each other. Never be lazy, but work hard and serve the Lord enthusiastically. Rejoice in our confident hope. Be patient in trouble, and keep on praying. When God's people are in need, be ready to help them. Always be eager to practice hospitality. Bless those who persecute you. Don't curse them; pray that God will bless them. Be happy with those who are happy and weep with those who weep. Live in harmony with each other. Don't be too proud to enjoy the company of ordinary people. And don't think you know it all! Never pay back evil with more evil. Do things in such a way that everyone can see you are honourable. Do all that you can to live in peace with everyone. Dear friends, never take revenge. Leave that to the righteous anger of God. For the Scriptures say, "I will take revenge; I will pay them back," says the*

LORD. Instead, If your enemies are hungry, feed them. If they are thirsty, give them something to drink. In doing this, you will heap burning coals of shame on their heads." Don't let evil conquer you, but conquer evil by doing good."

(Romans 12: 9 – 21 NLT)

The room at the Cross is not for truants. You must be a soldier of the Cross, and to this calling, you must abide. God expects you to be law-abiding at all times so that you will not bring His name and yours to shame. This is a show of reverence to God who establishes all authorities and to which we are accountable. Your relationship with God does not confer on you the right to act in defiance to the norms. Instead, it compels you to submit to all authority at all times. Make sure that in no situation are you found wanting so that you will not suffer the consequences. Follow God's command to love your neighbour so that in doing so, you would have met His expectation to obey His commandments and to live above board. As you live with others who enjoy with you the unmerited love of God, make sure you are focused on the end, which is when your Master will return to reward His servants. The day is actually at hand as most of all He has warned will take place in advance of His return are already happening around you.

Make every preparation to see to it that you qualify for His commendation. To qualify, you must "strip off every weight that slows us down, especially the sin that easily trips us. And let us run with endurance the race God has set before us" (Hebrews 12: 1a). Let godliness and godly living be like second nature to you. Avoid all that seems exciting and acceptable to the world as you live in non-conformity with the world. Be united with all who share with you in the Grace of Jesus Christ and let no one and no situation tear you apart from them. Remember you are one body with them, and nothing will gladden the Lord's heart more than your unity; for it is He who is deserving of your loyalty having given His life for you on the Cross and also having taken it back through His resurrection.

"This is all the more urgent, for you know how late it is; time is running out. Wake up, for our Salvation is nearer now than when we first believed. The night is almost gone; the day of Salvation will soon be here. So remove your dark deeds like dirty clothes, and put on the shining armour of right living. Because we belong to the day, we must live decent lives for all to see. Don't participate in the darkness of wild parties and drunkenness, or in sexual promiscuity and immoral living, or in quarrelling and jealousy. Instead, clothe yourself with the presence of the Lord Jesus Christ. And don't let yourself think about ways to indulge your evil desires."

(Romans 13: 11 – 14 NLT)

All who stay with you in the room at the Cross are your brothers and sisters, so you must look after them and yourself. Your focus must be how all of you will arrive safely at the New Jerusalem. Let it not be to your debt that someone loses his or her reward. Do all you can to see to it that no one stumbles or falls due to your action or inaction. Your lifestyle must be guided by what is for the greater good of your brother or sister. Anything short of this will be against the spirit of the room at the Cross. Do all you can to be as accommodating as possible and make sure that you do not allow customs and traditions to cause disharmony amongst you. Set an example of "a life of goodness and peace and joy in the Holy Spirit" (Romans 14:17b) and be guided by your genuine convictions and conscience all times for when you go against the leading of your inner spirit, you end up sinning by going against the law of God. Follow the example of Christ who put the sinner ahead of Himself so that He could offer His life as a ransom to save him. Do not be in league with those who want to be hero-worshipped, thereby ignoring the teaching of Jesus, which says the greatest must be the servant amongst His followers.

> *"We who are strong must be considerate of those who are sensitive about things like this. We must not just please ourselves. We should help others do what is right and build them up in the Lord. For even Christ didn't live to please himself. As the Scriptures say, "The insults of those who insult you, O God, have fallen on me." Such things were written in the Scriptures long ago to teach us. And the Scriptures give us hope and encouragement as we wait patiently for God's promises to be fulfilled."*

(Romans 15: 1-4 NLT)

The room at the Cross is a metaphor for what Jesus did to save you from eternal damnation. The room at the Cross describes the life He has called you to live for Him. It is a life redeemed and which was made possible by the death of Jesus at the Calvary Cross. It is a life of reformation where the "room" occupants are to live as prescribed by Jesus so that they can reign with Him when He returns. Jesus is standing on the balcony of one of the rooms, waving frantically at passersby to draw their attention and get them to come in to meet with Him. He wants to share His meal with you as a friend; all you need to do is to answer His call. He has done so much for you on the Cross, and you can only gain access to what He "finished" when you join others in the room at the Cross.

Jesus died to fulfil the scriptures. His death was a confirmation that God keeps His words, and nothing will hold Him back from doing what He says He will do. God in His wisdom gave Prophet Isaiah the revelation of the future coming of Jesus so that all who love Him will be expectant and not miss Him when He arrives.

> *"But it was the LORD's good plan to crush him and cause him grief. Yet when his life is made an offering for sin, he will have many descendants. He will enjoy a long life, and the LORD's good plan will prosper in his hands."*
>
> (Isaiah 53: 10 NLT)

Jesus died as a sacrifice for sin to break the power of the devil. He made the devil's power over death ineffective. He took this power hitherto held by the devil to set us free and give us freedom.

"Because God's children are human beings — made of flesh and blood — the Son also became flesh and blood. For only as a human being could he die, and only by dying could he break the power of the devil, who had[a] the power of death. Only in this way could he set free all who have lived their lives as slaves to the fear of dying."

(Hebrews 2: 14 – 15 NLT)

Jesus died so that all can be united together as one in Him. His death brings about the cancellation of all forms of segregation in the body of Christ.

"There is no longer Jew or Gentile, slave or free, male and female. For you are all one in Christ Jesus."

(Galatians 3: 28 NLT)

Jesus died so that each one who comes to Him can have direct access to God without any intermediary. There is no longer any mediator between man and His Creator. Nothing can stand between you and your maker except that which is self-made like sin and disobedience.

"Now, all of us can come to the Father through the same Holy Spirit because of what Christ has done for us."

(Ephesians 2: 18 NLT)

Jesus died, and so cancelled the power of sin. He provided the transformational power that will change our mortal bodies to an immortal one. Through His death, Jesus terminated the power of sin that brings permanent death to man. He has therefore defeated, through His death, the power of sin that causes death.

*"Then, when our dying bodies have been trans-
formed into bodies that will never die, this
Scripture will be fulfilled: "Death is swallowed
up in victory. O death, where is your victory? O
death, where is your sting?" For sin is the sting
that results in death, and the law gives sin its
power. But thank God! He gives us victory over
sin and death through our Lord Jesus Christ.
So, my dear brothers and sisters, be strong and
immovable. Always work enthusiastically for
the Lord, for you know that nothing you do for
the Lord is ever useless."*

(1 Corinthians 15: 54 – 58 NLT)

Jesus died to show to us that there is no limit to our commitment to obey and to love God. He endured all things to
the point of laying down His life to set the perfect example
for us to follow after Him.

*"He humbled himself in obedience to God and
died a criminal's death on a cross."*

(Philippians 2: 8 NLT)

Jesus died to provide a Salvation package for all and
from all sin. He died because of the inadequacy of the old
redemption plan.

*"For Christ died to set them free from the penalty
of the sins they had committed under that first
covenant."*

(Hebrews 9: 15b)

Jesus died so that the separation caused by sin that led
to enmity between man and God will come to an end. His
death, therefore, brought reconciliation and peace to all
who accept His gift of Salvation.

"For God in all his fullness was pleased to live in Christ, and through him, God reconciled everything to himself. He made peace with everything in heaven and on earth by means of Christ's blood on the cross. This includes you who were once far away from God. You were his enemies, separated from him by your evil thoughts and actions. Yet now he has reconciled you to himself through the death of Christ in his physical body. As a result, he has brought you into his own presence, and you are holy and blameless as you stand before him without a single fault."

(Colossians 1: 19 – 22 NLT)

Jesus died so that the debt that each person born of a woman owes will no longer be demanded of him or her. He paid the death penalty due to you and me for our sinful nature. You are no longer indebted in any way, and so are free to gain eternal life through Him.

"For God in all his fullness was pleased to live in Christ, and through him, God reconciled everything to himself. He made peace with everything in heaven and on earth by means of Christ's blood on the cross."

(1 Peter 1: 18 – 19 NLT)

Jesus died so that you can have access to healing in your body from every manner of disease and sickness. He proved beyond any shadow of a doubt that all power on earth and in heaven is with Him. At the name of Jesus, every knee must bow!

"Yet it was our weaknesses he carried; it was our sorrows that weighed him down. And we thought

his troubles were a punishment from God, a punishment for his own sins! But he was pierced for our rebellion, crushed for our sins. He was beaten so we could be whole. He was whipped so we could be healed."

(Isaiah 53: 4 -5 NLT)

Jesus died as part of God's plan and rose again, leading finally to His ascension. He, therefore, made way for the arrival of the Holy Spirit to whom we owe our power, counsel, and discernment.

"Now he is exalted to the place of highest honour in heaven, at God's right hand. And the Father, as he had promised, gave him the Holy Spirit to pour out upon us, just as you see and hear today."

(Acts 2: 33 NLT)

Jesus died and presented to us a perfect way of relating to God and having access to Him. God saw the need for a new and more glorifying covenant, and so did not hold back His best to give us access to it. Jesus is the mediator of the new covenant that all must go through if they want to gain eternal life.

"Before the way of faith in Christ was available to us, we were placed under guard by the law. We were kept in protective custody, so to speak, until the way of faith was revealed. Let me put it another way. The law was our guardian until Christ came; it protected us until we could be made right with God through faith. And now that the way of faith has come, we no longer need the law as our guardian."

(Galatians 3: 23 – 25 NLT)

Dearly beloved, Jesus has done so much for you on the Cross. His Salvation package came with so many extras, a few of which I have shared with you. All these and more are available in the room at the Cross – all for your sake. Everything about the Cross and the room Jesus made available free of charge is personalized. It's about you and Him alone. Jesus is God's best for you, and there is none other like Him. The room at the Cross can accommodate whosoever will come, but there is no compulsion by the Son of God. The room, according to the inspiration received by Ira Stanphill, is a shelter where you can hide, providing for you a fountain deep and wide. Stanphill saw Grace that is sufficient even if millions are in the room at the Cross. He affirmed that he knows that the Saviour can accommodate several million and that His gates are still open to welcome a sinner before it is too late. Stanphill concluded that "the hand of my Saviour is Strong and the love of my Saviour is long; Through sunshine or rain, through loss or in gain, the blood flows from Calvary to cleanse every stain." Why don't you come over to Jesus today? He is waiting for you!

The Ultimate Prize

"Look, I am coming soon, bringing my reward with me to repay all people according to their deeds. I am the Alpha and the Omega, the First and the Last, the Beginning and the End."

(Revelation 22:12 – 13. NLT)

Sometime in the first half of the year 1996, I found myself working in Aba in Abia State, South-East Nigeria. I attended a Baptist church on the outskirts of the city on the way to Ikot Ekpene. It had as its pastor, a young man who was starting in ministry. I always enjoyed the worship service even though the size of the congregation was about 25; it reminded me of my home as I was born into a Baptist family. I remember vividly that even in that small church, we had a very active choir of about 4 or 5 members. Every Sunday, the choir would lead the procession of the pastor and other officiating ministers, often singing a song I found to be very thought-provoking; the piece is I AM RUNNING THE RACE TO MEET MY REDEEMER – HEAVENLY RACE. It reminded all worshipers that life's journey is a race to meet our Redeemer.

Talking about a race, the Yorubas have a saying that coming to the world is like a journey, but heaven is the ultimate home of all humanity; our experiences in life confirm this truism daily. Some time ago, while riding in a car with my wife and my driver, God ministered something to me about my life; He made me see that except I received more grace, I barely had 23 years left of my life – 70 years minus 47 years as it were at that time. I thought genuinely about how short 23 years were, and I realised that time was running out for me if I saw heaven as the ultimate retirement home for all. When I shared this reality with other occupants of the car, there was an extended period of silence and reflection; maybe even fear and concern, with both of them agreeing with me that life is very short. The truth is that every day, the clock is ticking away, and no one knows the hour or time.

> *"Look, I will come as unexpectedly as a thief! Blessed are all who are watching for me, who keep their clothing ready so they will not have to walk around naked and ashamed."*
>
> *(Revelation 16:15. NLT)*

The purpose of this reflection is to deliver what I consider the best gift to you as a human being. I will like to encourage you to focus more on what I know is the ULTIMATE PRIZE. In the course of man's journey on earth, he may have had the privilege of many accomplishments. Whatever the achievements, whether it is in business, politics, academics, etc., none can compare with gaining the ultimate prize. Living as Jesus lived is undoubtedly the only access route to the ultimate prize! Paul encompassed this position in his letter to the people of Philippi when he wrote;

> *"I was circumcised when I was eight days old. I am a pure-blooded citizen of Israel and a member of the tribe of Benjamin—a real Hebrew if there ever was one! I was a member of the Pharisees,*

who demand the strictest obedience to the Jewish law. I was so zealous that I harshly persecuted the church. And as for righteousness, I obeyed the law without fault. I once thought these things were valuable, but now I consider them worthless because of what Christ has done. Yes, everything else is worthless when compared with the infinite value of knowing Christ Jesus, my Lord. For his sake, I have discarded everything else, counting it all as garbage, so that I could gain Christ and become one with him. I no longer count on my own righteousness through obeying the law; rather, I become righteous through faith in Christ. For God's way of making us right with himself depends on faith. I want to know Christ and experience the mighty power that raised him from the dead. I want to suffer with him, sharing in his death, so that one way or another I will experience the resurrection from the dead!"

(Philippians 3: 5 – 11. NLT)

The ultimate prize is not cheaply available. It requires three essential D's of Decision, Determination & Discipline and relates to a story I love so much in the Bible. It is probably one of the shortest parables. It shows the importance of this ultimate prize; Jesus referred to it as a treasure, which it is – CERTAINLY.

"The Kingdom of Heaven is like a treasure that a man discovered hidden in a field. In his excitement, he hid it again and sold everything he owned to get enough money to buy the field. Again, the Kingdom of Heaven is like a merchant on the lookout for choice pearls. When he discovered a pearl of great value, he sold everything he owned and bought it!"

(Matthew 13: 44 – 46. NLT)

The ultimate prize is a treasure comparable to a thing of great value - like pearls. Though Salvation is a gift, it is not available on a platter of gold. To get it, one must make the necessary sacrifice, just like the man who sold everything he had to acquire this treasure.

The ultimate prize is not only for you when you accept it, but it is also meant for those around you, especially if you are old enough to influence others. God expects us to make a spiritual impact in the homes He has led us into, in our communities and the world at large. It is a critical responsibility of a man or woman, and God does not want us to toy with it. It is one of the things that we have to give an account of at the judgement throne. The songwriter Charles C. Luther also epitomises this position in his song – MUST I GO EMPTY HANDED? A favourite song by Evangelist Funmi Aragbaye also emphasises the need to focus on life's accountability and the ultimate prize. The song goes like this;

Ijobaorunkudede, araiyeeyipa, onidajoaiyenbo, ti o berelowo re, bawo lo se lo, igbesiaiye re (The kingdom of heaven is near, all must repent because the one to judge the world is coming and He will require you to give an account of your life).

God expects us to live in a particular way, along with specific guidelines. A time is coming when we will all sit and give an account. No one can evade that session.

"And just as each person is destined to die once and after that comes judgment."
(Hebrews 9:27. NLT)

In life, success is desirable by all. I have never seen any man or woman who does not desire recognition and reward. Many people sacrifice a lot to get to the top to be revered and admired. The truth is, nothing is wrong with that. It is even good to be ambitious, to desire good, and see to its achievement. The critical issue, however, is that we must place these achievements where they belong – mundane things that have value only here on earth where we will spend just a little part of our total existence. What then does it mean to be successful? Who should be most admired by all men? I believe this man or woman is the one who is living to gain the ultimate prize. Jesus was very clear and definitive about the ultimate prize when He spoke to a crowd saying;

"And what do you benefit if you gain the whole world but lose your own soul? Is anything worth more than your soul?"
(Mark 8: 36 – 37. NLT)

The ultimate prize is all about the life hereafter. To focus on it, one must consecrate himself or herself. It is a life that sets you apart in the world, making you fix your gaze on things above. It does everything possible to see to it that there is non-conformity with things of this world. It denies itself, taking up the cross DAILY, following the Master – JESUS; THE AUTHOR AND FINISHER OF OUR FAITH (Hebrews 12:2).

"Since you have been raised to new life with Christ, set your sights on the realities of heaven, where Christ sits in the place of honour at God's right hand. Think about the things of heaven, not the things of earth. For you died to this life, and your real life is hidden with Christ in God. And when Christ, who is your life, is revealed to the whole world, you will share in all his glory."

(Colossians 3:1-3. NLT)

Focus on the ultimate prize prescribes that you forsake all others just as it is usually recommended at marriages AND CLING TO YOUR SAVIOUR. You must be ready to do away with all in your current life that is at variance with your new Master's expectation till death or when the Master returns. The challenge begins here, but there is no alternative in the matter; you have to abandon the way of the world for God.

"So put to death the sinful, earthly things lurking within you. Have nothing to do with sexual immorality, impurity, lust, and evil desires. Don't be greedy, for a greedy person is an idolater, worshipping the things of this world. Because of these sins, the anger of God is coming. You used to do these things when your life was still part of this world. But now is the time to get rid of anger, rage, malicious behaviour, slander, and dirty language. Don't lie to each other, for you have stripped off your old sinful nature and all its wicked deeds. Put on your new nature, and be renewed as you learn to know your Creator and become like him. In this new life, it doesn't matter if you are a Jew or a Gentile, circumcised

or uncircumcised, barbaric, uncivilised, slave, or free. Christ is all that matters, and he lives in all of us."

(Colossians 3: 5-11. NLT)

Again the ultimate prize can be related to the parable of the ten virgins. The difference in the two sets of virgins was in their lamps – the foolish ones with not enough oil, which allowed their fires to go out. The lamps provided light, and the Bible tells us that Jesus is the Light of the world. A virgin without this light, therefore, cannot meet the bridegroom. This lesson is particularly relevant for all those born into Christian families. You maybe like the virgins in the parable, but the critical issue is that anyone without the Light of the world (Jesus) is like the virgins with no oil in their lamps to provide light. Such a person is not a Christian and will not qualify to meet Jesus on the last day - just like the virgins who lost out when the bridegroom returned. No wonder Jesus said, "not all those who call me Lord Lord shall enter the Kingdom of God"(Matthew 7:21).

"But while they were gone to buy oil, the bridegroom came. Then those who were ready went in with him to the marriage feast, and the door was locked."

(Matthew 25:10. NLT)

For those who want to focus on the ultimate prize, they must ask themselves this question every day; WHAT IF I DIE TODAY? It is a question that I believe all who consider life to be transient must always ask and daily too. During a recent study of the Bible in my local church, someone brought to the fore the reality that many times the young will die before the old; therefore, everyone must be ready. Nobody knows the hour or time that his or her death will come; it will happen as the action of a thief in the night, sudden and unannounced. Jesus was so concerned about our failure to receive this ultimate prize that He gave us a warning;

> *"When the Son of Man returns, it will be like it was in Noah's day. In those days before the flood, the people were enjoying banquets and parties and weddings right up to the time Noah entered his boat. People didn't realise what was going to happen until the flood came and swept them all away. That is the way it will be when the Son of Man comes "Two men will be working together in the field; one will be taken, the other left. Two women will be grinding flour at the mill; one will be taken, the other left. So you, too, must keep watch! For you don't know what day your Lord is coming. Understand this: If a homeowner knew exactly when a burglar was coming, he would keep watch and not permit his house to be broken into. You also must be ready all the time, for the Son of Man will come when least expected. A faithful, sensible servant is one to whom the master can give the responsibility of managing his other household servants and feeding them. If the master returns and finds that the servant has done a good job, there will be a reward. I tell you the truth; the master will put that servant in charge of all he owns. But what if the servant is evil and thinks, 'My master won't be back for a while, and he begins beating the other servants, partying, and getting drunk? The master will*

return unannounced and unexpected, and he will
cut the servant to pieces and assign him a place
with the hypocrites. In that place, there will be
weeping and gnashing of teeth."

(Matthew24:37 – 51. NLT)

I often think about the ultimate prize. I do also think of death, something most people tend to shy away from, but it is a reality we cannot ignore. One of the benefits of God's Grace upon my life is that I always consider the things of God deeply. David made the point that only a foolish man would say in his heart that there is no God. It is Grace that allows a man to be sensitive to God's word or message because the required action can only come after conviction. Some people hear God's Word, and it bounces off them without recourse to it. They consider themselves all-knowing and not requiring this help, but alas, when the end comes, it will be too late. Death is so decisive and terminal that after it, there is no remedy. No wonder the preacher said;

"Whatever you do, do well. For when you go to
the grave, there will be no work or planning or
knowledge or wisdom."
(Ecclesiastes 9: 10. NLT)

On my fortieth birthday in the year 2005, I was led to write a tract reflecting on my life. Though I was still struggling with God's will at that time, He was gracious enough to give me a message entitled – how old are you? I understood God to be asking me how much of my 40 years I had dedicated to Him? He wanted me to compare my secular and spiritual achievements over the first four decades of my life, to see how I had fared. The outcome of the comparison was so disgraceful that I wondered if I deserved all the faithfulness of God in my life - for I had not done well in the things of God. God made me realise that the achievements that were valuable to Him are not all those niceties found with religious people, but instead, He was interested ONLY in the act of bearing fruits;

> *"When you produce much fruit, you are my true disciples. This brings great glory to my Father."*
>
> (John 15:8. NLT)

> *"So every tree that does not produce good fruit is chopped down and thrown into the fire."*
>
> (Matthew 9:19. NLT)

One very thoughtful quote that I added to the tract I wrote was one that I picked up in the Punch Newspaper of Wednesday, 26th October 2005. In its review of the Bell-view crash of the same year, the newspaper stated thus; "In the morning, you may be bubbling with life; you may be threatening to deal with your neighbour for insulting you. But in the night, the ultimate reality may call." The ultimate is for us to be ready when the Master comes.

I want to close with a story of two prominent men and leaders of their time in the Bible who had access to God's Word. Unfortunately, they did not benefit from it.

Marcus Julius Agrippa was the eighth and last king of the family of Herod the Great, the Herodians. He was the son of the first and better known Herod Agrippa.[1] He had the privilege of hearing God's Word during the trial of

Apostle Paul, but alas did not take advantage of it. Marcus Antonius Felix, who was the Roman Procurator of Iudaea Province 52 - 58 in succession to Ventidius Cumanus[2]; he wanted more time, which is not always available. May God help you and me not to toy with our opportunities in Jesus' name.

"Agrippa interrupted him. "Do you think you can persuade me to become a Christian so quickly?"

(Acts 26:28. NLT)

"A few days later Felix came back with his wife, Drusilla, who was Jewish. Sending for Paul, they listened as he told them about faith in Christ Jesus. As he reasoned with them about righteousness and self-control and the coming Day of Judgment, Felix became frightened. "Go away for now," he replied. "When it is more convenient, I'll call for you again."'

(Acts 24:24. NLT)

I implore you to prayerfully reflect on what you have read so far and ask God to help you do the needful in the areas of your life that require His touch.

As you go on in your life's journey, do remember the counsel of Solomon below;

"Please remember your creator before the silver cord is severed, and the golden bowl is broken; before the pitcher is shattered at spring, and the wheel broken at the well, and the dust returns to the ground it came from, and the spirit returns to God who gave it. "Everything is meaningless" says the Teacher, "completely meaningless"."

(Ecclesiastes 12: 6 - 8. NLT)

You must focus on the ultimate prize and nothing else!

The Solid Rock

"For no one can lay any foundation other than the one we already have—Jesus Christ."

(1 Corinthians 3:11. NLT)

Edward Mote was a pastor and hymn writer. Born in London on 21st January 1797, his parents managed a pub and often left Edward to his own devices playing in the street.[1] He worked in London for many years and was a cabinet maker. Later he entered the ministry and was pastor at Rehoboth Baptist Church in Horsham, West Sussex, for 26 years.[2] He was a favourite of his congregation in Horsham, and they once gave him the church building as a gift. Mote instead preferred the simple access to the pulpit and so turned down the offer. He passed on, on the 13th of November 1874, and was laid to rest in the churchyard at Rehoboth Church. One of his famous hymns is "My Hope Is Built on Nothing Less," which captures the lessons in Jesus' Parable of the Wise and the Foolish Builders, with its refrain 'On Christ the solid Rock I stand, all other ground is sinking sand.' [3] The hymn, initially titled the gracious experience of a Christian, was written in 1834. The completed hymn text originally consisted of six stanzas. Expressions from portions of these two omitted stanzas are fascinating to observe:

"My hope is built on nothing less than Jesus' blood and righteousness; 'Midst all the hell I feel within, on His completed work I lean. I trust His righteous character, His council, promise, and His power; His honour and His name's at stake, to save me from the burning lake."[4]

It is worth pondering over what was responsible for the turnaround in Edward Mote's life? Who gave him a second chance when all he knew was a background from ungodly parents running a beer parlour? Where did he get this inspiration? How did Jesus become so important to him? Why is Jesus still so crucial to humanity today?

The parable referred to above was Jesus' attempt to summarise a sermon he had preached for several days – the Sermon on the Mount. His message epitomises all in Christian living recorded by Matthew in only three chapters of his account of the life of Jesus. Jesus makes it very clear that obedience to His word is the panacea to a successful life. In the end, He made an effort to simplify all He had said by using the analogy of a solid foundation – wise builders who do a good job and the foolish ones who do not. Jesus reminded His listeners that both groups would not end with the same result.

"Anyone who listens to my teaching and follows it is wise, like a person who builds a house on solid rock. Though the rain comes in torrents and the floodwaters rise, and the winds beat against that house, it won't collapse because it is built on bedrock. But anyone who hears my teaching and doesn't obey it is foolish, like a person who

builds a house on sand. When the rains and floods come, and the winds beat against that house, it will collapse with a mighty crash."'

(Matthew 7:24-27. NLT)

What does Jesus want us to note? Recently, I had a sudden and burning desire to tell someone very close to me about Jesus. He is someone who is still fighting against the truth. The truth is that life will not end here on earth and that humanity will go forward to another place – in other words, life is a continuum, either to eternal life or eternal condemnation. The young man is very successful and full of life. He is a well-paid professional who feels on top of the world. Unlike him, I see the emptiness in this world; he considers the fullness. At the same time, I think of the hereafter, while he thinks of the present, and while I think of non-conformity with the world, my friend feels life is fun. In contrast, I think of posterity; he thinks of prosperity. I believe that God gave me this message not only for him, and so I do wish to share it with you too. I employ you to please read on with an open heart. I pray that God will minister to you profound things through these words.

Jesus Is The Alpha & Omega

God's love for humanity has never been in question. Since the fall of man shortly after creation, God had put together several rescue packages for man to drag him from the pit of destruction to the solid ground. Though this plan started with the prophets, the culmination of all these efforts is the final offer of God's best to humanity. It is an offer that is freely available to all who want to be genuinely free. It is the offer that ended with Jesus giving His life as a ransom for the sins of the world. Jesus is the Solid Rock who provided man with the much sought after victory over death. Christ is God's royal heir and was with His Father at creation. He manifests the person of God, and after completing the perfect work on the Cross is exalted above all.

> *"And now in these final days, he has spoken to us through his Son. God promised everything to the Son as an inheritance, and through the Son, he created the universe. The Son radiates God's own glory and expresses the very character of God, and he sustains everything by the mighty power of his command. When he had cleansed us from our sins, he sat down in the place of honour at the right hand of the majestic God in heaven. This shows that the Son is far greater than the angels, just as the name God gave him is greater than their names."*
>
> (Hebrews1:2 - 4. NLT)

Jesus was relevant at the beginning and is more so today! Why are you looking elsewhere for assistance?

Jesus Rules & Reigns

Man is interested in associating with the high and mighty, which in itself is not wrong if the purpose is right – godly to achieve what is good. We may decide to aspire for personal greatness, but again the goal must be to advance what will be pleasing to God. The opportunity that is available to us whenever we have the privilege is to do good and nothing else. Jesus must rule and reign in our lives, and this refers to having total dominion; nothing should come between you and this Jesus. His values become yours, and for all practical purposes, you do not have a life other than the one ordered by Him. This lordship of Jesus is permanent, and no one can contend with it. The lordship will guide you and keep you on the path of safety and security.

> *"But to the Son, he says, "Your throne, O God, endures forever and ever. You rule with a sceptre of justice. You love justice and hate evil. Therefore, O God, your God has anointed you, pouring out the oil of joy on you more than on anyone else." He also says to the Son, "In the beginning, Lord, you laid the foundation of the earth and made the heavens with your hands. They will perish, but you remain forever. They will wear out like old clothing. You will fold them up like a cloak and discard them like old clothing. But you are always the same; you will live forever."'*

> *(Hebrews 1: 8 – 12. NLT)*

Jesus is sufficient to guide and guard your life. Why do you depend on someone else to do it for you?

Jesus' Judgment Is Inevitable

I want you as my friend to appreciate as part of this discourse that life is transient and designed to achieve a purpose. Each one is allowed to play his or her role according to God's script. Unlike in a play where an artist may get an opportunity to go back to the stage after correction and counsel, in life, upon exit, there is no re-entry to the scene that the earth represents. All actors on the planet must take heed of God's word and remember that it is not enough to know what He expects of us without doing the same.

> *"So we must listen very carefully to the truth we have heard, or we may drift away from it. For the message God delivered through angels has always stood firm, and every violation of the law and every act of disobedience was punished. So what makes us think we can escape if we ignore this great Salvation that was first announced by the Lord Jesus himself and then delivered to us by those who heard him speak? And God confirmed the message by giving signs and wonders and various miracles and gifts of the Holy Spirit whenever he chose."*
>
> (Hebrews 2: 1 -4. NLT)

Jesus does not want you to throw away your life. Why are you toying with it?

Jesus Is The Only Route To Salvation

Since creation, man has sought fellowship and relationship with his Creator. Though Adam, with his exit from the Garden of Eden, lost what could be the ideal state of friendship that man can have with God, further evidence in his life shows that he never saw himself as being completely independent of God. He continued to ascribe many special blessings one after the other to God Almighty. As the years went by, man continued to search for God to build a relationship with Him. He identified various means or vehicles as he sought to draw closer to his Creator. Even today, as science takes over the world, there is a drive for understanding and knowledge of spiritual things that bother on man's desire to fill a gap in his life. Today there are over 20 religious groups all over the world. Man is in dire need of a soul medication that he needs to thrive.

> *"God, for whom and through whom everything was made, chose to bring many children into glory. And it was only right that he should make Jesus, through his suffering, a perfect leader, fit to bring them into their Salvation."*

(Hebrews 2:10. NLT)

Jesus is the ideal leader for you. Why are you looking for redemption where there is none?

Jesus Offers You Freedom

The difference between a Christian and a non-Christian is that a Christian has forsaken his sins and clung to the righteousness of Jesus to take him over to the other "side" while the other person still lives in sin. The other side, in this case, is a place of quiet rest where all who have lived a life prescribed by Jesus will receive the Crown that never fades. One other distinction is that as Christians – please note I did not say true Christians because there is nothing like that; there is no condemnation for us whatsoever because of our relationship with Christ. We do not fear death because of the victory that Jesus has won over death and the assurance that this victory is available to us too. Christ died for our sins, was buried, and He rose from the dead on the third day. He rose as the first of the great harvest; then all who belong to Christ will be resurrected when He returns. The freedom we have through Him is the absence of death fear, which comes to those who have this hope of resurrection.

> *"Because God's children are human beings — made of flesh and blood — the Son also became flesh and blood. For only as a human being could he die, and only by dying could he break the power of the devil, who had the power of death. Only in this way could he set free all who have lived their lives as slaves to the fear of dying."*
>
> (Hebrews 2:14 – 15. NLT)

This freedom of Christ is available to all who come to receive it. Why are you holding back?

Jesus Must Not Be Ignored

The whole purpose of life in time is to gain merit for eternity. Jesus has preached this message along with the apostles and other messengers of the Gospel for over 2000 years. In His time, Jesus spoke in a manner suggesting that His coming is close - is at hand. Today after 20 centuries, we are still being told that Jesus is coming soon. It is natural for the heart to grow weary when there is a delay in reaching the desired point, and even the Bible agrees with this, but the same Bible talks about watching and praying so that we are not caught unawares like the foolish virgins. Enough evidence abounds today, confirming the soon return of Jesus. Therefore since after death, there is no recourse to any matter; today, then is the time to accept

Jesus. To ignore the Saviour of the world will amount to playing poker with your most valuable treasure – your soul.

> *"And so, dear brothers and sisters who belong to God and are partners with those called to heaven, think carefully about this Jesus whom we declare to be God's messenger and High Priest. For he was faithful to God, who appointed him, just as Moses served faithfully when he was entrusted with God's entire house. But Jesus deserves far more glory than Moses, just as a person who builds a house deserves more praise than the house itself. For every house has a builder, but the one who built everything is God. Moses was certainly faithful in God's house as a servant. His work was an illustration of the truths God would reveal later. But Christ, as the Son, is in charge of God's entire house. And we are God's house if we keep our courage and remain confident in our hope in Christ."*
>
> *(Hebrews 3: 1 –6.NLT)*

Jesus is God's messenger and High Priest; why do you keep ignoring him?

Jesus Appeals To You

Today is the day of Salvation; tomorrow may be too late is a typical end of sermon phrase used by ministers of the Gospel. They make appeals to you as God's ambassadors to become reconciled to Him. They do so not for their interest but so that the unsaved listener may evade eternal condemnation if he repents and accepts Jesus as Lord. I learned of the story of a young man during one of the

Hour of Divine Mercy programmes. He was persuaded by his mother to attend a crusade. The mother loved him so much and knew that his soul was heading for destruction. She offered a monetary incentive for his attendance and gave notice to the preacher about the decay in her son's life. The preacher prayerfully prepared for the sermon and delivered a powerful message focusing on redemption. After several alter calls lasting more than usual, the young man still did not take the step forward. He left the programme before completion and died in an automobile accident on his way home. He, therefore, lost the opportunity of his Salvation.

> *"That is why the Holy Spirit says, "Today when you hear his voice, don't harden your hearts as Israel did when they rebelled when they tested me in the wilderness. There your ancestors tested and tried my patience, even though they saw my miracles for forty years. So I was angry with them, and I said, 'Their hearts always turn away from me. They refuse to do what I tell them.' So in my anger, I took an oath: They will never enter my place of rest."*
>
> *(Hebrews 3: 7 – 11. NLT)*

The catchphrase tomorrow may be too late is a reality, whether we like it or not. It is something that all who want to enter God's place of rest must take seriously. Are you taking it seriously?

Jesus Appeals To You a Second Time

Commercial properties are built in the world to earn income. I am yet to find a landlord who is unbothered when his house remains uninhabited. Jesus is like anyone of these landlords, though having much bigger estates in the New Jerusalem. These are estates that He has built hoping that you and I will inhabit the houses therein. He told us when He was here physically that He is going to prepare a place for us with the sole purpose that we can be with Him in the life hereafter. The only caveat is that ONE SINGLE UNCLEAN THING CANNOT FIND ITS WAY INTO THAT ESTATE. Most servants of God making appeals for the lost almost always sound like a broken record to those who are spiritually undiscerning. They are concerned that as the clock ticks away, so many of the mansions built by Jesus remain empty and looking like they will be unoccupied.

> *"Be careful then, dear brothers and sisters. Make sure that your own hearts are not evil and unbelieving, turning you away from the living God. You must warn each other every day, while it is still "today," so that none of you will be deceived by sin and hardened against God. For if we are faithful to the end, trusting God just as firmly as when we first believed, we will share in all that belongs to Christ. Remember what it says: "Today when you hear his voice, don't harden your hearts as Israel did when they rebelled."'*

> (Hebrews 3:12 -15.NLT)

There is a key to one of these mansions available just for you. Will you respond to Jesus' appeal this second time?

Jesus' Promise Is Not For All

The hope of eternal life is not for all, as painful as it may sound, and this is irrespective of the fact that God is LOVE.

The reality is that God has His standards that cannot be compromised under any circumstance. God hates sin and all forms of uncleanliness. He is LIGHT, and no darkness can come near Him and remain – it will be extinguished. The Bible teaches us to follow only the Narrow Way, which leads to eternal life and not the broad, all-comers' road that leads to death. For you to gain access to one of the houses in the New Jerusalem estate, you must pay for the title deed. Payment is with the quality of life you live here on earth. You cannot gain access to it in any other way. His standard is clear for all to see, and there is no partiality. The way we make choices in our secular lives is the way we must make decisions, too, in our spiritual lives. A life that honours God is rewarded with entering His rest, while one that dishonours Him is punished with eternal damnation. The choice, as they say, is always ours to make; please make a WISE decision.

> *"God's promise of entering his rest still stands, so we ought to tremble with fear that some of you might fail to experience it. For this good news — that God has prepared this rest — has been announced to us just as it was to them. But it did them no good because they didn't share the faith of those who listened to God. For only we who believe can enter his rest. As for the others, God said, "In my anger, I took an oath: 'They will never enter my place of rest,'" even though this rest has been ready since he made the world. So God's rest is there for people to enter, but those who first heard this good news failed to enter because they disobeyed God. So God set another time for entering his rest, and that time is today.*

God announced this through David much later in the words already quoted: "Today, when you hear his voice, don't harden your hearts."'

(Hebrews 4: 1- 3, 6 – 7.NLT)

Jesus Sees Into Your Closet

The songwriter who composed the song – "You can never hide it from God, you can never hide it from God, you may cover your sins that no one else could know, you can never hide it from God," was speaking the reality of God's omnipresence. Today, hypocrisy is so much the order of the day that not many Christian leaders can ask to be emulated like Apostle Paul. I once heard a shocking story of a pastor who travelled to South Africa with a colleague at work. Upon arrival, the pastor was making advances at every woman they came across in the course of their engagements. The astonished and baffled colleague called the pastor to order but surprisingly got the shock of his life; the Pastor told his colleague in clear terms that he left his pastoral status at the departure hall of the Murtala Mohammed International Airport in Lagos. According to him, he is free to do anything he chooses while in another man's country. The truth is that our dear pastor's life mimics that of several people in the world today. But is the Almighty fooled? No, never! God sees what we do even in our closets, and as such, we are inescapable to His judgement of truth.

"For the word of God is alive and powerful. It is sharper than the sharpest two-edged sword, cutting between soul and spirit, between joint

and marrow. It exposes our innermost thoughts and desires. Nothing in all creation is hidden from God. Everything is naked and exposed before his eyes, and he is the one to whom we are accountable."

(Hebrews 4: 12 -13. NLT)

All that you have done in secret will one day be revealed at the judgement throne of God. Why don't you come clean with your Creator?

Jesus Is The Chosen One of God

In a world where man seeks for perfection or the perfect solution, it is not out of place for spiritual matters to come under in-depth scrutiny. As man attempts to find and know his Creator more, he continues to look for a mediator who will help him forge a closer tie with God. The elusive search for this mediator went on until God decided to put together a perfect plan. That perfect plan unfolded with the birth of Jesus Christ in a little town called Bethlehem. Jesus completed that plan on the Cross of Calvary by offering Himself as a ransom for our souls. He finished the work of Salvation, and on the third day, He rose again. There is no other one chosen by God to carry out this mediation assignment, and there is no other sacrifice acceptable to God than that offered by Jesus on the Cross of Calvary.

"And no one can become a high priest simply because he wants such an honour. He must be called by God for this work, just as Aaron was. That is why Christ did not honour himself by

assuming he could become High Priest. No, he was chosen by God, who said to him, "You are my Son. Today I have become your Father."

(Hebrews 5: 4 – 5. NLT)

"Even though Jesus was God's Son, he learned obedience from the things he suffered. In this way, God qualified him as a perfect High Priest, and he became the source of eternal Salvation for all those who obey him. And God designated him to be a High Priest in the order of Melchizedek."

(Hebrews 5:8 – 10.NLT)

The work of Salvation has been completed freely for you. Why are you not taking advantage of it?

Jesus Warns You Not To Look Back

One of the most popular stories of looking back with its attendant consequence was that of Lot's wife. Though not named in the Bible, her life's report represents an excellent example of the result of disobedience. The chief purpose of Christ's coming is that you and I can come to the saving knowledge of the truth. It is essential to know that once we reach this stage of new birth, we must remain there till the end of our race. We must be mindful of the fact that the forces that wage war against us will not want us to persevere to the end. The good news is that the One who has called us into His service is ready to see us to the very end. Our resolve must be not to look back AGAIN by giving the devil a foothold in our lives.

"For it is impossible to bring back to repentance those who were once enlightened—those who have experienced the good things of heaven and shared in the Holy Spirit, who have tasted the

goodness of the word of God and the power of the age to come— and who then turn away from God. It is impossible to bring such people back to repentance; by rejecting the Son of God, they themselves are nailing him to the cross once again and holding him up to public shame."

(Hebrews 6: 4 – 6.NLT)

Since you have received this extraordinary gift, why are you letting down your guard to allow the devil to steal your birthright?

Jesus Has a Good Plan For You

The Prophet Jeremiah spoke about God's plan to give His children a future and a hope. Jesus offered His disciples a better lot when He promised them mansions above. The worrying thing about humans is that because of the reason of delay; we are quick to forget that God honours His Word more than His name and that heaven and earth may pass away, but not a single word uttered by God will fail to come to pass or accomplish its purpose. God also promised to bless Abraham and multiply his descendants beyond his imagination. Even though it was past the time of childbearing for his wife, God still delivered on His promise. The deliverance of the Israelites from Egypt is another proof that God has a plan for His children and that He keeps His words.

"So God has given both his promise and his oath. These two things are unchangeable because it is impossible for God to lie. Therefore, we who have fled to him for refuge can have great confidence as

> *we hold to the hope that lies before us. This hope is a strong and trustworthy anchor for our souls. It leads us through the curtain into God's inner sanctuary."*

(Hebrews 6: 18 – 19.NLT)

Jesus has said to you that He is coming back to take you home. Why don't you trust Him to do as He says He will?

Jesus Is Sufficient For You

The life of a man is transient. Sometimes I try to review my own experience concerning how time has flown. A few years ago, I was in the university getting a degree, not too long after that; marriage came, then children. I still remember the day of my older daughter's dedication; it was like yesterday. Today the same baby is doing her national service. At my work life, the time has also flown with the speed of light. The same way, the day of the most significant reckoning will come and quickly too. The matter to consider is after this life, what next? Does it all end here? Most humans believe that our sojourn here on earth is temporary and that we shall someday give an account of our stewardship. Most people also believe that God will judge humanity to separate those who have done good from the bad – the sheep from the goats, as the Bible puts it. Some believe in prophets and what they can do or achieve on their own to please God. The truth is that man cannot do enough by himself to please God or meet God's expectation. Jesus offers the only route to God premised on the fact that man is inherently unable to lead a righteous life without help. God provided this best help – His

Son, because of the limitations in the old plan of redemption, which was "weak and useless"(Hebrews 7:18). This Jesus plan is the only available route to live a life acceptable to God and which will lead to eternal life. To pursue another option, especially one based on adherence to the law is a gateway to destruction.

> *"So if the priesthood of Levi, on which the law was based, could have achieved the perfection God intended, why did God need to establish a different priesthood, with a priest in the order of Melchizedek instead of the order of Levi and Aaron? And if the priesthood is changed, the law must also be changed to permit it. For the priest, we are talking about belongs to a different tribe, whose members have never served at the altar as priests. What I mean is, our Lord came from the tribe of Judah, and Moses never mentioned priests coming from that tribe. This change has been made very clear since a different priest, who is like Melchizedek, has appeared. Jesus became a priest, not by meeting the physical requirement of belonging to the tribe of Levi, but by the power of a life that cannot be destroyed. And the psalmist pointed this out when he prophesied, "You are a priest forever in the order of Melchizedek." Yes, the old requirement about the priesthood was set aside because it was weak and useless. For the law never made anything perfect. But now we have confidence in a better hope, through which we draw near to God. This new system was established with a solemn oath. Aaron's descendants became priests without such an oath, but there was an oath regarding Jesus. For God said to him, "The Lord has taken an oath and will*

not break his vow: 'You are a priest forever.'"
Because of this oath, Jesus is the one who guar-
antees this better covenant with God. There were
many priests under the old system, for death pre-
vented them from remaining in office. But because
Jesus lives forever, his priesthood lasts forever.
Therefore he is able, once and forever, to save
those who come to God through him. He lives for-
ever to intercede with God on their behalf. He is
the kind of high priest we need because he is holy
and blameless, unstained by sin. He has been set
apart from sinners and has been given the highest
place of honour in heaven. Unlike those other
high priests, he does not need to offer sacrifices
every day. They did this for their own sins first
and then for the sins of the people. But Jesus did
this once for all when he offered himself as the
sacrifice for the people's sins. The law appointed
high priests who were limited by human weak-
ness. But after the law was given, God appointed
his Son with an oath, and his Son has been made
the perfect High Priest forever."

(Hebrews 7:11 – 28. NLT)

Jesus is sufficient for you. What else are you looking for?

Jesus Offers You a New Covenant

The gift of Salvation offered to humanity by God is available in only Jesus. He paid the full price for our redemption, so the ball is no longer in His court. Again we must note that the offer of Jesus came because of the inadequacy that God saw in His old arrangement – man still maintained a gap between himself and his Creator. God gave us a perfect sacrifice in Christ who left His glory above and offered His blood – in place of the blood of goats and calves as a ransom for you and me. The choice you have to make is whether to receive or reject Him. It is a free choice that God allows you to make, but not without its consequences. Elvina M Hall in 1865 was inspired by God to remind us about the full and comprehensive sacrifice of Jesus on the Cross in her song – Jesus Paid it all. Jesus has paid a full price for our Salvation, and yet some people are willing to throw away such an exceptional gift not available elsewhere. What folly if you miss this offer?

"So Christ has now become the High Priest over all the good things that have come. He has entered that greater, more perfect Tabernacle in heaven, which was not made by human hands and is not part of this created world. With his own blood— not the blood of goats and calves—he entered the Most Holy Place once for all time and secured our redemption forever. Under the old system, the blood of goats and bulls and the ashes of a heifer could cleanse people's bodies from ceremonial impurity. Just think how much more the blood of Christ will purify our consciences from sinful deeds so that we can worship the living God. For by the power of the eternal Spirit, Christ offered himself to God as a perfect sacrifice for our sins. That is why he is the one who mediates a new covenant between God and people; so that all who are called can receive the eternal inheritance God has promised them. For Christ died to set them free from the penalty of the sins they had committed under that first covenant."

(Hebrews 9:11-15. NLT)

If indeed Jesus has paid it all and we know this to be true, why are you still pursuing righteousness based on the law which cannot help you?

Jesus Indeed Paid It All For You

Again I must not fail to warn you that there is no other alternative to Jesus. You can search from now till kingdom come, Jesus has no substitute. If you accept Him, good for you; if you reject Him, it does not change Him. It is indisputable that man lacks something that only God can provide, and he continues to search after God's heart. Those who know the truth, embrace Jesus, and they find peace in close fellowship with God. Some others keep groping in the dark and, unfortunately, die still seeking the truth. God's perfect plan is already available to you through Christ, and I plead with you not to ignore it. I am also a living testimony of someone who finally accepted this gift, albeit after a long delay and procrastination. It was not easy at first because the devil wanted to destroy my life, but thank God because the whole essence of the Cross is mercy available to all who come to the Saviour - Jesus. Just like the thief on the right side of the Cross who out of compassion received Salvation, you too can get yours today. Life without Jesus is meaningless and heading nowhere. I can assure you that when you have finished enjoying your life, judgement will come. What then will be your fate if you have rejected God and His Son, who paid for your Salvation?

"Then he said, "Look, I have come to do your will." He cancels the first covenant in order to put the second into effect. For God's will was for us to be made holy by the sacrifice of the body of Jesus Christ, once for all time. Under the old covenant, the priest stands and ministers before the altar day after day, offering the same sacrifices again and again, which can never take away sins. But our High Priest offered himself to God as a single sacrifice for sins, good for all time. Then he sat down in the place of honour at God's right hand. There he waits until his enemies are humbled and made a footstool under his feet. For by that one offering he forever made perfect those who are being made holy. And the Holy Spirit also testifies that this is so. For he says, "This is the new covenant I will make with my people on that day, says the Lord: I will put my laws in their hearts, and I will write them on their minds." Then he says, "I will never again remember their sins and lawless deeds." And when sins have been forgiven, there is no need to offer any more sacrifices."
(Hebrews 10: 9 – 18. NLT)

Jesus' offer of a once and for all sacrifice is for you. You must take advantage of it TODAY!

Jesus Offers You Freedom From Old Guilt

One of the problems with the old covenant apart from its inadequacy is that it does not provide you freedom from old sin. Since all Christians have a past, filled with sin, there is a tendency sometimes to feel guilty about it. You have the assurance of forgiveness and justification in the new covenant, and so you must believe it – provided you utterly forsake your sins. On the contrary, the old covenant prescribes for continuous sacrifice – year after year, and they are never able to provide perfect cleansing for those who came to worship. Freedom from old guilt is a unique benefit available to all who accept Jesus into their lives. Even when the liar (devil) reminds you of your sinful past, you must quickly and continuously tell him that Jesus has paid for it all.

> *"And since we have a great High Priest who rules over God's house, let us go right into the presence of God with sincere hearts fully trusting him. For our guilty consciences have been sprinkled with Christ's blood to make us clean, and our bodies have been washed with pure water. Let us hold tightly without wavering to the hope we affirm, for God can be trusted to keep his promise. Let us think of ways to motivate one another to acts of love and good works. And let us not neglect our meeting together, as some people do, but encourage one another, especially now that the day of his return is drawing near."*

> (Hebrews 10: 21 – 25. NLT)

Jesus Requires You To Stop Sinning

The new covenant that God offers you through Christ requires you to accept Jesus as your personal Lord and Saviour. This requirement means that you completely turnaround from the way you were living before that point and face a new direction under the leadership of Christ. The old must go away, and the new must begin. The new is a life of holiness prescribed by Christ for all His followers. The prescription is a never-changing standard of God's expectation for all humanity right from creation. He never wavers in this position and does not care whose ox is gored when applying sanctions to all who fail to keep in line. Today, man has manufactured all kinds of variants of godly living that one begins to wonder if there is more than one God. God cannot be mocked and is unchanging in His ways. It is you and I who must accept Him or go our separate ways from Him. Holiness and Christian living gladden God more than anything – I believe even more than praise. When the Bible says God inhabits the praise of his people, I am sure here we are talking about His obedient people and not just anyone. After all, what makes us God's people is the relationship we have with Him through obedience to His words – obedience they say is better than sacrifice. There is no easy way to God; there is only ONE WAY. Do not be deceived so that on the last day, weeping and gnashing of teeth will not be your portion. "And the door was shut "(Matthew 25:10) is what the Bible told us in the parable of the ten virgins; again, the Bible provides a predetermined response to those living in sin on the last day – "depart from me you workers of iniquity; I know you not"(Matthew 7:23).

"Dear friends, if we deliberately continue sinning after we have received knowledge of the truth, there is no longer any sacrifice that will cover these sins. There is only the terrible expectation of God's judgment and the raging fire that will consume his enemies. For anyone who refused to obey the Law of Moses was put to death without

mercy on the testimony of two or three witnesses. Just think how much worse the punishment will be for those who have trampled on the Son of God, and have treated the blood of the covenant, which made us holy, as if it were common and unholy, and have insulted and disdained the Holy Spirit who brings God's mercy to us. For we know the one who said, "I will take revenge. I will pay them back. "He also said, "The Lord will judge his own people." It is a terrible thing to fall into the hands of the living God."

(Hebrews 10: 26 – 31. NLT)

Today you are hearing the voice of God. Why not harken to him?

Jesus Is Coming Soon

This subject is arguably the most treated with levity, disdain, or made a mockery of the most. This promise of Jesus is already over 2000 years old. Though the Bible says delay makes the heart grow weary, we must not allow this to be our case concerning this subject. For one thing, we have been made sure of the soon arrival of Jesus by the many happenings that He predicted will take place before His return; many have come to pass, and more are being so. Even with all these happenings, the question is whether we can trust Jesus. We can choose to say to ourselves that these happenings that Jesus predicted are mere coincidences, and there is no link to His return or even that there is no planned return at all. Jesus told us in advance about His going to the Cross to die, and on the third day, He will be raised back to life. Even though some of the disciples did not believe it and asked for proof, Jesus died and rose as He promised. Many can doubt Jesus as same was the case during His time, but this does not change anything. The Word of God is yea and amen. Jesus is coming back again. He is coming soon as He has promised; He has gone to prepare a place for His friends. The preparatory period for the arrival of Jesus for every individual on this earth ends when he or she breathes their last – you must be prepared for this to avoid the consequence of His meeting you unprepared.

> *"So do not throw away this confident trust in the Lord. Remember the great reward it brings you! Patient endurance is what you need now so that you will continue to do God's will. Then you will receive all that he has promised. "For in just a little while, the Coming One will come and not delay. And my righteous ones will live by faith. But I will take no pleasure in anyone who turns away. "But we are not like those who turn away from God to their own destruction. We are the faithful ones, whose souls will be saved."*

(Hebrews 10: 35 – 39.NLT)

Don't give up. Jesus is coming soon to take you home someday.

Jesus Demands That You Put Your Faith In Him

The life offered to you is one based on faith. It originates in faith, continues to work in faith, and ends up in faith. Jesus is the epitome of this faith in the sense that He showed complete trust in His Father by leaving His throne in heaven to actualise His Father's project. This faith in God required that He left His Spirit in His Father's hand as He gave up His life on the Cross of Calvary for you and me. It is a life you have to live trusting Jesus to lead you safely on. It believes in the all-sufficiency of Jesus and has absolute trust in Him. This life is one in which you lean entirely on the Master because your righteousness is like filthy rags. In this experience – if you allow it, Jesus takes you literarily on His wings and carries you through life's journey. It requires you to humble yourself in a close walk with Him and look up to Him all the time. He is your strength from day to day without Him; you will fail. He demands that you trust Him and never lean on your understanding. That way, you will never fail, and you will see God.

> *"It was by faith that Abraham obeyed when God called him to leave home and go to another land that God would give him as his inheritance. He went without knowing where he was going. And even when he reached the land God promised him, he lived there by faith—for he was like a foreigner, living in tents. And so did Isaac and Jacob, who inherited the same promise. Abraham was confidently looking forward to a city with eternal foundations, a city designed and built by God. It was by faith that even Sarah was able to have a child, though she was barren and was too old. She believed that God would keep his promise. And so a whole nation came from this one man who was as good as dead—a nation with so many people that, like the stars in the sky and the sand on the seashore, there is no way to count*

them. All these people died still believing what God had promised them. They did not receive what was promised, but they saw it all from a distance and welcomed it. They agreed that they were foreigners and nomads here on earth. Obviously, people who say such things are looking forward to a country they can call their own. If they had longed for the country they came from, they could have gone back. But they were looking for a better place, a heavenly homeland. That is why God is not ashamed to be called their God, for he has prepared a city for them."

(Hebrews 11: 8 -16. NLT)

Are you desirous of living in the New Jerusalem? You must first believe it and then pursue it.

Jesus Must Be Your Only Focus

Some years ago, I delved into the background of a wealthy Nigerian who is now late. As a young man, he was privileged to have travelled abroad for studies, but while there, he used part of his school fees to invest in real estate, slaving, and sacrificing all the way. He was driven by the principle of delayed gratification and so focused on his goal to acquire wealth, and ultimately he made it. In his story, he had to avoid certain pitfalls that could have derailed him and make him miss his target. In a Christian's life, the focus is also on a future goal that is attainable only when "we strip off every weight"(Hebrews 12:1), and certain pitfalls are avoided. It is the ultimate in delayed gratification. For you to reach your heavenly goal, you must run away from sin and discipline yourself in the race you have chosen, making Jesus your ONLY FOCUS.

"Therefore, since we are surrounded by such a huge crowd of witnesses to the life of faith, let us strip off every weight that slows us down, especially the sin that so easily trips us up. And let us run with endurance the race God has set before us. We do this by keeping our eyes on Jesus, the champion who initiates and perfects our faith. Because of the joy awaiting him, he endured the cross, disregarding its shame. Now he is seated in the place of honour beside God's throne. Think of all the hostility he endured from sinful people; then you won't become weary and give up. After all, you have not yet given your lives in your struggle against sin."

(Hebrews 12: 1- 4. NLT)

If Jesus could give His life for the goal of saving you, why can't you avoid sin and discipline yourself to receive your crown from Him?

Jesus Demands Holiness From You

Apostle Paul describes the message of the Cross as foolishness to those who are perishing! But we who are saved know it as the power of God. The truth about Christian living is that without holiness, it is impossible to see God. Any other counsel is an absolute falsehood. Several versions of Christian living exists today, but only the one which prescribes holiness as a corner piece of the Christian life is acceptable to God. Man has proffered many variants of so-called acceptable teachings, all amounting to heresy in the sight of God. God being no respecter of persons, continues to laugh at man's attempt to create different versions of His message. The church, as is constituted today in the world, continues to pursue a crowd generating agenda to make rich. Fortunately, God is not mocked; His ways are not our ways. We must conform, or He spits us out of His mouth; the choice is ours always to make.

"Work at living in peace with everyone, and work at living a holy life, for those who are not holy will not see the Lord.
(Hebrews 12: 14. NLT)

Will God change His standard to accommodate anyone? No, never; He will not.

Jesus Warns You To Listen To Him

I want to thank God that you have the privilege of reading this book. It is a privilege that is not available to all. You must, therefore, seize the opportunity if your life is not right with Christ. It may also be possible that you have previously given your life to Christ but have found yourself backslidden with one or more parts of this book addressing an area of your life. One thing is obvious – while our God is love, He also is a consuming fire. The Bible is clear that God does not want anyone to perish but only to come to the saving knowledge of the truth. That opportunity to be saved is available to you now because you are reading this book. All you need to do is to confess your sins, ask for forgiveness, and invite Jesus into your life. The Bible says all have sinned and went ahead to remind us that the wages of sin is death. The same Bible says that if we forsake our sins and come to Him (Jesus), He will never cast us away. All you need to do is to retire to a quiet place and take the steps above, and His Spirit will renew your life; after that, you must join up with a Bible-believing church to begin your growth. I must warn that this invitation to you is not available forever, and it comes with a consequence when rejected.

> *"Be careful that you do not refuse to listen to the One who is speaking. For if the people of Israel did not escape when they refused to listen to Moses, the earthly messenger, we will certainly not escape if we reject the One who speaks to us from heaven! When God spoke from Mount Sinai, his voice shook the earth, but now he makes another promise: "Once again I will shake not only the earth but the heavens also." This means that all of creation will be shaken and removed so that only unshakable things will remain."*

> *(Hebrews 12: 25 – 27. NLT)*

God's plan is for you to be saved. Please do not turn your back on Him.

Jesus Is The Solid Rock

The Solid Rock we are talking about is the One that can resist the storm because it will surely come. This Rock is Jesus and is available to those who not only hear the words but also do them. He promises that no amount of storm will overwhelm them. I want you to genuinely reflect over and over again, on the contents of this book. It has reached you by the Grace of God and through the leading of the Holy Spirit. I offer you JESUS THE SOLID ROCK as the foundation for your life here and hereafter. There is nothing good you can make out of life without this Rock. If you allow Him, He will build for you a mansion in the New City of God. My dearest friend, Jesus, is coming this way towards you today. Will you this moment receive Him? I plead with you to remember this short line all the days of your life;

> *"For this world is not our permanent home; we are looking forward to a home yet to come."*
>
> *(Hebrews 13:14.NLT)*

I present Jesus to you today as every other ground is sinking sand. My prayer for you is that you will know Him and the power of His resurrection, amen.

Divine Mercy

The gospel of Jesus Christ brings you a second chance. Jesus offers us the opportunity to start anew - clean and fresh. No matter how badly we've blown it, no matter how many times we've failed, we can start all over. Today is the day for a fresh start. Get back in the game! The second half has just begun.[1]

One of the most influential and insightful songs that shows the divine mercy of God was by Elvina Mable Reynolds Hall and is entitled "Jesus Paid it all." Mrs Hall was born in Alexandria, Virginia, on the 4th day of June 1822. She was the daughter of Captain David Reynolds. Elvina married Richard Hall of Westmoreland County, Virginia, and, after his death, Thomas Meyers, a Methodist minister of the Baltimore, Mary-land conference. She attended the Monument Street Methodist Church in Baltimore for four decades. She died on the 18th of July, 1889 in New Jersey.[2]

Going through the lyrics of the song written close to 150 years ago, one cannot fail to be inspired by the words. Even as I listen to the piano tune of the music playing on my laptop, I cannot but appreciate Jesus so much. Elvina was inspired to write this song from the Word of God as revealed to the Prophet Isaiah, the Apostle Peter and John the beloved.

"'Come now, let's settle this," says the LORD. "Though your sins are like scarlet, I will make them as white as snow. Though they are red like crimson, I will make them as white as wool."

(Isaiah 1:18 NLT)

"For you know that God paid a ransom to save you from the empty life you inherited from your ancestors. And it was not paid with mere gold or silver, which lose their value. It was the precious blood of Christ, the sinless, spotless Lamb of God."

(1 Peter 1:18 -19 NLT)

"And from Jesus Christ. He is the faithful witness to these things, the first to rise from the dead, and the ruler of all the kings of the world. All glory to him who loves us and has freed us from our sins by shedding his blood for us. He has made us a Kingdom of priests for God his Father. All glory and power to him forever and ever! Amen."

(Revelation 1:5 -6 NLT)

Although Mrs Hall was credited with few songs when compared to the very popular, more talented and much inspired Fanny Crosby, I believe this song touched the lives of so many and led them to a return to God. God is again speaking to you and me today through this excellent song, and if only we would carefully examine our lives and make a U-turn away from sin, it will be well with us. Jesus knocks on the door of your heart even today as you read this book; He wants you to appreciate His sacrifice and turn to Him for good. Jesus paid it all, so we do not owe anyone our Salvation. All we need to do is to come to

Him, and He will welcome us with open arms. He alone can do the perfect job of washing us clean even though we may think it impossible because of the depth of our despair.

> *"The next day John saw Jesus coming toward him and said, "Look! The Lamb of God who takes away the sin of the world!"*
>
> (John 1:29 NLT)

Jesus is available to you for free; He has paid it all. Hall saw man the way he has become after throwing away his birthright in the Garden of Eden. Man no longer has the strength to help himself; he is weak and helpless, needing someone to take the load off his shoulders. By paying the full ransom for our sins, Jesus offers us an escape route from destruction - if only we will find in Him our all in all. She saw that in man there is nothing good if he stands by himself without recourse to Christ whose blood it is that can wash away our sins.

Crimson, which is used to describe the colour of sin in our lives, is an intense, deep red colour, inclining to purple.[3] It originally meant the shade of the Kermes dye produced from a scale insect, Kermes vermilion but the title now refers to a generic term for slightly reddish-blue tones that are between red and rose.[4] It certainly can not be easy to achieve a conversion of this colour to white like snow. This change is a reflection of what Jesus brings to bear in the lives of those who accept Him. Although a leopard can't change its spots, God promises us that we can overcome all our weaknesses with the help of Jesus.

He alone can rescue and save us. His awesome power can melt a heart of stone according to the inspiration received by Elvina.

"This means that anyone who belongs to Christ has become a new person. The old life is gone; a new life has begun!"
(2 Corinthians 5:20 NLT)

"And I will give you a new heart, and I will put a new spirit in you. I will take out your stony, stubborn heart and give you a tender, responsive heart."
(Ezekiel 36:26 NLT)

The reality is that without Jesus, you cannot make anything useful out of your life. You may end up inheriting the whole world, but when Christ returns, you will have nothing to show for the talents He had left with you. You cannot have access to God's Grace freely given if you do not come to Jesus in submission. He alone can save you from the eternal condemnation that awaits all who ignore His offer of Salvation. The blood of Jesus, which pours out of Calvary's tree, will wash your garments clean. Jesus died to save our souls, and it is only in accepting this truth that one can be made entirely whole. Be prepared to stand before His throne and give an account one day. Do not let God's words sent to you through this inspirational song be in vain in your life.

"The Lord isn't really being slow about his promise, as some people think. No, he is being patient for your sake. He does not want anyone to be destroyed, but wants everyone to repent."
(2 Peter 3:9 NLT)

The Yoruba language translations of the song Jesus Paid it all, is so powerful and revealing of the magnitude of the Jesus effort. It vividly describes the depth of His sacrifice to pay our debts. He suffered and died so that you can be free and by doing so, completed the work of redemption. I see in the unsaved, a wearied soul man, labouring aimlessly; aimlessly because Jesus has already provided that which he strives to accomplish. Why then are you travelling this long distance in search of emptiness? Just imagine yourself in a shopping mall staring at many unaffordable items on display. Someone unknown to you now invites you to go on a shopping spree on his or her credit card; I am sure most of us will shop till we drop. Jesus has paid for your Salvation "shopping spree" not with a credit card but with His blood. How fortunate you are to have access to this divine mercy!

> *"When Jesus had tasted it, he said, "It is finished!" Then he bowed his head and released his spirit."*
>
> (John 19:30 NLT)

One of the demonstrations of the divine mercy of God to humanity occurred many years ago near a city called Jericho. Jericho is a city close to the Jordan River in the West Bank. It is the administrative seat of the Jericho Governorate.[5] Jericho's name in Hebrew, Yeriho, is thought to derive from Canaanite word Reah ("fragrant"). However, an alternative theory holds that it is derived from the word meaning "moon" (Yareah) in Canaanite since the city was an ancient centre of worship for lunar deities. Jericho's

Arabic name, Hariha, means "fragrant" and derives from the same Canaanite word Reah, of the same meaning as in Hebrew.[6,7,8,9]

Matthew, Mark & Luke all tell of Jesus healing a blind man near Jericho, shortly before going to Jerusalem. The Mark story is about a particular Bartimaeus who met Jesus on the outskirts of Jericho, thereby taking advantage of His passing to receive his miracle. Matthew, on the other hand, gave an account of two blind men healed outside of Jericho but offered no names. Luke, however, tells of an unknown blind man but gave the impression that he met Jesus with Jericho just in sight.

These healings together would be the second of two miracles of blind men performed by Jesus on His journey from His travels starting in Bethsaida (in Mark 8:22 -26). It is very likely, though not sure that Bartimaeus heard about the first healing, and so knew of Jesus' reputation.

The divine mercy of God comes with certain preconditions before it can be accessible. The stories in the Bible about the people of Noah's days, Sodom & Gomorrah and Nineveh show very distinctly that even when the door of divine mercy is left open by God if we fail to act by going through the door, we cannot have access to God's gift. Amongst these three groups, only the people of Nineveh appreciated that God's open door of divine mercy is not left open indefinitely. They took the right decision and action to forsake their sins and turned back to God.

"The people of Nineveh believed God's message, and from the greatest to the least, they declared a fast and put on burlap to show their sorrow. When the king of Nineveh heard what Jonah was saying, he stepped down from his throne and took off his royal robes. He dressed himself in burlap and sat on a heap of ashes. Then the king and his nobles sent this decree throughout the city: "No one, not even the animals from your herds and flocks, may eat or drink anything at all. People and animals alike must wear garments of mourning, and everyone must pray earnestly to God. They must turn from their evil ways and stop all their violence. Who can tell? Perhaps even yet, God will change his mind and hold back his fierce anger from destroying us." When God saw what they had done and how they had put a stop to their evil ways, he changed his mind and did not carry out the destruction he had threatened."

(Jonah 3:5 -10 NLT)

Jesus is calling us to repentance today; we must seize the opportunity and not turn our backs on Him!

The name Bartimaeus is a hybrid word from Aramaic bar = "son," and Greek timaios = "honourable."[10] Though the Bible has referred merely to its meaning as the son of Timaeus, the import of his life's story is the divine mercy of God which is available ONLY THROUGH JESUS TO ALL WHO ACCEPT HIM. The lessons from the Bartimaeus encounter with Jesus find relevance in our lives today, and we must strive to take these to heart for us to gain the advantage of God's divine mercy.

Divine Mercy

The Crowd, The Distractions & The Shout

I have tried to imagine the scenario on that day as Bartimaeus found and went through the door of divine mercy. Jesus was available in the neighbourhood, but with so much distraction from a large crowd, Bartimaeus could have missed his opportunity. Even for an average person, a gathering which usually generates so much noise is a formidable obstacle to overcome. The Bible records that Bartimaeus began to shout to overcome the obstacle. Probably if he had shouted once, he would not be heard. To start to shout means that Bartimaeus continued to generate the noise level required to get the Master's attention. He pressed on with his effort to attract Jesus even when the crowd challenged him to keep quiet. The crowd represented an obstacle on his route to divine mercy - BUT BARTIMAEUS OVERCAME THAT OBSTACLE. Today many distractions stand between us and God's plan and purpose for our lives. For most people, instead of taking a cue from the experience of Bartimaeus, they easily succumb to destiny thieves and give up before they reach their destinations. God does not want you to fail. He wants you to come to the saving knowledge of the truth. Why are you at the slightest hindrance or discouragement giving up hope and accepting what is not God's plan for your life? Why can't you fight for what is right and take hold of God's plan for your life?

"For I know the plans I have for you," says the LORD. "They are plans for good and not for disaster, to give you a future and a hope."

(Jeremiah 29:11 NLT)

Be Quiet!

The experience of blind Bartimaeus shows the evil plan of the devil. Though there is no mention of the duration of his blindness, apparently he was in severe distress and discomfort. Ideally, he should find help from the people around him; unfortunately, those who should offer him support stood at the door of his divine mercy insisting that he cannot go in. This scenario also plays itself out in our daily lives, and for those who are discerning, they must take the Bartimaeus option, ensuring that they do not give up no matter the situation. There are many things that God does not do for man even though His love for us is unquestionable. We must sow before we can reap. We must ask in faith before we can receive. We must knock on the door before it can be open. We must seek before we can find.

During one of the most memorable Jesus encounters in the Bible - at the tomb of Lazarus, the Master insisted that the stone is rolled away by those present before asking Lazarus to come forth. Why did Jesus do this? Jesus was sending us a message that to access God's divine mercy, we too have a role to play. You must not allow anyone or anything to stand in your way, no matter the situation or circumstance. The statement "Be quiet!" yelled at Bartimaeus by the crowd of people as he cried for help is an attempt to prevent his access to God's divine mercy. Bartimaeus resisted and became an overcomer; you must do likewise!

"The thief's purpose is to steal and kill and destroy. My purpose is to give them a rich and satisfying life."

(John 10:10 NLT)

Jesus Answers

There is a confident assurance that if we call, Jesus will answer. In normal circumstances, a blind beggar's voice cannot be heard over and above the noise of a large crowd. In Bartimaeus case, the crowd wanted him to keep quiet. Is it the loud shout of Bartimaeus that attracted Jesus or the gentle whisper from his heart? If we take a cue from the story of the woman with the issue of blood, we can see that Jesus who at that time felt just a gentle touch on the hem of His garment, can hear the whisper of the blind man even when there is a significant shouting crowd. It does not matter if we shout to God or whisper to Him; He will undoubtedly hear us and answer too. The experience of the blind man also confirms that God does not delay His answer provided our need is according to His will for us, and there are no hindrances in our lives, preventing Him from doing so. Bartimaeus received an immediate response to his request because he trusted that if he called to Jesus for help, he would get it.

"And Jesus said to him, "Go, for your faith has healed you." Instantly the man could see, and he followed Jesus down the road."

(Mark 10:52 NLT)

Cheer Up!

A close examination of this portion of the story will reveal the complete confidence that the crowd had in Jesus. Do you have this confidence in the Saviour? As unruly as the group was, they were in no doubt that it was decisive that Jesus had now agreed to attend to the blind man. The phrase "Cheer up" is a confirmation of the fact that they knew even at this stage that there was a certainty of a positive outcome to the Bartimaeus encounter with Jesus. Jesus' call to many today also comes with the assurance of a positive result. However many unlike the blind man in our story do nothing about the call; they remain in their irrational state not caring that there is a place of quiet rest near to the heart of the Lord Jesus. Even though the onlookers of the Bartimaeus' days knew Jesus to be of divine origin, they were only interested in the spectacle of the occasion. Many of us today are like the Jericho crowd. We focus on what is not essential and miss out of the divine touch of Jesus, which is freely available to all who want to receive it. We get quickly excited and distracted about happenings around us without focusing on what is essential; which is giving our life to the Master.

> *"When Jesus heard him, he stopped and said, "Tell him to come here." So they called the blind man. "Cheer up," they said. "Come on, he's calling you!"'*
>
> *(Mark 10:49 NLT)*

The Coat Thrown Away

I wonder why a blind man and a beggar with little or no resources will throw away his coat; probably his only jacket, when Jesus called out to him. I do believe that there are many symbolic meanings of the Bartimaeus coat. It is, in this case, a hindrance; when we come to Jesus, He expects that we leave behind all impediments. There should be no baggage in our lives that will prevent us from walking close to the Master. Jesus reminds us in Matthew 6:24 that it is impossible to serve two masters at the same time. Many do not understand, or they fail to appreciate that we cannot deceive God. They claim to be committed to God in public but still carry around several other little "gods" in private. Bartimaeus knew that if he came to Jesus unhindered, he was sure to receive his gift.

"Therefore, since we are surrounded by such a huge crowd of witnesses to the life of faith, let us strip off every weight that slows us down, especially the sin that so easily trips us up. And let us run with endurance the race God has set before us."

(Hebrews 12:1NLT)

Again, by throwing away his coat, Bartimaeus shows that his desire to meet Jesus is worth more than any material thing. Jesus wants us to prioritise our decisions and actions by seeking first the kingdom of God and His righteousness - AND EVERY OTHER THING SHALL BE ADDED UNTO US. Bartimaeus showed great faith in the Lord. By throwing away his coat as he approached Jesus, he was letting go of everything in preference for the more significant promise that Jesus offered. Bartimaeus sends a clear message to those who believe that leaving the things of the world to serve God will make them more miserable. This assumption is not correct at all.

"And this same God who takes care of me, will supply all your needs from his glorious riches, which have been given to us in Christ Jesus."

(Philippians 4:19 NLT)

Be Decisive

Bartimaeus was decisive and prompt. By jumping at Jesus' offer, he showed that he was happy with his decision. He was willing and ready to come forward. Many of us have heard powerful divinely inspired messages for many years, but instead of taking the step forward to walk with God, we are still procrastinating and waiting for the "best time". I pray that this so-called best time would not meet us in the grave. Others take sad-looking steps forward; steps that encourage many not to follow God, thereby leading them to stay away. The Bartimaeus example was a complete opposite. Jesus called to him, and he answered IMMEDIATELY.

"As God's partners, we beg you not to accept this marvellous gift of God's kindness and then ignore it. For God says, "At just the right time, I heard you. On the day of Salvation, I helped you." Indeed, the "right time" is now. Today is the day of Salvation."

(2 Corinthians 6:1-2 NLT)

Anything Is Possible

Many so-called messengers of the Gospel are known to arrange their miracles. They do so because they have no relationship with the power giving Jesus of Nazareth. This

Jesus that we are offering to you has no limitations whatsoever. He was, He is and is to come. He is the Eternal
Light of God that shines and makes the darkness not to
comprehend it. When you allow Him to shine into your
life, all the night that is represented by sin and evil will
disappear. Right from creation, Jesus has been doing miracles and is still doing the same today. I listened to a sermon
recently, which revealed that the Israelites that crossed the
red sea were more than a million (Exodus 12:37), and God
fed them twice a day for 40 years. I also know of a woman
of over 50 years who gave birth after all hope seemed lost.
Many still call upon Jesus' name today and are saved.
Bartimaeus did not doubt in his mind that with God, all
things were possible; you could say that he asked for the
impossible at that time - BUT YET HE ASKED FOR IT IN
FAITH. Jesus was probably not known to him as having
opened the eyes of the blind, especially as in the earlier
healing of the man born blind, Jesus encouraged the recipient of divine mercy to keep his experience secret. It is this
type of faith that is asked of all today, the faith as small
as a mustard seed that can move mountains. No wonder
William H. Bathurst said in his song: "O for a faith that
will not shrink, though pressed by every foe that will not
tremble on the brink of any earthly woe"! It is this faith
that distinguishes the men from the boys!

*"Jesus looked at them intently and said, "Humanly
speaking, it is impossible. But with God, everything is possible."'*

(Matthew 19:26 NLT)

He Followed Jesus

There is no one living being today that has not received one miracle or the other from Jesus. All of us are beneficiaries of God's divine and unmerited favour, yet we still find it difficult to follow the example of Bartimaeus. The fact that we even came out of our mother's womb and are still alive to read this is a big miracle - especially if you are living in a third world country. Bartimaeus did not delay in deciding to move forward; following Jesus is akin to moving forward. Many today upon receipt of divine mercy, opt to go on sabbatical leave, hoping to return to God at their convenient time. Unfortunately, time waits for no one, and no one knows the hour or the time when he or she will be called to give an account of his or her stewardship. Although Bartimaeus received a special gift of healing from God before he decided to follow Jesus, this does not mean that all must await such experience before they can act in like manner. Paul followed Jesus to the end even though he had unanswered prayers in his life, relying instead on God's Grace which is sufficient for all (2 Corinthians 12: 8 – 10). We too must accept that following Jesus is not contingent on the receipt of any prior benefit.

The divine mercy of God is available ONLY through Christ Jesus. It may come like that which was made available to Bartimaeus or may occur in a higher form as a gift of Salvation which leads to eternal life. Either way, the intended recipient must act to receive it. Today, God is asking you to go through His door of divine mercy so that you can receive the gift of Salvation far more significant than the mere grant of physical sight given to Bartimaeus. Jesus wants to open your spiritual eyes so that you will know the Truth and be free.

> *"Then Jesus told this story: "A man planted a fig tree in his garden and came, again and again, to see if there was any fruit on it, but he was always disappointed. Finally, he said to his gardener, 'I've waited three years, and there hasn't been a single fig! Cut it down. It's just taking up space in the garden.' "The gardener answered, 'Sir, give it one more chance. Leave it another year, and I'll give it special attention and plenty of fertiliser. If we get figs next year, fine. If not, then you can cut it down.'"'*
>
> (Luke 13: 6 – 9 NLT)

I want to encourage you to embrace the Word of God given to you by Christ. The reason is that no matter what you make out of this life, it will all end in waste leading to death. I want to plead that you leave all your wasted efforts at gaining Salvation; leave it at the feet of Jesus. Stay in Him alone, in perfection and glory. The story of the fig tree is very apt. The extra year offered by the gardener is what you are already enjoying today; there may not be another year for you. If you are ready to bear fruits as desired by your Creator, then you MUST submit to Him. HE ALONE IS ABLE BECAUSE HE HAS PAID IT ALL.

He Is Coming Soon

"There is more than enough room in my Father's home. If this were not so, would I have told you that I am going to prepare a place for you? When everything is ready, I will come and get you, so that you will always be with me where I am."

(John 14: 2- 3 NLT)

The above promise made by Jesus of Nazareth is now more than 2000 years old. Many have taken this promise to be a fairy tale, thinking it will not come to pass. Some even make a mockery of Jesus; they say He is unable to keep His promise or He has taken too long a time to do so. I recall an encounter with a very successful Nigerian businessman. I was led to draw his attention to the emptiness of this world by giving him a book written by Gbile Akanni entitled - Living with Eternity in View. The man was then about 78 years old and was living a life that I thought was focused only on the here and not the here-after. He was a very lovely happy go, lucky older man, and there was never a dull moment with him. Although he politely asked me to give the book to his assistant, he later joked that he didn't know that I was a preacher and asked if I believed that Jesus was going to come back someday. He sarcastically wondered that if I was Jesus, would I be ready to go back when the last time I visited the earth, I was crucified by my people - the Jews. I was not surprised as I knew what to expect from him. The man has since gone to meet his Creator to give an account of his sojourn on this planet. Another prominent Nigerian leader and elder statesman recently said that at 80 years, he was in the departure lounge of the world and was waiting to board his flight to eternity. The truth is that not only the old are in this lounge. Once you are born, you are admitted and depending on the time on your "boarding pass"; you will leave someday sometime. The critical issue is not whether we are in the departure lounge or what time is on our boarding pass; it is whether we are ready for our flight. To be prepared for a typical trip, you must have checked in your luggage, and you must not have any prohibited item in your carry-on bags. Unlike the travel situation, where you will be told to meet the conditions before boarding your flight, with eternity when the flight is called, you must board whether you meet the criteria or not. The difference, however, is in the destination you go; either to eternal life or eternal condemnation; depending on what the Master finds in your life's luggage.

"Look, I am coming soon, bringing my reward with me to repay all people according to their deeds. I am the Alpha and the Omega, the First and the Last, the Beginning and the End."'

(Revelation 22:12 – 13 NLT)

Why should Jesus be believed? Someone who promised to do something, and it is now over 2000 years, and He has not done it. As a father, I know the import of making promises, especially to my children and sometimes my wife. It is almost always time-bound, and when there is a delay, doubt sets into their minds. Today many take the promise of Jesus' return as a myth, something that is not to be believed or taken seriously. Others, however, having received divine inspiration believe Jesus' coming to be an expected reality and take Him at His Word. The indefatigable songwriter Fanny J Crosby and the less so Leila Morris, another songwriter were two of many who were sure that Jesus would be faithful to His Word. Between them, they received inspiration to write over 9000 powerful songs that are still touching the lives of many people today. Leila spoke with assurance about His coming in power and love to reign. She saw that with the dominion of Satan being over, comes the disappearance of sorrow and sighing as Jesus returns to take His chosen bride. Though she claimed uncertainty of knowing His arrival time, Leila concluded that signs of His coming are multiplying every day. Fanny too said that the One who inspired her did not let her in on the time of Jesus' return. She was like her sister Leila very assured of Christ's coming again. She spoke about those Jesus will find watching when He comes; she called them blessed. Fanny & Leila had another thing in common. They both left this world after losing their physical eyes, but both retained their spiritual eyes to the end. They were able to see into the future and know that Jesus will keep His words. A clergyman once sympathetically remarked to Fanny, "I think it is a great pity that the Master did not give you sight when He showered so many other gifts upon you." She replied quickly, "Do you know that if at birth, I had been able to make one petition, it would have been that I should be born blind?" "Why?" asked the surprised clergyman. "Because when I get to heaven, the first face that shall ever gladden my sight will be that of my Saviour!"[1]

"After saying this, he was taken up into a cloud while they were watching, and they could no longer see him. As they strained to see him rising into heaven, two white-robed men suddenly stood among them. "Men of Galilee," they said, "why are you standing here staring into heaven? Jesus has been taken from you into heaven, but someday he will return from heaven in the same way you saw him go!"'

(Acts 1: 9 -11 NLT)

So, who is this Jesus? Before we can contemplate whether to believe Him or not, we at least must try to learn as much as we can about Him. Prophet Isaiah spoke about Jesus close to 700 years before His birth. God revealed to him the human impossibility of virgin birth and gave him the Saviour's name by revelation - IMMANUEL. Again God told the prophet that this child would be a Wonderful Counselor, Mighty God, Everlasting Father and Prince of Peace. His government and its peace will never end; He will rule for all eternity. Isaiah did not stop there; God said to him that this Prince would be despised and rejected. He will be pierced for our rebellion and crushed for our sins. He will also be beaten so we could be whole and whipped for us to be healed. The prophecy went ahead to say that God will lay on Him the sins of all. Isaiah saw in this vision that the coming Prince would be oppressed and treated harshly, He will be unjustly condemned and led away like a lamb to the slaughter; but in all this, He will be silent and never open His mouth to say a word.

> *"All right then, the Lord himself will give you the sign. Look! The virgin will conceive a child! She will give birth to a son and will call him Immanuel (which means 'God is with us')."*
>
> *(Isaiah 7:14 NLT)*

> *"For a child is born to us, a son is given to us. The government will rest on his shoulders. And he will be called: Wonderful Counselor, Mighty God, Everlasting Father, Prince of Peace. His government and its peace will never end. He will rule with fairness and justice from the throne of his ancestor David for all eternity. The passionate commitment of the Lord of Heaven's Armies will make this happen!"*
>
> *(Isaiah 9:6 – 7 NLT)*

> *"He was despised and rejected— a man of sorrows, acquainted with deepest grief. We turned our backs on him and looked the other way. He was despised, and we did not care. Yet it was our weaknesses he carried; it was our sorrows that weighed him down. And we thought his troubles were a punishment from God, a punishment for his own sins! But he was pierced for our rebellion, crushed for our sins. He was beaten so we could be whole. He was whipped so we could be healed. All of us, like sheep, have strayed away. We have left God's paths to follow our own. Yet the Lord laid on him the sins of us all. He was oppressed and treated harshly, yet he never said a word. He was led like a lamb to the slaughter. And as a*

sheep is silent before the shearers, he did not open his mouth. Unjustly condemned, he was led away. No one cared that he died without descendants, that his life was cut short in midstream. But he was struck down for the rebellion of my people. He had done no wrong and had never deceived anyone. But he was buried like a criminal; he was put in a rich man's grave. But it was the Lord's good plan to crush him and cause him grief. Yet when his life is made an offering for sin, he will have many descendants. He will enjoy a long life, and the Lord's good plan will prosper in his hands. When he sees all that is accomplished by his anguish, he will be satisfied. And because of his experience, my righteous servant will make it possible for many to be counted righteous, for he will bear all their sins. I will give him the honours of a victorious soldier because he exposed himself to death. He was counted among the rebels. He bore the sins of many and interceded for rebels."

(Isaiah 53: 3 – 12 NLT)

The prophecy of Jesus did not stop there. A few years earlier, God again spoke about Jesus through the prophet Micah. Micah said the root of David would come from one of Judah's smallest cities - Bethlehem Ephrathah. He saw in Jesus, a Ruler who came from a distant past. Micah also confirmed that the birth would be of a virgin origin. Jesus, according to him, will lead with the Lord's strength, in the majesty of the name of the Lord His God. In agreement with Isaiah, he called Jesus the source of peace who will be highly honoured around the world.

"But you, O Bethlehem Ephrathah, are only a small village among all the people of Judah. Yet a ruler of Israel, whose origins are in the distant past, will come from you on my behalf. The people of Israel will be abandoned to their enemies until the woman in labour gives birth. Then, at last, his fellow countrymen will return from exile to their own land. And he will stand to lead his flock with the Lord's strength, in the majesty of the name of the Lord his God. Then his people will live there undisturbed, for he will be highly honoured around the world. And he will be the source of peace."

(Micah 5: 2 – 5 NLT)

Two hundred years later, God again confirmed all that was said about Jesus through another prophet - Zechariah. God put His reputation at stake along with that of Jesus by referring to what we now celebrate every year in Christendom; the triumphant entry of Jesus to Jerusalem which we refer to as Palm Sunday. Zechariah referred to Jesus as a humble King riding on a donkey. Jesus was, therefore, acting God's script when He got a donkey for His use in entering Jerusalem.

"Rejoice, O people of Zion! Shout in triumph, O people of Jerusalem! Look, your king is coming to you. He is righteous and victorious, yet he is humble, riding on a donkey— riding on a donkey's colt."

(Zechariah 9: 9 NLT)

"As Jesus and the disciples approached Jerusalem, they came to the town of Bethphage on the Mount of Olives. Jesus sent two of them on ahead. "Go into the village over there," he said. "As soon

you enter it, you will see a donkey tied there, with its colt beside it. Untie them and bring them to me. If anyone asks what you are doing, just say, 'The Lord needs them,' and he will immediately let you take them." This took place to fulfil the prophecy that said, "Tell the people of Jerusalem, 'Look, your King is coming to you. He is humble, riding on a donkey— riding on a donkey's colt.""

(Matthew 21:1 -5 NLT)

The messages of the prophets confirm the divine origin of Jesus as someone on a predetermined mission. All that was prophesized about Him did come to pass. If all that was said about Jesus by Old Testament prophets has come to pass, why does humanity think that what He has said about Himself will go unfulfilled?

Jesus came as was foretold according to God's plan. His arrival was heralded by the voice of one crying in the wilderness. John came to prepare the way for the Lord and to clear the road for Him. He acknowledged the mightiness of Jesus when he said he is not worthy to untie the lace of His shoes. Not minding this, Jesus showed unrivalled humility by presenting Himself to John for baptism. Here was the Son of God who came to take away the sins of the world, allowing a lesser person who could only baptise with water to do so to Him who baptises with water and the Holy Spirit. Everything Jesus did was according to the purpose of His father, who sent Him.

"Then Jesus went from Galilee to the Jordan River to be baptised by John. But John tried to talk him out of it. "I am the one who needs to be baptised

> *by you," he said, "so why are you coming to me?"*
> *But Jesus said, "It should be done, for we must*
> *carry out all that God requires." So John agreed*
> *to baptise him."*

> (Matthew 3:13 – 15 NLT)

He showed great obedience to His father by leaving His
heavenly home to come to the world to carry out the will
of the One who sent Him. No wonder He said;

> *"My nourishment comes from doing the will of*
> *God, who sent me, and from finishing his work"".*

> (John 4:34 NLT)

The Saviour of the world was born in a manger. This
happened because there was no available room for Him
at the inn. God's plan for Jesus still went ahead. Nothing
could stop it. Today most people do not have space for
Jesus in their lives; notwithstanding this, God's good
plan continues to manifest in the lives of those few who
are willing to allow it. At the presentation of Jesus, God
confirmed that all He had revealed about Him through
the prophets were true and THAT ALL WILL COME TO
PASS. After eight days, He was circumcised and given the
name advised by angel Gabriel. His parents brought Him
to Jerusalem for the dedication. God spoke to a righteous
and devout man called Simeon, confirming the status of
Jesus as the Messiah.

> *"Sovereign Lord, now let your servant die in*
> *peace, as you have promised. I have seen your Sal-*
> *vation, which you have prepared for all people.*
> *He is a light to reveal God to the nations, and he*
> *is the glory of your people Israel!"*

> (Luke 2: 29 – 32 NLT)

The Apostle John, who was also known as the Beloved, did an excellent job of introducing Jesus. It is essential to see a bit more about Jesus before we examine His return claim which He made such a long time ago and to which many are no longer tuned. John told us that Jesus was with God at the beginning of creation and that He is the Word of God through which everything was created. Jesus gave life to all creation, and His life brought light to everyone. The Jesus light extinguishes the darkness of sin anywhere it is resident with the import being that anyone who opens the door of his heart to Him will receive this Eternal Light of God which darkness cannot comprehend. Jesus is full of unfailing love and faithfulness. He expressed this in no small measure in the life of Lazarus, a man of whom Jesus said that his sickness would not end in death. At that time, too, just like now, many did not believe Jesus. Even Martha, though very close to Jesus, did not believe Him. She had a limited understanding of the power of God in Jesus. The rest is history. Jesus went on to call out Lazarus from the dead after four days in the tomb.

> *"Jesus was still angry as he arrived at the tomb, a cave with a stone rolled across its entrance. "Roll the stone aside," Jesus told them. But Martha, the dead man's sister, protested, "Lord, he has been dead for four days. The smell will be terrible." Jesus responded, "Didn't I tell you that you would see God's glory if you believe?" So they rolled the stone aside. Then Jesus looked up to heaven and said, "Father, thank, you for hearing me. You always hear me, but I said it out loud for the sake of all these people standing*

*here so that they will believe you sent me." Then
Jesus shouted, "Lazarus, come out!" And the dead
man came out, his hands and feet bound in grave
clothes, his face wrapped in a headcloth. Jesus
told them, "Unwrap him and let him go!"'*

(John 11: 38 – 44 NLT)

Jesus promised to send an Advocate to His disciples.
This gift is only available to those who show love to Jesus
by obeying His commandments. This Advocate will come
from God and will abide with God's children forever. He
will lead all Jesus' disciples into all truth and is a confirmation of the promise of Jesus not to abandon them. You
must, however, be warned that to retain the presence of
the Advocate, you must not be severed from the Vine
- Jesus the True Vine. This Advocate is the Holy Spirit.
Jesus again kept His promise to send the Holy Spirit. He
insisted that the disciples stay together in Jerusalem and
wait to receive Him.

*"On the day of Pentecost, all the believers were
meeting together in one place. Suddenly, there
was a sound from heaven like the roaring of a
mighty windstorm, and it filled the house where
they were sitting. Then, what looked like flames
or tongues of fire appeared and settled on each
of them. And everyone present was filled with
the Holy Spirit and began speaking in other lan-
guages, as the Holy Spirit gave them this ability."*

(Act 2: 1 – 4 NLT)

God's purpose of sending His Son is for all to receive
Him and be saved. The death and resurrection of Jesus
are one of the focal points of the Salvation package. Jesus

predicted His death and resurrection when He told the disciples that He must suffer many terrible things and be rejected by the elders, the leading priests and the teachers of religious law. He promised that He would rise from the dead precisely three days after being killed. Peter, as one of the vocal and passionate disciples, could not understand all these and tried to discourage Him. Jesus, however, had a higher focus and was prepared to go along with His Father's plan for the benefit of humanity. Jesus went to Jerusalem to keep His promise to offer Himself as a ransom for the sins of the world. He was crucified on the Cross of Calvary and on the third day He rose from the dead. Hallelujah!

"Jesus knew that his mission was now finished, and to fulfil Scripture, he said, "I am thirsty." A jar of sour wine was sitting there, so they soaked a sponge in it, put it on a hyssop branch, and held it up to his lips. When Jesus had tasted it, he said, "It is finished!" Then he bowed his head and released his spirit."

(John19:28 – 30 NLT)

"Then, the angel spoke to the women. "Don't be afraid!" he said. "I know you are looking for Jesus, who was crucified. He isn't here! He is risen from the dead, just as he said would happen. Come see where his body was lying. And now, go quickly and tell his disciples that he has risen from the dead, and he is going ahead of you to Galilee. You will see him there. Remember what I have told you." The women ran quickly from the tomb. They were very frightened but also filled with great joy, and they rushed to give the

disciples the angel's message. And as they went, Jesus met them and greeted them. And they ran to him, grasped his feet, and worshipped him. Then Jesus said to them, "Don't be afraid! Go tell my brothers to leave for Galilee, and they will see me there."'

(Matthew 28: 5 - 10 NLT)

On His way to the Cross, Jesus took His disciples to Jerusalem, and they had a wonderful time with Him in an upper room. Jesus shared many truths of God's Word with them and prayed for them. This prayer of Jesus also extends to us today if we believe the message of Salvation and accept Jesus as Lord and Saviour.

"'I am praying not only for these disciples but also for all who will ever believe in me through their message."

(John 17:20 NLT)

Jesus told His disciples in advance that Judas Iscariot will betray Him while Peter will also deny Him. The two events came to pass as He said it would even though Peter vehemently protested that he would rather die than deny Jesus. Judas in connivance with the Jewish religious leaders took the easy way out by proceeding to do that which he has purposed in his mind. Peter, on the other hand, fought the battle but ultimately failed. He was able to embrace repentance because Jesus had prayed for him. In His final message, Jesus warned His disciples that a time would come in the world when Christians will be killed and those doing so will claim that they are doing it for God. Is it not happening today and all over the world too?

"'I have told you these things so that you won't abandon your faith. For you will be expelled from the synagogues, and the time is coming when those who kill you will think they are doing a holy service for God. This is because they have never known the Father or me. Yes, I'm telling you these things now, so that when they happen, you will remember my warning. I didn't tell you earlier because I was going to be with you for a while longer."

(John 16: 1 – 4 NLT)

Jesus has told us He is coming back again. The question is this; should we trust Him to be faithful to His words, or do we ignore Him and take Him for a liar? The Bible reported that those who fought against Jesus called Him a liar and an impostor, claiming that His disciples plan to steal His body and say that He has risen. Perhaps that is why Jesus appeared to many and even showed them His wounds. He appeared to Mary Magdalene outside the tomb and later to the other disciples. Again He appeared to Thomas alone and then Peter beside the Sea of Galilee. Luke also reported that Jesus appeared to two of His disciples on the way to Emmaus. He ate with His disciples and spent about 40 days confirming His resurrection before ascension.

"'Why are you frightened?" he asked. "Why are your hearts filled with doubt? Look at my hands. Look at my feet. You can see that it's really me. Touch me and make sure that I am not a ghost because ghosts don't have bodies, as you see that I do." As he spoke, he showed them his hands and his feet. Still, they stood there in disbelief,

filled with joy and wonder. Then he asked them, "Do you have anything here to eat?" They gave him a piece of broiled fish, and he ate it as they watched."

(Luke 24: 38 – 43 NLT)

The fact that Jesus is coming back again is the very essence of Christian living. Apostle Paul gave an insight into this when he told the people of Corinth that if our hope in Christ is only for this life, we are more to be pitied than anyone in the world. Paul's message confirms that there is another life, and we must begin to prepare for it. Jesus is involved in that other life. Jesus took the issue of His return very seriously. In choosing to tell His disciples about events preceding His return, Jesus again confirms to us the certainty of His second coming.

"Later, Jesus sat on the Mount of Olives. His disciples came to him privately and said, "Tell us, when will all this happen? What sign will signal your return and the end of the world." Jesus told them, "Don't let anyone mislead you, for many will come in my name, claiming, 'I am the Messiah.' They will deceive many."

(Matthew 24: 3 – 5 NLT)

Jesus is undoubtedly coming back at the end of the world to take with Him, His own whom He loves so much. He, therefore, decided to provide milestones for His return. The wise ones are those who will be prepared and ready when the Bridegroom cometh; for they will have noted the accounts of Jesus about the future events and be prepared for HIm.

*"At midnight they were roused by the shout,
'Look, the bridegroom is coming! Come out and
meet him!'"*
(Matthew 25:6 NLT)

Jesus emphasised the suddenness of His return to us. He wanted us to be sensitive and careful with how we spend each day. It is important to note that only through constant feeding on God's Word, can we be sensitive to heavenly matters. It is not possible to do this by ourselves. The nature of man is such that he is more inclined to be controlled by the flesh, but when the Spirit in God's Words is allowed to take control through constant study and meditation, then there is the suppression of the flesh by the Spirit. You cannot have a connection to God except through His Word. Those who daydream and forget what matters do so not because they want to but because there is control from someone or somewhere which they cannot resist. I pray for you as you read this that the hunger for God's Word will overcome you and cause you to thirst for it every day. The suddenness that Jesus talked about is a reality. You need the Grace of God not to be caught unawares.

"'When the Son of Man returns, it will be like it was in Noah's day. In those days before the flood, the people were enjoying banquets and parties and weddings right up to the time Noah entered his boat. People didn't realise what was going to happen until the flood came and swept them all away. That is the way it will be when the Son of Man comes."
(Matthew 24: 37 – 39 NLT)

Jesus talked about deceit in the years to come. He spoke about wars and threats of wars - Nation against Nation and also warned there would be famine and earthquakes in many parts of the world. He told us also that Christians will be hated, arrested, persecuted and killed, because of their association with Him. Again there will be back-sliding and in some cases, a complete turn away from God. Jesus talked about the appearance of false prophets and the acceptance of sinful living as the order of the day. The gauge for His return will, however, be that the message of Salvation will have to be preached throughout the world - and then the end will come.

The deceit that Jesus was talking about here is the continued efforts in the world today to preach a message different from that sent out by Him. The message of Salvation, Holiness and Christian living with strict non-conformity to the world is fast disappearing. Today we are told the lie that we can be in friendship with the world in a certain way and still not offend God. This is a complete falsehood, and all who believe that Jesus is coming soon must reject this message.

> *"You adulterers! Don't you realise that friendship with the world makes you an enemy of God? I say it again: If you want to be a friend of the world, you make yourself an enemy of God."*
>
> *(James 4:4 NLT)*

I don't know how old you are, but in my over five decades on this planet, I have witnessed the passing of several of the Jesus return milestones. When I was a young child, I took a great interest in signs when travelling

134

between two cities. Together with my siblings, we usually sang through our travel, indicating distances left to drive with my dad at the steering wheel. It kept us awake and got us ready for arrival at our destination. The message to us today is that we MUST do likewise in the journey of life. Jesus has provided us with critical milestones we can only ignore to our peril.

I recall an occurrence years ago in Aba, south-east of Nigeria. A young man who I sincerely hope has now reconciled himself to God told us a story. He had gone to bed with his girlfriend and then had a dream. In the dream, Jesus came back as He had promised and unfortunately found him in sin. According to him, he was so terrified because he knew the END HAD COME AND HE WAS NOT IN GOOD STANDING WITH GOD. When he woke up, he was hugely relieved that it was only a dream. A day is, however, going to come when a similar occurrence will take place, and it will not be a dream. On that day when Jesus appears, there will be no opportunity to make amends. It is what He meets us doing that will determine our fate. Anyone found in sin will have the door shut against him.

> *"But while they were gone to buy oil, the bride-groom came. Then those who were ready went in with him to the marriage feast, and the door was locked. Later, when the other five bridesmaids returned, they stood outside, calling, 'Lord! Lord! Open the door for us!' "But he called back, 'Believe me, I don't know you!' "So you, too, must keep watch! For you do not know the day or hour of my return."*
>
> *(Matthew 25: 10 – 13 NLT)*

The purpose of His milestones, therefore, is to keep us alert and ensure that we are not found wanting. You may not have been old enough to witness the world wars or even seen the Nigerian Civil war, but you must have read about them and also seen on television numerous wars and conflicts all other the world. Now and then one country or group of nations take up arms against the other(s) in fulfilment of the Jesus prophecy. Today the world is for all practical purposes in a constant state of war as signified by the post-September 11, 2001, declaration of war on terror by the US and its allies. Again there is the newer ISIS waging war in the Middle East and the Boko Haram group causing mayhem in Nigeria; Al-Qaeda has been in existence for over 27 years and is still active even after the death of Bin Laden. The world is now a place where same-sex marriage is encouraged, western countries are pushing for legalising homosexuality, and gay bishops are being ordained. In the year 2004, at least 230,000 people were killed or missing in 14 countries bordering the Indian Ocean as a result of a Tsunami. Also, nearly 260,000 people died during the famine that hit Somalia from 2010 to 2012. An Open Doors statement in 2015 has approximated that 100 million Christians were persecuted worldwide, making them one of the most oppressed religious groups in the world. In 2014, the world witnessed, in the Ebola Virus, an example of the plague milestone Jesus referred to in the Gospel. The eccentric preacher - The Reverend Jim Jones of the famed Guyana tragedy misled 913 people in 1978 to take their lives; an example of the false messiahs mentioned by Jesus. All these wars, famine, earthquakes, persecution, plagues, false prophets and abominable sin more than confirm the prophecy of Jesus to be accurate and that He is coming and coming very soon too.

"'For in just a little while, the Coming One will come and not delay."
(Hebrews 10:37 NLT)

My dear friend, all that was said about Jesus is true and is coming to pass. Events happening around us also confirm that His return is imminent. If Jesus is coming soon and He has also told us what He is coming to do, then the wise among us must prepare to meet Him. The purpose of sharing this with you is to draw your attention to this reality. You must make yourself ready before He comes. The return of Jesus is one of the most significantly talked about subjects in the world today. God, Himself has driven this message because He does not want anyone to perish but ONLY TO COME TO THE SAVING KNOWLEDGE OF THE TRUTH (1 Timothy 2:4). You are one of those that God has determined to reach through this passionate appeal. Do not miss this opportunity of repentance or rededication. Learn from the experiences of the days of Noah and get into "the boat" before it is too late.

"Seek the Lord, all who are humble, and follow his commands. Seek to do what is right and to live humbly. Perhaps even yet the Lord will protect you — protect you from his anger on that day of destruction."
(Zephaniah 2:3 NLT)

I pray that you will not suffer the fate of the foolish virgins who missed the arrival of the Bridegroom. God bless you.

Pleasing God

"I am old now; I have lived a long time, but I have never seen good people abandoned by the Lord or their children begging for food."

(Psalms 37:25 NLT)

I sometimes wonder with the testimony given by David above why man fails to heed God's call to live as dictated by Him. I for one and for a long time was chief amongst those who were not serious about God and so lived a life that did not mirror the truth contained in the words of David. David was one of God's very close friends. The testimony of the Creator about him was that he was a man after His own heart. David lived for only 70years, and though he had his ups and downs in his relationship with Jehovah, God in being faithful was able to reveal to David the truism of the above text. One of the lies that the devil says to man to drag him as far as possible from God is that one needs to "help" himself in this world if one wants to succeed. To help themselves, many subscribe to the philosophy that one must cut corners and do things in the way of the world to make a success out of life. Again, David says his experience is a big no to that myth.

"Even strong young lions sometimes go hungry, but those who trust in the LORD will lack no good thing."

(Psalms 34:10 NLT)

Although David in the above Psalms tried to simplify the benefits of pleasing God to only what we can get out of Him, apparently this is not the only purpose of satisfying our Creator. David was succeeded by his son Solomon who was reputed to be one of the wisest kings of Israel. Solomon ruled for 39 years and died at a ripe age of 80 years. Solomon having lived a life of success many can only dream of, concluded that the purpose of life is to fear God and obey His commandments. Why did these two reputable men think so much about God? Why did they believe that life without putting God in the right place will become unprofitable?

> *"That's the whole story. Here now is my final conclusion: Fear God and obey his commands, for this is everyone's duty. God will judge us for everything we do, including every secret thing, whether good or bad."*

> *(Ecclesiastes 12:13 – 14 NLT)*

One of the most learned and reputable apostles of Jesus was Paul of Tarsus. Paul started as a chief persecutor of the church, and he did an excellent job of it. He was involved in the violence that took the life of Stephen. The story went that it was on the way to Damascus to continue in his persecution agenda against Christians that the divine mercy of God was made available to him. He acknowledged that though he by birth was not of lowly status, Christ, and the opportunity to follow Him is the all in all.

> *"I was circumcised when I was eight days old. I am a pure-blooded citizen of Israel and a member of the tribe of Benjamin — a real Hebrew if there*

ever was one! I was a member of the Pharisees, who demand the strictest obedience to the Jewish law. I was so zealous that I harshly persecuted the church. And as for righteousness, I obeyed the law without fault. I once thought these things were valuable, but now I consider them worthless because of what Christ has done. Yes, everything else is worthless when compared with the infinite value of knowing Christ Jesus, my Lord. For his sake, I have discarded everything else, counting it all as garbage, so that I could gain Christ and become one with him. I no longer count on my own righteousness through obeying the law; rather, I become righteous through faith in Christ. For God's way of making us right with himself depends on faith. I want to know Christ and experience the mighty power that raised him from the dead. I want to suffer with him, sharing in his death, so that one way or another I will experience the resurrection from the dead!"

(Philippians 3: 5 – 11. NLT)

Paul saw and affirmed that following Christ is what should matter to all men. He understood that Christ should be the centrepiece of his life and existence. He went on to live that life, making many to follow suit.

"For I fully expect and hope that I will never be ashamed, but that I will continue to be bold for Christ, as I have been in the past. And I trust that my life will bring honour to Christ, whether I live or die. For to me, living means living for Christ, and dying is even better. But if I live, I can do more fruitful work for Christ. So I really don't know which is better. I'm torn between two desires: I long to go and be with Christ, which

would be far better for me. But for your sakes, it is better that I continue to live. Knowing this, I am convinced that I will remain alive so I can continue to help all of you grow and experience the joy of your faith. And when I come to you again, you will have even more reason to take pride in Christ Jesus because of what he is doing through me."

(Philippians 1: 20 – 26. NLT)

One of the frontal challenges faced by man today is the struggle between pleasing God and self. Although some people who have sold their souls to the devil may not experience this struggle as they are already on an expressway to destruction, most reasonable people go through this challenge day in day out. Even early Christians as alluded to by Apostle Paul were not free from this everyday phenomenon.

"So the trouble is not with the law, for it is spiritual and good. The trouble is with me, for I am all too human, a slave to sin. I don't really understand myself, for I want to do what is right, but I don't do it. Instead, I do what I hate. But if I know that what I am doing is wrong, this shows that I agree that the law is good. So I am not the one doing wrong; it is sin living in me that does it. And I know that nothing good lives in me, that is, in my sinful nature. I want to do what is right, but I can't. I want to do what is good, but I don't. I don't want to do what is wrong, but I do it anyway. But if I do what I don't want to do, I am not really the one doing wrong; it is sin living in me that does it. I have discovered this principle of life—that when I want to do what

*is right, I inevitably do what is wrong. I love
God's law with all my heart. But there is another
power within me that is at war with my mind.
This power makes me a slave to the sin that is
still within me. Oh, what a miserable person I
am! Who will free me from this life that is dominated by sin and death? Thank God! The answer
is in Jesus Christ, our Lord. So you see how it is:
In my mind, I really want to obey God's law, but
because of my sinful nature, I am a slave to sin."*

(Romans 7: 14 – 25. NLT)

I also have a similar experience. The struggle I have
every day is how to remain on the right side of God; free
from sin and sinful living. I believe that many will want to
please God with their lives. The truth is that they usually
don't because of the cost of doing so and all that it entails.
To do the will of God is not a piece of cake. It requires
that not only must one make a choice, but he or she must
be prepared for costs and consequences. The trouble is
that many, even though they desire it, are not prepared
to pay the price. In our earlier references, we talked about
a father and his son – David & Solomon. Both contended
with this struggle with varying degrees of success; both
lives confirming that this battle for the control of man's
soul is a reality.

*"Then he said to the crowd, "If any of you wants
to be my follower, you must turn from your selfish
ways, take up your cross daily, and follow me."*

(Luke 9:23 NLT)

Again there is the spiritual angle to the challenge of
pleasing God. The prince of this world orchestrates this

143

constant battle that goes on in our lives. He has been defeated and condemned to destruction; he is looking for many to take along with him. The more significant fact is that He that is with us is greater than he that is in the world and this same Person has given us the power to overcome all things, both physical and spiritual. We must, therefore, apply the weapons He has given us every day to win the warfare that we face.

> "A final word: Be strong in the Lord and in his mighty power. Put on all of God's armour so that you will be able to stand firm against all strategies of the devil. For we are not fighting against flesh-and-blood enemies, but against evil rulers and authorities of the unseen world, against mighty powers in this dark world, and against evil spirits in the heavenly places. Therefore, put on every piece of God's armour so you will be able to resist the enemy in the time of evil. Then after the battle, you will still be standing firm. Stand your ground, putting on the belt of truth and the body armour of God's righteousness. For shoes, put on the peace that comes from the Good News so that you will be fully prepared. In addition to all of these, hold up the shield of faith to stop the fiery arrows of the devil. Put on Salvation as your helmet, and take the sword of the Spirit, which is the word of God. Pray in the Spirit at all times and on every occasion. Stay alert and be persistent in your prayers for all believers everywhere."
>
> (Ephesians 6: 10 –18 NLT)

For those who are desirous of living a successful life, a life that pleases God is inevitable. Although some may think that the only thing that matters is what they make out of their existence on this planet, they are far from the truth as life is a continuum. It is therefore instructive that one must be guided in the heavenly direction. In the course of my discovery of this truth, I have found for myself several guiding lights, and these must all be embraced if one is intent on pleasing his Creator.

The Truth – Guiding Light to Pleasing God 1: Avoid False Teachers

It is important to note that to please God, one must know what He expects of us at all times. God's mind was revealed to us by the prophets of old and later on by Jesus, His disciples and apostles. God expects that we keep His words in our heart so that we do not sin against Him. Today the Word of God has been so mutilated by all and sundry for one reason or the other. While some do it for varying personal gains, others do not bother to study and meditate and instead pass on whatever their minds tell them God is saying to His people. The widely held and very popular obedience to the law teaching, instead of that of Salvation by Grace through Christ, is the flagship of this false teaching. Jesus made it very clear that many false teachers will arise and we must be mindful of them. It is impossible to learn to please God if we do not know Him through His words.

"When I left for Macedonia, I urged you to stay there in Ephesus and stop those whose teaching is contrary to the truth. Don't let them waste their

time in endless discussion of myths and spiritual pedigrees. These things only lead to meaningless speculations, which don't help people live a life of faith in God."

(1 Timothy 1: 3 – 4 NLT)

The Truth – Guiding Light to Pleasing God 2: Faith & Conscience

The Bible gives value to the importance of faith in our relationship with God. It singled out giants as examples for us to follow. In this group were the likes of Abel, Enoch, Noah, Abraham, Sarah, Isaac, Jacob, Moses & even Rahab. Again, the Bible in placing a value to faith tells us that if we do no show the prescribed level of faith, we cannot please God – or should I say, God will not be happy with us. Paul saw the need to quickly pass on the importance of faith to Timothy very early in his letter. The word "cling" which Paul has used means hold on tightly. It shows the importance of faith and indicates the possibility of losing it. Conscience, which is a person's moral sense of right and wrong is also important to God. It is so important that God sent the Holy Spirit to play the role of influencing our conscience – if only we will allow Him. Paul's counsel to keep one's conscience clear merely is that we should not run afoul of the standard of God concerning doing right all the time – including our thoughts.

"Timothy, my son, here are my instructions for you, based on the prophetic words spoken about you earlier. May they help you fight well in the Lord's battles. Cling to your faith in Christ,

*and keep your conscience clear. For some people
have deliberately violated their consciences; as a
result, their faith has been shipwrecked."*

(1 Timothy 1: 18 -19 NLT)

The Truth – Guiding Light to Pleasing God 3:
Intercession

Jesus reminded His disciples in one of His lessons that
the two most significant commands are tied to love and
related to the love of God and that of our fellow brethren.
It is essential if we want to please God that we intercede
on behalf of others. This mediation should be focused on
knowing the truth and gaining Salvation. While not dis-
counting the importance of praying for the needs of others,
Paul makes us understand that they are mundane and less
pleasing to God than the Salvation of their souls. Again to
live in peace, we must not forget to pray for our leaders.

> *"I urge you, first of all, to pray for all people. Ask
> God to help them; intercede on their behalf, and
> give thanks for them. Pray this way for kings
> and all who are in authority so that we can live
> peaceful and quiet lives marked by godliness and
> dignity. This is good and pleases God our Savior,
> who wants everyone to be saved and to under-
> stand the truth."*
>
> *(1 Timothy 2: 1 – 4 NLT)*

The Truth – Guiding Light to Pleasing God 4:
One Mediator

In the letter of Apostle Paul to the people of Galatia, he
broached this subject to the people. The way the world

is religiously structured today, it is easy for someone to be misled into thinking that obeying the law and having high moral standards are enough to please God. Paul was evident "that a person is made right with God by faith in Jesus Christ, not by obeying the law" (Galatians 2:6). He emphasised the same to his student Timothy as it remains pivotal for anyone who seeks the truth. Jesus gave this testimony of Himself when He said "I am the Way, the Truth, and the Life. No one can come to the Father except through Me." Because our righteousness is as filthy rags, we need this Mediator whose righteousness is adequate and sufficient for us. Jesus is that one Mediator and He offers Salvation by Grace through faith – lest anyone should boast.

> *"For, There is one God and one Mediator who can reconcile God and humanity—the man Christ Jesus. He gave his life to purchase freedom for everyone. This is the message God gave to the world at just the right time."*
>
> *(1 Timothy 2: 5 – 6. NLT)*

The Truth – Guiding Light to Pleasing God 5: Holiness

Holiness is one of the fast disappearing sermon topics in the church today. In times gone by, it was the order of the day as this was the defining legacy of the scripture union days. Although the Word of God is true that He will build His church and the gates of hell shall not prevail against it, we must warn ourselves that if we do not stand up to be counted, God will raise stones to replace us. God does not compromise His standards, and so holiness remains pivotal to Him. One of the lessons from the seven Revelation churches is that anyone who circumvents God's standard shall receive due punishment. The writer of Hebrews was even more definitive in saying that "without holiness, no one will see the Lord"(Hebrews 12:14). Jesus promised His disciples that He would send them a Comforter – this Spirit only inhabits holy places. If you want Him in your life, you must prepare a place habitable to Him.

"In every place of worship, I want men to pray with holy hands lifted up to God, free from anger and controversy."
                                            (1 Timothy 2: 8 NLT)

The controversy I believe Paul was referring to has to do with doing things that will make people question our standing in Christ. I remember the advice a man of God gave me one day. He said, "do not disappoint God". We disappoint God when we attract controversy to the body of Christ by living in a way contrary to our calling as Christians.

The Truth – Guiding Light to Pleasing God 6: Modesty & Decency

One of the ways evil has taken hold of the world is through the manipulation of man to engage in all manner of dress sense. In today's world, the craziest and inappropriate is appreciated and copied by many. In an account of three supernatural visits to heaven and hell written by Michel Thomas Sambo, Jesus reminded His servant that all that takes place in the world today is a contest between God's will and that of the prince of this world. It was revealed to Sambo that Satan orchestrates several changes and evolutions in this world in his grand desire to draw many to his abode – Hell. All these Solomon has long described as vanity, but unfortunately for those who are perishing, it is modernity, fun and excitement. The Bible has already made it clear to us that though we are in the world, we MUST not be of the world. Why then can't we embrace modesty and decency that will honour God and save our souls? Again there is too much emphasis by a man on the outward. The inner which defines the outward and is more critical is left unattended to leading to its ruin. The inner which lives forever is ignored in favour of the outer, which is mortal. How unwise of man who has received power to have dominion over all things!

> *"And I want women to be modest in their appearance. They should wear decent and appropriate clothing and not draw attention to themselves by the way they fix their hair or by wearing gold or pearls or expensive clothes. For women who claim to be devoted to God should make themselves attractive by the good things they do."*

> *(1 Timothy 2: 9 -10 NLT)*

The Truth – Guiding Light to Pleasing God 7: Christian Leadership

The Bible teaches that as Christians, we MUST be the light and salt of the world. That means Christians must set the example for others to follow in any area of life they find themselves. Many who are called by HIS NAME do not resemble the Lord in any way. They are only Christians by name, partying with the devil at the slightest opportunity. God's standard of truth, righteousness and holiness cannot be changed for any race, people or generation. It is either we accept it by aligning with Him and then enjoy the benefits, or we do not, and He spits us out of His mouth. The type of example that God expects is not one that is just talked about but is lived and can be copied by others. It must be consistent and not one that is put forward only for others to see. It reflects the innermost being of the person and must impact his or her relationship with others. The Bible goes on to provide specifics in Christian leadership that we must note and not compromise regardless of efforts by many in the church today to do away with them.

> *"This is a trustworthy saying: "If someone aspires to be an elder, he desires an honourable position." So an elder must be a man whose life is above reproach. He must be faithful to his wife. He must exercise self-control, live wisely, and have a good reputation. He must enjoy having guests in his home, and he must be able to teach. He must not be a heavy drinker or be violent. He must be gentle, not quarrelsome, and not love money. He must manage his own family well, having children who respect and obey him. For if a man cannot manage his own household, how can he take care of God's church?"*
>
> *(1 Timothy 3: 1 – 5 NLT)*

The Truth – Guiding Light to Pleasing God 8: Godly Training

The mindset of someone who wants to please God must be that he or she is a sojourner here on earth and that heaven is his or her ultimate destination. Paul, in his first letter to the people of Corinth, compared the Christian race to that of an athlete. In doing so, he tried to make his audience appreciate the need for an athlete to make sacrifices based on the prescribed training guidelines required to win the prize set before him or her. In a similar vein, the life of a Christian can typify that of a race which is conducted based on biblical training guidelines. The Christian who is intent on receiving a commendation at the end of his life must prepare to win the Christian race. It is clear from their testimonies that many in the Bible who fell by the wayside failed to equip themselves in a godly way. The Scripture recommends the belt of truth, the body armour of God's righteousness, the peace that comes from the good news, the shield of faith, Salvation helmet and the Sword of the Spirit as requirements to ensure that we remain standing after the battle that will inevitably come to all believers (Ephesians 6:14–17). Godly training comes from immersing yourself in the Word of God.

> *"Do not waste time arguing over godless ideas and old wives' tales. Instead, train yourself to be godly. "Physical training is good, but training for godliness is much better, promising benefits in this life and in the life to come." This is a trustworthy saying, and everyone should accept it. This is why we work hard and continue to struggle, for our hope is in the living God, who is the Savior of all people and particularly of all believers."*
>
> *(1 Timothy 4: 7 – 10 NLT)*

The Truth – Guiding Light to Pleasing God 9: Bearing Fruits

In his account of the gospel of our Lord and Saviour Jesus Christ, John reported Jesus as giving great prominence to bearing fruits. Jesus talked about all the efforts He has made and continues to make through the Word to ensure that we are fruit-bearing Christians. Jesus did not stop there. He went ahead to warn that as a part of Him, we have no choice but to be productive. He described in details all efforts He continues to make to ensure that we are capable of reproducing ourselves. He told His listeners that only a permanent connection to Him as the Source would guarantee our being able to produce much fruit, making it clear that once we sever that relationship, we can do nothing. Jesus has deposited so much in us that we cannot afford to fail Him and ourselves. For Him, while He has recourse to replacing us – even with stones, we are left with nothing if we do not produce our kind. He concluded by saying that bearing fruits is the only confirmation that we are His disciples. How then can we give what we do not have? Many who are not genuinely connected to Jesus are unwilling and unable to pursue the number one agenda of the Lamb of God. They instead wallow in spiritual poverty all their lives and end up going to meet their Saviour empty-handed. Little wonder again Apostle Paul was so concerned about bearing fruits that he admonished Timothy to watch how his life impacts on the Salvation of others.

"Keep a close watch on how you live and on your teaching. Stay true to what is right for the sake of your own Salvation and the Salvation of those who hear you."

(*1 Timothy 4: 16 NLT*)

The Truth – Guiding Light to Pleasing God 10: Love & Respect

One of the vivid and unforgettable parables of Jesus is the parable of the Good Samaritan. This parable is unique in that Jesus used it to confront some of the holier than thou religious leaders of His day. Jesus was trying to teach love through the context of good neighbourliness. Just like it was easy for the spiritual leader who approached Jesus to feign ignorance of who his neighbour is, many today also tow that line by burying their head in the sand; pretending that they are oblivious of what God expects of them. The story is very striking in that Jesus used both the leaders and followers to show the bad example that pervades Christendom today. God has set the standard through His Son, who left His glorious mansion to offer His life as a ransom for us. This example is for us to follow daily if indeed we are His disciples. Christianity simply is about followership and nothing more; man as the follower of Jesus of Nazareth. The show of love scene by the "lowly" Samaritan is practical from all ramifications. Caring for those we do not know is the standard, and this we must seek to do all the time. The care we offer to our own though compulsory is of lesser value than that we give to those unknown to us.

"Never speak harshly to an older man, but appeal to him respectfully as you would to your own father. Talk to younger men as you would to your own brothers. Treat older women as you would, your mother, and treat younger women with all purity as you would your own sisters. Take care of any widow who has no one else to care for her. But if she has children or grandchildren, their first responsibility is to show godliness at home and repay their parents by taking care of them. This is something that pleases God."

(1 Timothy 5: 1 - 4 NLT)

The Truth – Guiding Light to Pleasing God 11: Christian Work

Jesus showed His readiness to please God by His approach and commitment to the work of His Father. No wonder He said; we must quickly carry out the tasks assigned us by the One who sent us. The night is coming, and then no one can work (John 9:4). The Saviour also typified the importance of doing God's assignment in the parable of the talents. In portraying the importance of doing this work, Jesus told a story of a man who went away on a long journey and left his servants with some work to do. In the example of Jesus and that of the parable, the emphasis is on the work to be done. Both cases show a clear indication that time is of the essence; the night and day analogy of Jesus and the return of the master in the parable. Each one of us has been given one assignment or the other by our Creator - according to his talents. The truth is that all work will be evaluated one day. Apostle Paul in his letter to the church at Corinth, made this point very clear. He spoke not only about the importance of doing God's work but also that whatever work we do will be assessed by an examiner. If we desire to please God, then we must make sure that our performance is good enough for Him.

> *"Anyone who builds on that foundation may use a variety of materials — gold, silver, jewels, wood, hay, or straw. But on the judgment day, fire will reveal what kind of work each builder has done. The fire will show if a person's work has any value. If the work survives, that builder will receive a reward. But if the work is burned up, the builder will suffer great loss. The builder will be saved, but like someone barely escaping through a wall of flames."*

(1 Corinthians 3:12 – 15 NLT)

It is essential that as Christians, our approach to our secular work must be different from others. The concept of non-conformity with the world which all followers of Christ must embrace and is non-negotiable truly sets us apart, and we must live by it. Paul, in his letters to the people of Colossae and Ephesus, was very emphatic about this teaching. Many believers bring dishonour to the name of Christ by the way they conduct themselves at work. I recall many years ago while working as an intern in a hospital in Kano; one of the Christian pharmacists using part of her work time to read her Bible and other Christian literature. Jesus was clear in advising us to be law-abiding – by giving unto Caesar what is Caesar's.

> *"Slaves, obey your earthly masters with deep respect and fear. Serve them sincerely as you would serve Christ. Try to please them all the time, not just when they are watching you. As*

slaves of Christ, do the will of God with all your heart. Work with enthusiasm, as though you were working for the Lord rather than for people. Remember that the Lord will reward each one of us for the good we do, whether we are slaves or free. Masters, treat your slaves in the same way. Don't threaten them; remember, you both have the same Master in heaven, and he has no favourites."

(Ephesians 6: 5 – 9 NLT)

The Truth - Guiding Light to Pleasing God 12: Godliness & Contentment

The new living translation of the bible equates Godliness and contentment to great wealth. In order words, anyone who seeks fulfilment must be content with what he or she has and also pursue a life of close walk with God. I recall an encounter that Jesus had with a wealthy man. This man, the Bible tells us despite his riches still discovered that he lacked something. During Jesus' time, many who came to Him were looking for solutions to problems they were unable to solve by themselves or by the help of other persons. I know that a rich man at any time in history has access to limitless resources of diverse nature. However, he was still able to identify that something was missing in his life – something higher than his riches. The Bible tells us that he was so committed to his search for the better life (eternal life) that he had been diligent to keep all the commandments of Moses from a young age, but all were to no avail. No wonder the Bible says – there is a way that seems right to a man, but the end thereof is destruction (Proverbs 14:12). Although it is good to keep these commandments, how far does our righteousness take us? The Bible calls it filthy rags. Jesus wanted him to appreciate the futility of earthly wealth and instead recommended for him to store treasure in heaven, but he would have none of it. He wanted to receive from God but was not ready to let go of things in his hand that will not allow him to be blessed. How come he tried to get the most expensive product on earth – Salvation, freely given and yet he is unwilling to share his wealth with the poor? I have come to terms with the life that God expects me to live when it comes to the things of the world. As much as they are important, God wants us to see them as secondary to the wealth He has made available to us in and through Jesus Christ.

> *"Yet true godliness with contentment is itself great wealth. After all, we brought nothing with us when we came into the world, and we can't take anything with us when we leave it. So if we have enough food and clothing, let us be content. But people who long to be rich fall into temptation and are trapped by many foolish and harmful desires that plunge them into ruin and destruction. For the love of money is the root of all kinds of evil. And some people, craving money, have wandered from the true faith and pierced themselves with many sorrows."*

> *(1 Timothy 6: 6 – 10 NLT)*

The Truth – Guiding Light to Pleasing God 13: Wealth Application

The Bible gives us two seemingly contrasting messages about money. On the one hand, money is essential and desirable because it is the answer to all things while on the other hand, the love of this same money is the root of all evil. Some then despise it and go to the extent of seeing wealth as not to be desired by Christians. In the church today, one may readily see two divides - those who focus so much on prosperity and others who see the seeking of wealth as a no go area for Christians. But again, the same Bible which says that it is God that gives us the power to make wealth goes ahead to say that he who gives to the poor lends to God. We can go on and on and dig up Bible messages about money without stopping. My mind quickly goes to a man who was reputed to be the richest in the history of humanity. God gave him extraordinary wisdom so we can learn a lot from him. According to the Bible, the Israelite monarchy gained its highest splendour and wealth during Solomon's reign of 40 years. In a single year, according to 1 Kings 10:14, Solomon collected tribute amounting to 666 talents (39,960 pounds) of gold. This amounts to about $1.2b in today's money. The striking thing about Solomon was that with all this wealth at his disposal, he never saw money as anything – he called all of it VANITY! I believe that it is in the purpose and application of funds that God wants us to be different from the world. No wonder we reminded ourselves earlier that we came to the world with nothing and will also return with nothing. The disciple Matthew gives one of the greatest money lessons that we must imbibe – storing our treasures where thieves cannot get to them and where CERTAINLY we can access them after we leave this planet.

"Teach those who are rich in this world not to be proud and not to trust in their money, which is so unreliable. Their trust should be in God, who richly gives us all we need for our enjoyment. Tell

*them to use their money to do good. They should
be rich in good works and generous to those in
need, always being ready to share with others. By
doing this, they will be storing up their treasure
as a good foundation for the future so that they
may experience true life."*

(1 Timothy 6: 17 – 19 NLT)

The Truth – Guiding Light to Pleasing God 14: Protecting your Salvation

One of the saddest parables in the bible was the one told
by Jesus of a rich man and Lazarus. One cannot but feel
pity for the poor man who was longing for scraps from the
rich man's table with dogs coming to lick his wounds. The
picture painted by Jesus is very vivid today and typifies
what we find in our society. The rich man, after crossing
to the great beyond met with his judgment which in his
case was eternal condemnation. What a great pity! The
bible is very clear that – there is appointed unto man a
time to die and after which there is judgment (Hebrews
9:27). Many choose to forget this truth and reality; they go
on in their lives as if that day will never come. They ignore
God's clear message which says He cannot be mocked and
also that whatever we sow, we will reap. Many know this
story of weeping and gnashing of teeth by the hitherto
rich man who the Bible described as always splendidly
clothed in purple and fine linen and who lived each day
in luxury. The sadness is the absence of any opportunity
for repentance – something that is only available here on
earth. Jesus said that He is coming soon, but some laugh it
off and continue to wallow in sin and godless living. The

warnings in the days of Noah are there for all to see. Let him who has ears listen to what God is saying through this medium. For those who have accepted Jesus and have become saved, we must protect our Salvation, but for those who are still playing poker with their lives, Jesus is tenderly calling you today.

> *"Timothy, guard what God has entrusted to you. Avoid godless, foolish discussions with those who oppose you with their so-called knowledge. Some people have wandered from the faith by following such foolishness. May God's Grace be with you all."*
>
> *(1 Timothy 6: 20 – 21 NLT)*

The Truth – Guiding Light to Pleasing God 15: Be Faithful & Courageous

The Christian life begins with faith but continues on a journey of faithfulness, passing through several challenges and difficulty but making sure that one keeps his eyes on the target and ends with reaching the goal. Although it is helpful to have a good beginning, it is what one achieves at the end that matters. Little wonder the Bible says, better the end of a matter than the beginning (Ecclesiastes 7:8). Apostle Paul did not start well; he was a chief persecutor of Christ through his antagonism to the Gospel. However, he took advantage of the mercy of God received on the way to Damascus and went on faithfully to the end. Many of his assistants abandoned him along the way, and he faced many difficulties that only the courage given to him by God helped him to overcome. Being faithful requires that one becomes a champion of the message of Good News which all Christians must pursue without fail. Faithfulness and courage are essential ingredients for soldiers of the Cross who are expecting their Master's commendation at the end. *I come quickly, and My reward is with Me* was the promise of Jesus (Revelation 22:12). Indeed He will keep all His words.

> *"That is why I am suffering here in prison. But I am not ashamed of it, for I know the one in whom I trust, and I am sure that he is able to guard what I have entrusted to him until the day of his return. Hold on to the pattern of wholesome teaching you learned from me — a pattern shaped by the faith and love that you have in Christ Jesus. Through the power of the Holy Spirit, who lives within us, carefully guard the precious truth that has been entrusted to you."*
>
> (2 Timothy 1: 12 – 14 NLT)

The Truth – Guiding Light to Pleasing God 16: Endure Suffering

It is an irony for the message of Christ to be called the Good News, yet we are being encouraged to endure suffering. The reality is there are no two ways about it. Jesus Himself set the ball rolling by giving up His majestic glory to come here to die for His friends – you and I. Sometimes ago I was exposed to the principle of delayed gratification. I read about the experience of someone whose wealth foundation was built when he sacrificed a lot as a student in the UK. The message of the Cross is not so much different from this. Jesus has provided for us free Salvation by Grace; He expects us to hold firmly to this gift until He comes again. The assurance we have in Him is that He is there for us, even to the end. He did not hide from us the fact that we will face trials in this world, but He has overcome the world for us. Our focus is to please God, making sure that we are not suffering for the wrong reasons. Peter encouraged us that our sufferings make us partners with Christ – so we should rejoice. He warned that no Christian must suffer for murder, stealing, causing trouble or prying into other people's affairs (1 Peter 4:15). Peter's disposition was that all Christians must celebrate their sufferings because according to him "for then the glorious Spirit of God rests upon you" (1 Peter 4:14).

"Endure suffering along with me, as a good soldier of Christ Jesus. Soldiers don't get tied up in the affairs of civilian life, for then they cannot please the officer who enlisted them. And athletes cannot win the prize unless they follow the rules. And hardworking farmers should be the first to enjoy the fruit of their labour. Think about what I am saying. The Lord will help you understand all these things. Always remember that Jesus Christ, a descendant of King David, was raised from the dead. This is the Good News I preach. And because I preach this Good News, I am suffering and have been chained like a criminal. But the word of God cannot be chained. So I am willing to endure anything if it will bring Salvation and eternal glory in Christ Jesus to those God has chosen. This is a trustworthy saying: If we die with him, we will also live with him. If we endure hardship, we will

reign with him. If we deny him, he will deny us. If we are unfaithful, he remains faithful, for he cannot deny who he is."

(2 Timothy 2: 3 – 13. NLT)

The Truth – Guiding Light to Pleasing God 17: Godly Conduct

The purpose of Jesus' coming is to show us the way to the Father. Man could not still find his way even after all Old Testament efforts by his Creator to show him the road to redemption. Jesus was the perfect plan put together by God to offer us a last chance to His Kingdom. He came to give His life as a ransom for our souls and to show us a way to God – godly conduct. This holy conduct is the narrow road manual that tells us how to live in a way pleasing to God. Matthew's gospel account tells us that we can enter the kingdom of God ONLY through this Narrow Gate (Matthew 7:14). He differentiates this Narrow Way from another which he called a highway, which is broad and its entrance is wide. This highway, which I prefer to call an expressway accommodates unrepentant sinners. It is designed to take the many who will eventually use it. It is an expressway to hell and eternal condemnation.

Matthew warns that the Narrow Way which is to eternal life is difficult and only a few will find it. The idea of godly conduct takes me back memory lane. As a student, I can describe my experience in two folds – the early days when I was not so focused on my studies and the later years when I was prepared to give all for my books.

In both situations, I wanted to succeed, but by failing to follow the success manual, the earlier me never achieved his potential as a student. This made me adopt the success manual, which helped me in later years. The life of a Christian requires that we apply the godly manual. The narrow road - highway admonition in Matthew were the direct words of Jesus, which we must not take with levity. The holy conduct keeps you watching and waiting so that when Jesus comes, He will find you worthy of commendation. Fanny Crosby said this much in her song – will Jesus find us watching?

> *"In a wealthy home, some utensils are made of gold and silver, and some are made of wood and clay. The expensive utensils are used for special occasions, and the cheap ones are for everyday use. If you keep yourself pure, you will be a special utensil for honourable use. Your life will be clean, and you will be ready for the Master to use you for every good work. Run from anything that stimulates youthful lusts. Instead, pursue righteous living, faithfulness, love, and peace. Enjoy the companionship of those who call on the Lord with pure hearts."*
>
> *(2 Timothy 2:20 – 22 NLT)*

The Truth – Guiding Light to Pleasing God 18: Remember the Last Days

It is important to remember the last days to get prepared for the bridegroom. In the parable of the ten virgins, we see the perfect example of unpreparedness and its consequence. Both sets of virgins knew that they were going to meet the Bridegroom, but not all were fully prepared. Many Christians and non-Christians alike can tell what the signs are of the last days. But the question is, what are they doing about it? The truth today is that we are already in the last days, and the only thing we cannot say for sure is how long gone are we into the last days. The wisdom that we MUST apply is given to us by King Solomon in Ecclesiastes 7:14 – A wise person thinks a lot about death while a fool thinks only about having a good time. Again David, who had a close walk with God, said in Psalm 90:12 – Teach us to realise the brevity of life so that we may grow in wisdom. The import of the last days made Jesus spend time with His disciples on the Mount of Olives to warn them not only to remember the last days but also to be prepared for it. Jesus warned us to be on the lookout for false messiahs so that they will not steal our crown. He also warned that the end of the last days would be His SUDDEN return pleading that we should be ready all the time. Parables and analogies were also given by Jesus to drive home His message. Many will not see the physical coming back of Jesus, but all will face His Judgment. Jesus is an incorruptible Judge that will separate the sheep from the goats. We are CERTAINLY in the last days and MUST prepare ourselves for the coming of Messiah.

> *"You should know this, Timothy that in the last days there will be very difficult times. For people will love only themselves and their money. They will be boastful and proud, scoffing at God, disobedient to their parents, and ungrateful. They will consider nothing sacred. They will be unloving*

and unforgiving; they will slander others and have no self-control. They will be cruel and hate what is good. They will betray their friends, be reckless, be puffed up with pride, and love pleasure rather than God. They will act religious, but they will reject the power that could make them godly. Stay away from people like that!"

(2 Timothy 3: 1- 5. NLT)

"I solemnly urge you in the presence of God and Christ Jesus, who will someday judge the living and the dead when he comes to set up his Kingdom: Preach the word of God. Be prepared, whether the time is favourable or not. Patiently correct, rebuke, and encourage your people with good teaching. For a time is coming when people will no longer listen to sound and wholesome teaching. They will follow their own desires and will look for teachers who will tell them whatever their itching ears want to hear. They will reject the truth and chase after myths. But you should keep a clear mind in every situation. Don't be afraid of suffering for the Lord. Work at telling others the Good News, and fully carry out the ministry God has given you. As for me, my life has already been poured out as an offering to God. The time of my death is near. I have fought the good fight, I have finished the race, and I have remained faithful. And now the prize awaits me — the crown of righteousness, which the Lord, the righteous Judge, will give me on the day of his return. And the prize is not just for me but for all who eagerly look forward to his appearing."

(2 Timothy 4: 1 – 8 NLT)

My dear brothers and sisters, I have been led to share with you these words, encouraging you to focus your life on pleasing God, for it is to your benefit. God has paid the ultimate price for you through the offering of His only begotten Son. All that remains for man is to chart the course for his life. My passionate appeal is that you look in the direction of this Saviour Jesus and not the other way. Living a life that pleases God should be a daily continuum.

> *"But you, Timothy, are a man of God; so run from all these evil things. Pursue righteousness and a godly life, along with faith, love, perseverance, and gentleness. Fight the good fight for the true faith. Hold tightly to the eternal life to which God has called you, which you have declared so well before many witnesses. And I charge you before God, who gives life to all, and before Christ Jesus, who gave a good testimony before Pontius Pilate, that you obey this command without wavering. Then no one can find fault with you from now until our Lord Jesus Christ comes again. For, At just the right time, Christ will be revealed from heaven by the blessed and only almighty God, the King of all kings and Lord of all lords. He alone can never die, and he lives in light so brilliant that no human can approach him. No human eye has ever seen him, nor ever will. All honour and power to him forever! Amen."*

> *(1 Timothy 6:11 – 16 NLT)*

I pray that you shall know Him and the power of His resurrection.

He Is Able

"Therefore, God elevated him to the place of highest honour and gave him the name above all other names, that at the name of Jesus every knee should bow, in heaven and on earth and under the earth, and every tongue declare that Jesus Christ is Lord, to the glory of God the Father."

(Philippians 2: 9 – 11 NLT)

Jesus can do exceedingly greater than you require of Him, even if your situation requires a last-minute miracle. He spent His time on earth exhibiting the tremendous power of God deposited in Him – the power to save and to heal. He came to the rescue of a man on the Cross. The man needed redemption for his soul and got it from the Saviour just at the right time. Jesus is doing the same today in any instance that help is called out to Him with an open and sincere heart. Charles Carroll Luther was a journalist and lay evangelist before being ordained as a Baptist minister in 1886. Though not a prolific composer, he authored an extraordinary hymn in 1877 when he heard a certain Rev. A.G. Upham relate to him the story of a young man who was about to die. The young man had known Christ for only one month. Though thankful to the Lord for granting him Salvation during his final hour, he was nevertheless grieved that he had no opportunity to serve the Lord nor to share Him with others. He explained, "I am not afraid to die; Jesus saves me now. But must I go empty-handed?"[1]

Upon hearing this account, Luther wrote the very popular hymn – Must I go an empty-handed? It is a song of sincere regret. It tells us that there is a better time to know Jesus, early in our lives and that after meeting Him, work must be done as demanded by Him. Jesus is the most important index in the life of a man. Anyone who ignores Him does so at his or her peril. To know Him is the ultimate experience and to do His work is the only way to have treasure in heaven. The life of the young man in our story is one we must all be wary of – never to miss the early opportunity to follow the Master.

> *"Seek the LORD while you can find him. Call on him now while he is near."*
>
> *(Isaiah 55:6 NLT)*

The Jesus we are talking about is the One who was in the beginning, the Word: He was with God, and He is God. God created everything in the world through Jesus, and it was through Him that life was given to all of God's creation. The presence of Jesus brought light to everyone, and this light shines in the darkness, and the dark cannot extinguish it. Jesus is the Alpha and Omega; the Beginning and the End. He is the End because He is coming soon to bring an end to the world. He has all the power on earth and in heaven and everyone who accepts Him, He will give the power to become children of God. There came a time when it pleased God that the Word became flesh to dwell among us. He came to show forth God's unfailing love and faithfulness. God anointed Him with the Holy Spirit and power; He went about doing good and healing all who were oppressed by the devil, for God was with Him. No wonder the songwriter said;

He is able, abundantly able; to deliver and to save. He is able abundantly able; to deliver those who trust in Him.

The earthly story of Jesus began in a little town called Bethlehem. The Bible tells us that while shepherds were watching their flock one cold winter night, God announced the birth of His only begotten Son through one of His messengers. God confirmed the royal status of Jesus through the gifts of gold, frankincense and myrrh – given to the Saviour by the wise men. The purpose of Jesus coming was to save the world from their sins. To fulfil this purpose, Jesus in agreement with His Father manifested the power of God everywhere He went – so that the world will believe in Him and know that God, His Father, indeed sent Him.

> *"And you know that God anointed Jesus of Nazareth with the Holy Spirit and with power. Then Jesus went around doing good and healing all who were oppressed by the devil, for God was with him."*
>
> *(Acts 10:38 NLT)*

Jesus proved Himself not only to be sufficient to meet our spiritual needs but also to contend with all our cares and burdens. He asked that our requests and supplications be brought to His attention so that we won't have to carry them by ourselves. Jesus can meet all our needs – only if we trust Him. He is able to deliver and to save. Jesus is a living assurance of the solution to our problems –the more so because He is alive and Jessie Brown Pounds (1861 – 1921) reechoed this conviction in her song **"I know that my redeemer liveth."** Jesus provides credible proof, even to the sceptics that He is willing and able to meet the needs of those who come to Him.

"However, those the Father has given me will come to me, and I will never reject them."

(John 6:37 NLT)

One of the most compelling evidences of the all-sufficient power of Jesus took place in a city called Bethany, east of Jerusalem. I am moved to tears, every time I go through this portion of the Bible. I feel so proud of Jesus and also humbled by the privilege of my relationship with Him. I cannot but imagine the way the onlookers of the day would have felt if little me could feel this way every single time I read the account of my Saviour's intervention in the life of His friend. The message that is taken from this particular miracle is that He has power over life and death (John 10:17 -18). This explains why the grave could not also hold Him. Again His intervention assures us that no matter what holds us down in life as indicated by the four days Lazarus spent in the grave; Jesus has the power to bring us out and to UNWRAP us from our problems.

Though I am still at the "nursery" stages of the knowledge of the Word of God, I believe that this Bethany visit of Jesus, is arguably one of the most significant encounters of man with God; if not in the whole Bible, at least in the New Testament. This encounter also reveals another truism; that He and His Father are one and that God Himself sent Jesus to the world for a specific purpose; the import of this is that we too can connect to God through Jesus. Jesus knew the end of the Lazarus encounter with death from the beginning. He said, **"It happened for the glory of God so that the Son of God will receive glory from this"** (John 11:14). Jesus intentionally delayed for two days after hearing the news because He has control over everything. The significance of this delay is another proof that time does not affect Him. We should be ready to wait for God's time anytime we seek divine intervention.

Jesus was ready to return to a city where there was an earlier attempt on His life. He did this because of His love for man, in this case, the man Lazarus. Jesus was sure of the Lazarus sickness outcome; a positive result when he said; **"our friend Lazarus has fallen asleep, but now I will go and wake him up"** (John 11:11). The Lazarus miracle was Jesus' way of telling His disciples that He is THE WAY, THE TRUTH AND THE LIFE. Jesus clarified to them that He knew that Lazarus was already dead, which meant that His reference to waking him up was not the conventional tap on the shoulder to wake someone up from a nap. Jesus knew what had happened and also what was required of Him. Many of those around Him did not even know Jesus well, while those who knew Him, did not realise that there were no limitations to what He could do.

Martha in our story knew Jesus and the fact that He had a special relationship with God, she even acknowledged Him as Messiah and Son of God, but she too like most had a limited understanding of the power of God in Christ Jesus. She knew some of what the Word of God promises, but she did not know enough about the Master. Many languish in the Martha club with half-baked bread – not having the full knowledge of the Word of God under spiritual guidance. Jesus knew what Martha did not know and which many do not know today. Jesus was there when Lazarus was created. He knew him while he was still in his mother's womb. He knows better than the best what had taken place during those four days in that tomb, and most importantly, He knew how to reverse it. Jesus proved in the Lazarus encounter that He was with God at creation and so death has no power over Him and over those whom He loves. He showed that His promise of eternal life was no fluke and that anyone who pitches his tent with Him makes a wise decision. Mary too like her sister had limited knowledge of the Son of God. She knew He could have prevented her brother from dying through His healing power, but beyond that, her "Jesus" could not go any further.

The question then is which Jesus raised Jairus' daughter, or did the story not reach the two sisters? Maybe they thought that the four days in the tomb were just too much for Jesus to cope with or handle. The response "come and see" when Jesus asked where Lazarus was laid, gives the impression that they expected Jesus to only visit the tomb as a show of respect and love. The lack of understanding and little faith of the two sisters is prevalent even today. "Lord, he has been dead for four days. The smell will be terrible"(John 11:39) was the sisters' proof that they did not know the Messiah well enough. In the end, Jesus manifested the power and glory of God to all who were present at the tomb. The transformation that took place by reversing the body's decay after four days in the grave can only be imagined. Jesus indeed can deliver and save. All you need to do is to turn to Him for help anytime you need it.

"Then Jesus shouted, "Lazarus, come out! "And the dead man came out, his hands and feet bound in grave clothes, his face wrapped in a headcloth. Jesus told them, "Unwrap him and let him go!"'

(John 11:43 – 44 NLT)

The world that we live in is full of all manner of religious messages. These are available to man to help him build a relationship with the Supreme Being. At the last count, I would say there are at least 16 religious faiths and persuasions in the world. One significant thing that readily comes to my mind when I think of all these persuasions is what the Psalmist said in the Bible;

"The idols of the nations are merely things of silver and gold, shaped by human hands. They have mouths but cannot speak, and eyes but cannot see. They have ears but cannot hear, and mouths but cannot breathe. And those who make idols are just like them, as are all who trust in them."

(Psalm 135: 15 – 18. NLT)

You must always ask yourself this question. Can the God I serve save me? For those of us who preach the crucified and risen Christ, we do so because we believe that it is impossible to please God without faith and that anyone who wants to come to Him must believe that God exists and that He rewards those who diligently seek Him.

> *"And it is impossible to please God without faith. Anyone who wants to come to him must believe that God exists and that he rewards those who sincerely seek him."*
>
> *(Hebrews 11:6 NLT)*

While growing up, I was privileged to have been a member of the choir in my local Baptist church in Kano, northwest of Nigeria. It was an excellent opportunity to serve God and to enjoy good music. The power of God's music continues to play a vital role in my life today. One of the many powerful songs I learnt and loved to sing, which finds daily relevance is titled Peace! Be still, written by Mary Ann Baker in 1874. Ms Baker wrote thus in connection with the inspiration for writing the song; **"A very dear and only brother, a young man of rare loveliness and promise of character, had been laid in the grave, a victim of the same disease that had already taken father and mother. His death occurred under peculiarly distressing circumstances. He was more than a thousand miles away from home, seeking in the balmy air of the sunny South the healing that our colder climate could not give. Suddenly he grew worse. The writer was ill and could not go to him. For two weeks the long lines of telegraph wires** carried back and forth messages between the dying brother and his waiting sisters, ere the word came which told us that our beloved brother was no longer a dweller on the earth. Although we mourn not as those without hope, and although I had believed on Christ in early childhood and had always desired to give the Master a consecrated and obedient life, I became wickedly rebellious at this dispensation of divine providence. I said in my heart that God did not care for me or mine. But the Master's voice stilled the tempest in my unsanctified heart, and brought it to the calm of deeper faith and perfect trust."[2]

This song takes a bearing from one of the early Jesus' proofs that He is Able. Jesus and His disciples were in a boat on the Sea of Galilee when a storm came, and water was filling the boat, causing danger and great panic. They were on an evangelical mission, so their purpose was godly. The presence of Jesus, therefore, does not preclude the absence of problems. My confidence, however, is in the adequacy of Jesus to address our needs anytime we call upon Him. Again Jesus is not moved by difficulties and challenges as represented by the storm. He was in this instance in the midst of all panicky men; sleeping at a corner of the boat. The fact that Jesus was available in the boat meant that the people and the vessel had divine insurance; not the type that pays for damage and lost lives but one that protects and prevents evil from overcoming us. The fact that the storms were no respecter of Jesus means they will be no respecter of you and I. The only prescription we must apply is to have faith. In other to have access to help, we must have access to Jesus. Without Him being in our lives, we cannot call on Him and access His help. Jesus is always willing to come into our boat (our lives); the only thing that shuts Him out is sin. "The winds and the waves shall obey Thy will, Peace, be still!" These were the positive words in the song by Mary Ann Baker. Today this same Jesus is ready to rebuke the storms in our lives.

> *"The disciples went and woke him up, shouting, "Master, Master, we're going to drown!" When Jesus woke up, he rebuked the wind and the raging waves. Suddenly the storm stopped, and all was calm. Then he asked them, "Where is your faith?" The disciples were terrified and amazed. "Who is this, man?" they asked each other. "When he gives a command, even the wind and waves obey him!"'*
>
> *(Luke 8:24 – 25 NLT)*

On the same journey after safely crossing the sea, Jesus arrived in the region of Gerasenes. This area is a place on the eastern side of the Sea of Galilee located near the modern city of Jerash in Jordan. The Jesus intervention in this locality perhaps might have more significance in the African Continent where there are enormous acknowledgements and recognition of the power of darkness; something also attested to by the Bible. Jesus showed that His mere presence is a major calamity to demonic forces. Not only do they recognise His sovereignty over them, but they do also attest to His ability to do to them as He pleases.

Jesus can subdue any force no matter how daring and powerful it may portend to be. The young man, according to the Bible, had been in bondage "for a long time, he had been homeless and naked, living in a cemetery outside the town" (Luke 8:27). All efforts to calm and control him had failed – "even when he was placed under guard and put in chains and shackles, he simply broke them and rushed out into the wilderness, completely under the demon's power"(Luke 8: 29). However, when he met the KING OF KINGS & the LORD OF LORDS, there again was the confirmation to us that Jesus is able. The chief tormentor now becomes the chief beggar saying; "please I beg you, don't torture me" (Luke 8:28)! That Jesus is able was not in doubt. He continues to show Himself mighty to save and deliver from physical and spiritual harm. All Jesus' interventions are permanent; hence the fear of the tormenting spirit that he was heading to the bottomless pit, a point of no return which finally was his destination. Today the most common spirit in peoples' lives has to do with sin. Just as the demons controlled the Gerasenes man, many have built a permanent residence for sin to control their lives. They make no effort to come to Jesus for help and Salvation. Sin has taken control of their lives, such that they are powerless to help themselves. Jesus is visiting you today through this medium, and if you determine to present yourself to Him, He is willing and able to free you from sin slavery.

> *"People rushed out to see what had happened. A crowd soon gathered around Jesus, and they saw the man who had been freed from the demons. He*

was sitting at Jesus' feet, fully clothed and per-fectly sane, and they were all afraid. Then those who had seen what happened told the others how the demon-possessed man had been healed. The man who had been freed from the demons begged to go with him. But Jesus sent him home, saying, "No, go back to your family, and tell them every-thing God has done for you." So he went all through the town proclaiming the great things Jesus had done for him."

(Luke 8: 35 – 36 & 38 – 39 NLT)

The Jesus encounter with the people was far from over. As led, He crossed again to the other side of the lake. The Bible referred to a large crowd welcoming Him – they had been waiting for Him. Jesus is waiting for many today to answer His knock on the door to their hearts. Alas, they refuse to open and allow Him to come in and have a meal with them. The Son of God wants to dine with you; what a real privilege! He can walk into your life, but He will not do so uninvited. Why don't you turn the key and open up for Him to come in and do the miracle that will change your life for good?

Jairus was a fortunate man. Not only had he heard about this prophet from Nazareth who heals all manner of diseases, but he was also humble enough to go after Him in a large crowd and not being ashamed or proud "fell at Jesus' feet pleading with Him to come home with him. His only daughter, who was about twelve years old, was dying"(Luke 8:41- 42). Jairus was a leader of the local synagogue. This was an exalted position at a time when

Judaism held sway. Paul, it was, who said he counted everything he was or had obtained as loss, all for the surpassing purpose of knowing Christ (Philippians 3:8). Jairus did the same for the sole purpose of meeting Christ to request for help.

> *"Pride ends in humiliation, while humility brings honour."*
> *(Proverbs 29:23 NLT)*

> *"True humility and fear of the LORD lead to riches, honour, and long life."*
> *(Proverbs 22:4 NLT)*

In humbling himself, Jairus received a long life for his daughter and recognition by the visit of Jesus to his home. He demonstrated an extreme measure of faith by going to Jesus in the first instance and even when the news came that the child was dead, he did not heed the counsel of the messenger who brought the news saying; "there is no use troubling the Teacher now" (Luke 8:49). He chose to believe Jesus, who assured him that the child would be healed. How can a dead child be healed you will ask too? Is it possible that the messenger who was trusted did not know what he was saying? Again Jesus demonstrated to all that He can deliver in whatever circumstance. Though the crowd laughed at Him, Jesus' focus was, as always, to do the work of Him who has sent Him before the night falls. "My child, get up"(Luke 8:54) was all that was required in the physical for her life to return. I know that what Jesus did and is still doing is far beyond the physical. The battle in the spirit won by Jesus is confirmed physically for the Jairus family and the crowd to experience.

The control of the life of the dead child is seen in the choice of words that Jesus spoke. Jesus has this power because He was part of the creation process of Jairus' daughter and He alone could have reversed what had taken place. Today many laugh at Jesus directly and indirectly. They laugh because of unbelief in the Salvation and power of God available in Christ to their loss and detriment. You are reading this and must take advantage. Jesus' message is for you to avoid destruction. Jesus is available and able to help you to be free, indeed. He set the child free and can do so to you today.

> *"The house was filled with people weeping and wailing, but he said, "Stop the weeping! She isn't dead; she's only asleep."'*
>
> *(Luke 8:52 NLT)*

While the Jairus experience was a short-lived one which met with the power of Jesus, there are many today who have been carrying their cross of problems for several years. The power of Jesus is also able to surmount long drawn out issues. One exceptional case of long-term suffering was reported in detail by Mark's account of the life of Jesus. The person in question who the Bible did not name, was a woman who had a long-standing bleeding problem. According to Mark, this woman had suffered nonstop for twelve years. She had experienced a great deal from many doctors and over the years had spent everything she had to pay them without getting any result. The

Bible recorded that she had even become worse. Fortune finally smiled at her; she heard about Jesus! She believed that Jesus could deliver her since He had been healing all manner of diseases. She took a step of faith and did something unprecedented. Her experience tells me that there is no one single way to access the divine power of God; if only we believe. Her faith in Christ and His healing power was manifest immediately after she touched the hem of His garment. She had gone forward in faith to find Jesus not to speak to Him but to touch His robe. That is how simple it can be when we anchor our faith on the Son of God. It does not depend on any other thing. The end came to her twelve years of suffering and shame because of this unique encounter. Jesus not only healed her but knew immediately about this occurrence because He is all-knowing. There is nothing outside His sphere of control and knowledge. All we need to do is to come unto Him with all our problems. He is able to deliver and to save.

"And he said to her, "Daughter, your faith has made you well. Go in peace. Your suffering is over."'
(Mark 5:34. NLT)

In the world today and especially in the third world, people are so deprived that Jesus is offered to them only on a platter of material things. Jesus is not just there to meet our material needs. He said that man should not live by bread alone. However, many have material needs, and Jesus can meet them. He requires that we must follow His ways which are upright and not crooked and all His promises – both material and otherwise will be a reality in our lives, provided the needs are in sync with His plan and purpose for us at that time. Jesus' proof of His all-sufficient power was again manifested as He went about feeding the people with God's Word. In this instance, the Bible reported an audience of over 5000 men; not counting the women and children. Jesus had done enough to meet their spiritual needs and also wanted to attend to the physical demands of the crowd. This encounter throws up a lot of lessons for those who are intent on following Jesus.

Philip, in the account of John, took a position many including this writer, will take today. When Jesus asked for a solution to the feeding needs of the people, Philip remained in the physical and replied Jesus that **"even if we worked for months, we wouldn't have enough money to feed them"**(John 6:7)! Philip was working by sight and could not see a solution to the problem, no wonder Apostle Paul reminded the people of Corinth that as Christians we should live by believing and not by seeing (2 Corinthians 5:7). Andrew, like Philip, was unable to see beyond the challenge, although he was able to identify a young boy with five barley loaves and two fishes. He too concluded negatively by saying – **"but what good is that with this huge crowd"**(John 6:9). The propensity to express fear in the face of a problem is widespread in man. God, however, expects us as Christians to set a different example for others to follow as light & salt of the world. We, according to the Word of God, have not been given the Spirit of fear and timidity. The Spirit that we have is that of POWER!

"For God has not given us a spirit of fear and timidity but of power, love, and self-discipline."

(2 Timothy 1:7 NLT)

While reflecting on this encounter, my mind goes back to the boy who gave his food. The young boy demonstrated an uncommon action for which there was no regret. Many benefited from his generous response, and same brought up a great reward to him in the form of twelve leftover baskets. I want to believe that at the worst he would have been given back his seed meaning he helped so many people at no cost. Jesus demonstrated that He could meet our physical needs no matter the contending situation. The thing to do is not to emulate the lack of faith shown by Philip and Andrew – only focus on Jesus alone. Of course, ultimately, the people sat down as instructed by Jesus. They could not help themselves and were very hungry. The Apostles too were no better as they were still growing in their faith and knowledge of Jesus. The same is the case today, where you may find that some ministers of the Gospel may not be able to help you strengthen your faith. All you have to do is to look up to Jesus, the Author and Finisher of your faith. He can provide you with all your needs. Anyone who puts his trust in Him will not be put to shame.

"After everyone was full, Jesus told his disciples, "Now gather the leftovers, so that nothing is wasted." So they picked up the pieces and filled twelve baskets with scraps left by the people who had eaten from the five barley loaves."

(John 6:12 – 13 NLT)

The high and mighty also need Jesus. Though the Bible is clear that it is difficult for a rich man to enter the kingdom of God, Jesus always shows that God's love, available through Him, is for all. A centurion is a professional officer of the Roman army after the Marian reforms of 107 BC.[3] In ancient Rome the "centurion" meant "captain of 100", and the Roman centurion was captain of 100-foot soldiers in a legion. The centurion is loyal and courageous, beginning as a soldier in the army and working his way up the ranks. They were noticed by the general for their skill and courage in battle and were made officers. A centurion, therefore, is a principal military officer.[4]

Jesus' encounter with this centurion is not only significant because of the status of the man, but it is also important because the man demonstrated a type of faith that blew the mind of Jesus. The officer also showed love which is the focal point of the Good News. In Saint Luke's account, the centurion was reported to have built a good relationship with the Jewish elders such that he could request their help in reaching out to Jesus. He made this conscious effort to reach Jesus on behalf of his slave, though a highly valued one. For those of us who are students of history, we will recall that the relationship between the Roman occupiers and their Jewish hosts was never that cordial. This, however, did not prevent the centurion from going out of his way to building bridges; bridges he now had to pass through to get help from Jesus. He had a good reputation - "for he loves the Jewish people and even built a synagogue for us"(Luke 7:5). The slave too valued his work and his master and was dutiful enough to make him well appreciated; working as if unto God. Little wonder his master went out of his way to seek help for him.

> *"Slaves, obey your earthly masters in everything you do. Try to please them all the time, not just when they are watching you. Serve them sincerely because of your reverent fear of the Lord. Work willingly at whatever you do, as though you were working for the Lord rather than for people. Remember that the Lord will give you an inheritance as your reward and that the Master you are serving is Christ. But if you do what is wrong, you will be paid back for the wrong you have done. For God has no favourite. Masters, be just and fair to your slaves. Remember that you also have a Master—in heaven."*
>
> *(Colossians 3:22 – 25 & 4:1NLT)*

The Centurion & his servant both sowed, and when it was time to reap, God did not disappoint them. The centurion recognised the power of Jesus and showed exceptional humility even as an officer of the vast Roman army to decline Jesus to visit his home, claiming he was unworthy of such an honour. How unique indeed! Jesus proved that He is the Word, who was at the beginning with God, and through which God created everything and that He gave life to everything that was created. Unlike other miracles of Jesus where contact was made with the beneficiary or where He was near the one needing help, this encounter was one of the rare occasions where Jesus assisted afar as a consequence of man's faith in Him. You too can access God's mercy through Christ if only you believe. Jesus can meet your needs and is not affected by distance once you ask in faith.

"When Jesus heard this, he was amazed. Turning to the crowd that was following him, he said, "I tell you, I haven't seen faith like this in all Israel!" And when the officer's friends returned to his house, they found the slave completely healed."

(Luke 7:9 – 10 NLT)

The divine elevation of Jesus above all is none better exemplified than during the Capernaum healing of the paralytic man. Although Jesus' greatest miracle was done on the Cross when He through the sacrifice of His life, gave man access to eternal life, nevertheless He showed very early in His ministry concerning this miracle that all power has been given to Him by God Almighty. The Bible recounts the desperation of the man's friends who dug a hole through the roof to gain access to Jesus while ministering. They demonstrated massive faith in Jesus, leading to their gatecrashing the session. Jesus chose to stir up controversy instead of addressing the perceived immediate need of the helpless man. He proclaimed the forgiveness of his sin to show that He had the power and probably because in this case, that was the remote cause of the paralysis. Jesus not only gave the sick man freedom from the bondage of disease but also the more critical freedom from sin that could lead to a second death. Jesus has power over the body and the soul and can save us from the destruction of both.

"Jesus knew immediately what they were thinking, so he asked them, "Why do you question this in your hearts? Is it easier to say to the paralysed man 'Your sins are forgiven,' or 'Stand up, pick

up your mat, and walk'? So I will prove to you that the Son of Man has the authority on earth to forgive sins." Then Jesus turned to the paralysed man and said, "Stand up, pick up your mat, and go home!" And the man jumped up, grabbed his mat, and walked out through the stunned onlookers. They were all amazed and praised God, exclaiming, "We've never seen anything like this before!"'

(Mark 2: 8 – 12 NLT)

It is possible for you as a child of God to access God's throne of mercy, but this is only through the name of Jesus. Jesus must recognise you before He can give you access to Himself. All who have called upon His name have never been disappointed. Peter & John demonstrated that just like Jesus; they could exhibit the power of God but only in the name of Jesus. The young shall grow indeed as both gave the best that is available in the name of Jesus.

"Peter and John looked at him intently, and Peter said, "Look at us!" The lame man looked at them eagerly, expecting some money. But Peter said, "I don't have any silver or gold for you. But I'll give you what I have. In the name of Jesus Christ, the Nazarene, get up and walk!" Then Peter took the lame man by the right hand and helped him up. And as he did, the man's feet and ankles were instantly healed and strengthened. He jumped up, stood on his feet, and began to walk! Then, walking, leaping, and praising God, he went into the Temple with them. All the people saw him walking and heard him praising God. When they realised he was the lame beggar they had seen so often at the Beautiful Gate, they were absolutely

astounded! They all rushed out in amazement to Solomon's Colonnade, where the man was holding tightly to Peter and John."

(Acts 3: 4 – 11 NLT)

The Jesus that we present to you can wipe away any tear from your eyes. Stop crying and turn to Jesus. The experience of the widow of Nain is no fairy tale. She had lost hope. Her husband was no more, and her only son was about to be buried. Jesus came into her situation, and the tears dried up. He is ready to do the same for you if you will allow Him.

"When the Lord saw her, his heart overflowed with compassion. "Don't cry!" he said. Then he walked over to the coffin and touched it, and the bearers stopped. "Young man," he said, "I tell you, get up." Then the dead boy sat up and began to talk! And Jesus gave him back to his mother."

(Luke 7: 13 – 15 NLT)

Testimonies of Jesus' intervention in the lives of His friends are too many to mention here. I am encouraged to share one of those testimonies with you.

The testifier calls it DIVINE CONNECTION - HOW I MET MY HUSBAND. In her own words, the story goes thus; I gave my life to Christ in the year 1986 in Kano, Kano state, northwest of Nigeria at the National Evangelical Mission, Kano branch, where I heard the sound teaching of the Word of God and how to live a Christian life. In 1993 I left Kano for Lagos as a result of transfer at my place of work. Upon my arrival in Lagos, I went in search of a church where I could continue to receive the sound teaching of the Word of God. I joined a church where I spent over ten years. During this period, the church conducted many marriage ceremonies; the question many people in the church and my office were asking was when I would get married? But the answer was unknown to me, though I had pencilled down the type of person to marry. The desire to marry the very kind of person I had pencilled down was so intense that many considered me to be too selective, and I became a laughing stock both in the office, neighbourhood and church. Many people had written me off but God re-wrote me on!

On the 31st of December 2005, during the cross-over service, I joined the Calvary Army Ministries (aka Warfare Tent) in Ejigbo, Lagos State, southwest of Nigeria. The church is known for deliverance and expository teaching of the Word of God. The general superintendent of the church, who is a disciplinarian and God's General, focuses on the sound teaching of the Word of God. I attended the church for five years as a single sister. I was committed to all the church programmes and activities, growing both physically and spiritually. But the problem of when and whom to marry was paramount in my mind. The criteria I pencilled down were always fresh in my mind. The church usually observes its annual forty days fasting and prayer programme between October & November, every year. In the year 2010, when the programme was about to commence, the assistant general superintendent said to me, **"Use this year's programme to seek God's**

**face concerning your life partner. Stop moving by sight
and praying for materials things. Allow the will of God
in your life."** I was angry and replied, that I have been
praying for a life partner, but God has not revealed any-
body to me besides I had zeroed my mind to the fact that I
might not get married because my desire was yet to be met
and I became frustrated. She replied, "If you are a child of
God, one to three days is enough to get an answer from
God when you pray in faith." This was a challenge to me
as someone who had given her life to Christ Jesus a long
time ago, and I decided to take my annual leave so that I
could seek the face of God and also know my standing as
a child of God.

The programme commenced on the 10th of October
2010. On the first day, the general superintendent; Pastor
Gabriel Joseph preached on the topic: The Journey to the
Power House of God. After the service, I got home and
prayed; I said, "God, I resign myself to your will. O Lord,
let your will prevail in my life and my marriage." On the
second day, the sermon was on the same topic. One getting back home, I repeated the same prayer to God, but
there was no revelation, and as a result of this, I considered
changing my prayer point to something else. On the third
day, I planned to arrive at the church early to have time to
pray for the day's programme. At about 3:15 p.m., I was
feeling a bit weak, so I decided to wait for some minutes
before leaving for the programme. Suddenly, I fell into a
trance. In it, a purple coloured skirt was handed over to
me, but I could not identify the person who gave me the

skirt. After a while, I stood up, went to the church and narrated the vision to the assistant general superintendent. She advised that I need to pray more for God to reveal to me who brought the skirt. Between the fourth to the sixth day, I continued with my fasting and prayers, but there was no revelation about who gave me the skirt. On the seventh day, the general superintendent preached a message tagged HOLY GHOST AND HUMAN PROBLEM focusing on the scriptures below:

> *"Then God said, "Let there be light," and there was light."*
>
> *(Genesis 1:3 NLT)*

> *"He also says to the Son, "In the beginning, Lord, you laid the foundation of the earth and made the heavens with your hands."*
>
> *(Hebrews 1:10 NLT)*

> *"When I look at the night sky and see the work of your fingers— the moon and the stars you set in place."*
>
> *(Psalm 8:3 NLT)*

In the message by the general superintendent, he said: "The Holy Spirit creates light where there is darkness, darkness represents confusion and stagnation." He continued; "when people have written you off, all you need is the Holy Spirit. A man or woman who is baptised by the Holy Spirit will be a problem solver and will have insight into any matter." The message on the Holy Spirit and my prayer on the revelation about the skirt continued till November 11th, 2010. On this fateful day, the church had a crusade outside its premises in the evening. Immediately the programme ended at 9:00 p.m.; there was a torrential downpour. I headed home, and on getting to my house, behold the gate was closed, and there was nobody to open it for me. I was under the rain; my Bible and my choir book were both soaked. I stood in the rain for about one hour, and some minutes, before a neighbour came to assist in opening the door.

> *"Then the Lord God said, "It is not good for the man to be alone."*
>
> *(Genesis 2:18a NLT)*

I got into my apartment and discovered that rain had entered into my sitting room, and everywhere was flooded. I became frustrated and dejected that night, and I could not even thank God nor continue in the prayer concerning the revelation about the skirt. I climbed into my bed in tears, feeling lonely and slept off. At about 3:15 a.m. of 12th November 2010, I had a clear revelation of who the person was! The face was so bright, and God revealed specific details in advance about the life of the man, and this was confirmed when we finally met. Unfortunately, I had never seen the brother before in my local church. At this time, I decided not to disclose the revelation and the message to anyone as the face I saw was not in my church. The months of December and January rolled by, and the brother had not surfaced physically.

My advice is that, when you decide to get insight into a matter, take time out to seek God's face, engage the Holy Spirit, He will respond to all your yearnings.

> *'"Keep on asking, and you will receive what you ask for. Keep on seeking, and you will find. Keep on knocking, and the door will be opened to you.*

For everyone who asks, receives. Everyone who
seeks finds. And to everyone who knocks, the
door will be opened."
                                    (Matthew 7:7 -8 NLT)

In March 2011, the marriage committee of my church
invited me and said I should pray concerning a brother
who had seen a revelation about me. I asked if the brother
is a member of this church. They were reluctant to say yes
or no. Then I told them, if the brother is in this church,
he is not the person God revealed to me. The Committee
concluded that I should continue to pray.

My advice is that God is not an author of confusion
when He reveals things; He watches it pass. Never con-
fuse God's revelation with mental projection. Be very
sure you heard from God because the vision would be
tested.

"This vision is for a future time. It describes the
end, and it will be fulfilled. If it seems slow in
coming, wait patiently, for it will surely take
place. It will not be delayed."
                                    (Habakkuk 2:3 NLT)

It was during the same period on a particular Sunday
service; I was teaching in the Sunday school with my class
facing the entrance of the church. Behold the brother who
gave me the purple skirt in my revelation came in and
walked straight to the technical corner where the church
had its media gadgets and not too long afterwards he left.
At this moment, I lost concentration in my Sunday school
teaching. After the service that day I went home, and I

began to think; I hope the brother is not from the tribe I would wish not to marry. In April 2011, another brother in the church went to the marriage committee and told them that he had seen a revelation concerning me. The marriage committee, therefore, invited me again and this time, I had to disclose the full details of the series of revelations I have had and how the brother had come to work on the church media gadgets. It became astonishing because he is not a member of the church and nobody knows much about him and his Christian faith. At this juncture, the marriage committee decided to invite the brother I saw in my revelation for detailed discussion. They wanted to find out who the brother was; his Christian background, and his family background. After that, his Pastor was contacted to give more information about him; this exercise took a month. After the series of investigation and findings, on 1st June 2011, the marriage committee introduced us to each other. I then discovered that the brother is a Yoruba man, and this made me very sad. I was downcast, and I cried heavily to the extent that I was accompanied home by a sister in the church. I got home sobbing with a feeling that God had not met my needs as I desired. I had an inner voice asking me to read Isaiah 66:24. After reading this portion of the Bible, I started pleading for forgiveness, and I immediately cried to God saying that I have resigned from my desire and right away I heard an audible voice speak to me; "read Isaiah 55:8."

> *"And as they go out, they will see the dead bodies of those who have rebelled against me. For the worms that devour them will never die, and the*

fire that burns them will never go out. All who pass by will view them with utter horror."'

(Isaiah 66:24 NLT)

"'My thoughts are nothing like your thoughts," says the Lord. "And my ways are far beyond anything you could imagine."

(Isaiah 55:8 NLT)

It was evident to everyone that this is a divine connection. At this point, the marriage committee began its proper marriage counselling and other regularities as instituted by the church. On the 10th of March 2012, the wedding ceremony finally took place, three months shy of my 38th birthday. My husband is the perfect match I envisaged. He is my friend, brother and companion indeed. God instituted marriage in the Garden of Eden. He is still in the business of giving wives and husbands to those who give Him a perfect chance to select for them. Abandon your list of the type of husband or wife you want. Stop going by sight and cling to the selection God will make for you. God is the Porter; you are the clay, allow Him to mould you the way He wishes. Never struggle with Him. He knows who you are, and He is ready to meet your need accordingly. This concludes my testimony on Divine Connection to the glory of God.

It is not enough to know that Jesus is able. The miracles of His time and that of the sister above are available to all who depend on Him. To be known to Jesus means that if you knock on the door of His house, so to speak, He will open the door because you have surrendered your life to

Him. The disciples of Jesus received power to do what the Master had done in their own time. You too can receive power if you surrender your life to Jesus. These are not mere stories; they are real occurrences that can also happen in your life. Whatever you are passing through, Jesus can deliver and save you. I want to close with another miracle of Jesus. Jesus was in the district of Tyre and Sidon, where a Syrophoenician woman approached Him for help regarding her sick daughter. Although Jesus ultimately provided succour to her by healing her daughter after persistent pleading, He made it clear to her that she did not qualify for any help from Him because of her status. This is a lesson for all.

> *"Then Jesus said to the woman, "I was sent only to help God's lost sheep—the people of Israel." But she came and worshipped him, pleading again, "Lord, help me!" Jesus responded, "It isn't right to take food from the children and throw it to the dogs.""*
>
> *(Matthew 15: 24 – 26 NLT)*

The above encounter shows that His blessings are not for all. If you want to access them, you MUST establish a relationship with Him. Jesus is willing to make you a son or daughter today. Are you ready?

> *"But to all who believed him and accepted him, he gave the right to become children of God. They are reborn—not with a physical birth resulting from human passion or plan, but a birth that comes from God."*
>
> *(John 1: 12 – 13. NLT)*

Take advantage of this gift and go to the Saviour. He is waiting for you with open arms.

I Will Follow Him

"Then Jesus said to his disciples, "If any of you wants to be my follower, you must give up your own way, take up your cross, and follow me."

(*Matthew 16:24 NLT*)

Good Friday is a special day in Christendom. It is a day we remember the great love that God has towards humanity epitomised by sending His Son Jesus to die on the Cross of Calvary. Jesus arose, and so completed the work of Salvation. I usually spend my Good Friday mornings in church but this year 2016, our Easter morning programme was replaced with a night vigil. On the morning of Good Friday, I travelled to Iwo, near Ibadan, southwest of Nigeria, to visit my younger daughter at Bowen University. On my return, though I had planned to be in the church that night, I was too tired to go. To connect with the occasion, I spent my late evening before going to bed watching a Franco Zeffirelli produced version of the very popular film – Jesus of Nazareth. Being too tired to go to church, I expected to begin the movie and shortly fall asleep; this, however, did not happen. Though I was not watching the film for the first time, it produced such a remarkable impact on me that several scenes in the movie brought me to tears. I wept because of the effect the life of Jesus made on humanity. I saw in Him, someone who left no stone unturned to attend to the needs of the people, both physical and spiritual. I was moved by the fact that Jesus towered above all situations and problems. The fact that He brought succour to the oppressed and the hopeless made me very emotional as I went through the miracle scenes. Jesus' message of peace which He gives to us, not as the world gives was very pervasive all through His people encounters. I wept because it came across to me once again that Jesus is the best of God, offered to man and yet many still do not know this to be a fact. The tears that ran down my cheeks were because not only did I feel so proud of my Saviour, I was fortunate to know Him as I continue to try every day to model my life after His.

"And a voice from heaven said, "This is my dearly loved Son, who brings me great joy."'
(Matthew 3:17 NLT)

As I reflected on Jesus and all the good He brought to humanity, it became clear again to me that this Jesus is sufficient for me and following up on that I said to myself that whatever it will take, **"I will follow Him all through the rest of my life."** As I meditated upon this resolve and reaffirmation, something within me said that I must share with others the message of following Jesus and what it takes to be His disciple. Jesus spent a brief time on earth, and it was devoted to His purpose for coming to the world. His message was simple and straightforward for all who want to follow after Him. His commitment to doing the work of God was so unrivalled that we can learn many things from it, whether for our spiritual or secular lives. To follow Jesus is not a child's play. Though it is gratifying, it requires a complete abandonment of an existing way of life for another prescribed by the Master. Critically the one who follows Jesus will find many instances where he has to make choices – to choose to align with the flesh or the spirit, to consider immediate benefits or wait for the future gains and to build treasures on earth or in heaven.

> *"Then Peter said to him, "We've given up everything to follow you. What will we get?" Jesus replied, "I assure you that when the world is made new, and the Son of Man sits upon his glorious throne, you who have been my followers will also sit on twelve thrones, judging the twelve tribes of Israel. And everyone who has given up houses or brothers or sisters or father or mother or children or property, for my sake, will receive a hundred times as much in return and will inherit eternal life. But many who are the greatest now will be least important then, and those who seem least important now will be the greatest then."*
>
> *(Matthew 19:27 – 30 NLT)*

Jesus Prescribes a Life of Orderliness, Obedience and Humility

The coming of Jesus to the world was for a predetermined and definite purpose. It was to provide a final and adequate Salvation package for humanity. Jesus knew this plan and what was expected of Him at every stage. He knew that regardless of the lower stature of John the Baptist, He had to receive baptism from him at the Galilee end of the Jordan River. This orderly life of Jesus was maintained regardless of situation and circumstance. He knew the role of John in advance and the fact that He had to tow God's line obediently. He showed uncommon humility by allowing one who could only baptise with water to execute His baptism – He who could baptise with the Holy Spirit and fire. Jesus came in human form as a testimony of His humble nature. He left His glory to come as a servant to carry out work assigned to Him by God. All through His life, He walked the path of orderliness, obedience and humility. The laying down of His life and washing of disciples' feet were examples of obedience to the Father and humility to a fault. The life of a Christian cannot be complete without orderliness, obedience and humility.

> *"Then Jesus went from Galilee to the Jordan River to be baptized by John. But John tried to talk him out of it. "I am the one who needs to be baptized by you," he said, "so why are you coming to me?" But Jesus said, "It should be done, for we must carry out all that God requires." So John agreed to baptize him."*
>
> *(Matthew 3:13 – 15)*

Jesus Prescribes a Life of Holiness

In the early account of the ministry of Jesus, He faced a well-orchestrated plan by Satan to scuttle God's purpose for His life. A typical experience for an everyday Christian or person, the action to take is to use of Word of God to confront the devil. Jesus confirmed this position as in every instance of temptation; He overcame with the Word of God. The American songwriter Horatio Richmond Palmer clarified in his song – "Yield not to Temptation" that it is not the exposure to a temptation that disconnects us from God but our falling into it. The life of Joseph in Egypt while in Potiphar's house is a perfect example of how we should react to temptation – fleeing. Joseph left his cloak in the hands of Potiphar's wife as he ran from the house. Although this may have been used as evidence in chief against him, God never forsakes or abandons the faithful. The good thing about temptation is that "each victory will help you some other to win" according to Palmer's song. To overcome temptation, we need Jesus, and only Jesus can save. Jesus is the WORD that we must know and apply when temptations inevitably come to us. These temptations will be diverse, mostly targeting our weaknesses, but if we ask Jesus for help, He is willing to aid us and will carry us through. Jesus is what He is today because He was able to overcome temptation. We too can overcome with His help, and when we do, there is a reward for us. Palmer said: "to him that overcometh, God giveth a crown". The life of a Christian is a practical walk in the footsteps of Jesus. If Jesus can do it, you too can!

> *"Then Jesus was led by the Spirit into the wilderness to be tempted there by the devil. For forty days and forty nights, he fasted and became very hungry. During that time, the devil came and said to him, "If you are the Son of God, tell these stones to become loaves of bread." But Jesus told him, "No! The Scriptures say, 'People do not live by bread alone, but by every word that comes from the mouth of God.'" Then the devil took him to the holy city, Jerusalem, to the highest point of the Temple, and said, "If you are the Son of God,*

jump off! For the Scriptures say, 'He will order his angels to protect you. And they will hold you up with their hands so you won't even hurt your foot on a stone.' Jesus responded, "The Scriptures also say, 'You must not test the LORD your God.'" Next the devil took him to the peak of a very high mountain and showed him all the kingdoms of the world and their glory. "I will give it all to you," he said, "if you will kneel down and worship me." "Get out of here, Satan," Jesus told him. "For the Scriptures say, 'You must worship the LORD your God and serve only him." Then the devil went away, and angels came and took care of Jesus."

(Mathew 4: 1 – 11 NLT)

Jesus Prescribes a Life of Positive Difference

The followers of Jesus were first called Christians in Antioch; a city in present-day Turkey. They were so-called because of a lifestyle similar to that of Jesus seen in them. Jesus intended it to be so. He expects His followers to live as strangers in the world with a focus on a home above. This lifestyle is a life of positive impact to cause a change to occur. Jesus drove this message home by comparing His followers to salt and light – each having the clear and distinct effects that it brings to bear anytime it is exposed or made to come in contact with anything. Salt is essential for human life and plays many roles; common among them is that of flavouring and preservation. Jesus used the benefit of seasoning to depict what he expects His followers to be in the world – adding flavour to the world. Jesus goes further to liken His followers to light in the presence of darkness. The world, with its sin and corruption, represent darkness; Christians must provide a contrast to this darkness by shining their light into the world. A person, therefore, who professes to be His follower and does not give light or saltiness cannot claim to know Christ at all. Christians must lead a life that sets an example for others to follow. They must never be hidden from the world; instead, in humility, they are supposed to shine so that the world will become illuminated by the life that they have gained from Christ.

> *"You are the salt of the earth. But what good is salt if it has lost its flavour? Can you make it salty again? It will be thrown out and trampled underfoot as worthless. "You are the light of the world—like a city on a hilltop that cannot be hidden. No one lights a lamp and then puts it under a basket. Instead, a lamp is placed on a stand, where it gives light to everyone in the house. In the same way, let your good deeds shine out for all to see so that everyone will praise your heavenly Father."*
>
> (Matthew 5: 13 – 16 NLT)

Jesus Prescribes a Life of Faithfulness & Peace

Jesus knew early in His ministry that He needed to make clarifications concerning His mission and message. He knew that there was the likelihood of the people misunderstanding Him and the religious leaders taking advantage of it, which may still be the case today. Jesus gave full approval to the Ten Commandments but clarified that the context in which He wanted the people to view them was different. He emphasised that all the laws were equal and that obedience to all is not negotiable. To those who place greater emphasis on teaching the doctrine but less so on being doers of the law, Jesus warned that they would not enter the kingdom of heaven. He clarified that such people's understanding of the law was restrictive. He wanted His followers to know that God intended the statute to reach beyond the limited level the people had kept it. He gave insight to God's mind that murder, just like anger, malicious words and curses are all placed on the same pedestal of being against the law with no ranking whatsoever – all who are found wanting in any one of them "are in danger of the fires of hell"(Matthew 5:22). Jesus encouraged His followers to embrace a life of continuous reconciliation towards peace. He affirmed God's unwillingness to accept anyone who does not tow this line.

> *"'So if you are presenting a sacrifice at the altar in the Temple and you suddenly remember that someone has something against you, leave your sacrifice there at the altar. Go and be reconciled to that person. Then come and offer your sacrifice to God."*
>
> *(Matthew 5: 23 – 24 NLT)*

Jesus Prescribes a Life of Total Commitment

The purpose of Jesus coming is to help us gain merit for eternal life. To assist His followers in appreciating this the more, Jesus used the analogy of the sin of adultery. He taught that lustfully looking at a woman constitutes God's definition of adultery and gets its justification from the

Law of Moses, which warns against covetousness. Jesus told His followers that no price should be too high to pay for their Salvation. He warned that in many instances, His followers would be faced with opportunity cost situation for their Salvation. He counselled that even our most prized possessions should not come between us and our higher goal of reigning with Him. Jesus saw in advance the experiences of many today whose love for the things of the world has stolen their Salvation. This is why He talked about denying ourselves and taking up our cross.

> *"So if your eye; even your good eye causes you to lust, gouge it out and throw it away. It is better for you to lose one part of your body than for your whole body to be thrown into hell."*

(Matthew 5:29 NLT)

Jesus Teaches Against Divorce

One of God's most cherished and valued relationship is one that exists between a man and his wife. God set up this union very early at creation when He determined by Himself that it is not good for Adam to be alone. His expectation confirms the value placed by God on marriage that the two should become one after taking their vows. God's choice of man's partner is deemed good enough; hence his calling her – right for him. Jesus, who was part of the creation team, places the same value on matrimony and expects that in this relationship, no price should be too much to pay to keep it going. He demands that His followers establish a relationship with their spouses; same as exists between Him and His church. It is a relationship that made Him give His life for the church and for which the husband must do likewise if the situation calls for it. The wife too like unto God must submit to her husband. The relationship between Christ and the church is eternal. So He expects His followers to have a similar mindset in their marriages until death do them part – never finding any price too much to pay to achieve the purpose of God in marriage. Divorce, according to Jesus, is therefore never an option.

> *"But Jesus responded, "He wrote this command-ment only as a concession to your hard hearts. But 'God made them male and female' from the beginning of creation. 'This explains why a man leaves his father and mother and is joined to his wife, and the two are united into one.' Since they are no longer two but one, let no one split apart what God has joined together."'*
>
> *(Mark 10: 5 – 9 NLT)*

Jesus Prescribes a Life Distinction

The way we live our life matters so much to Jesus. He came to teach us a lifestyle that will glorify God and bring benefit to ourselves and others. Jesus led a simple life that was guided by strict adherence to the will of His Father. Little wonder He says His nourishment comes from doing the will of His Father. Many who have been adopted into the Christian family find it difficult to follow in the footsteps of Jesus. Jesus wants us to live a life that is driven by love for everybody. He is particular that our lifestyle should not be one that will show only reciprocal love but one which transmits love to persons who are willing, in some cases, to do us harm. His view of love is that we must be different from others and demonstrate that we are true children of God by loving our enemies. Christ also warns against exerting revenge in any way or form. Many do not see anything wrong in this because it is a human way of getting back at those who offend us. I recall a prominent pastor telling me years ago that she did not see anything wrong with retaliation – though that was before she became a Christian. The standard of God presented by Jesus was for His followers not to consider anything too significant to offer or give up for their faith. For Him, giving must be a part of the Christian life for it to be complete and meaningful. Jesus counselled that not only is the giving important, but the motive and mode of giving as well. He admonished all who give to do so secretly because God, who rewards all giving, sees everything we do either openly or secretly. He warned that the reward for doing good is lost once we expose our giving for others to commend us. Jesus will go on to pray for the forgiveness of those who crucified Him as proof that He does what He preaches.

> *"If you love only those who love you, what reward is there for that? Even corrupt tax collectors do that much. If you are kind only to your friends, how are you different from anyone else? Even pagans do that. But you are to be perfect, even as your Father in heaven is perfect."*
>
> (Matthew 5:46 – 48 NLT)

Jesus Teaches About Monetary Possessions

Jesus knows that as far as we are in the world, money will remain very important to us. He has asked us not to store up possessions here on earth but instead to focus on heavenly treasures. It was Solomon, reputed to be one of the wisest men ever to live that summed up all about this world as meaningless. He had lived a life full of the best of life's possessions, and yet he came up with the conclusion that all we struggle to grab in this world is not worth it AT THE END OF THE DAY!

> *"Don't store up treasures here on earth, where moths eat them and rust destroys them, and where thieves break in and steal. Store your treasures in heaven, where moths and rust cannot destroy, and thieves do not break in and steal. Wherever your treasure is, there, the desires of your heart will also be."*
>
> *(Matthew 6: 19 – 21 NLT)*

Jesus warned that the risk attached to storing wealth here on earth is very high. He suggested that the better thing to do is to put our possessions in heaven where it is safe and secure with zero risks. Jesus had a heavenly mandate which meant that His preoccupation was how to keep us focused on the life hereafter. He knows that to help us have and retain this focus, it will be better if our treasure is in heaven. To have treasure in heaven, you must serve God faithfully and be committed to doing all that Christ has commanded us to do. This way, God continues to keep our reward in the heavenly bank so that when we get there, we can cash the same. A wise person is one who does everything possible to qualify for a place in God's kingdom, having stored up treasures therein. Again Jesus made His followers realise that money must not compete with God in their lives. The things of God must remain pivotal to them and money seen and used only as a tool for the glory of God. In acknowledging God's supremacy, Jesus demands that His followers must depend on Him entirely for their sustenance and cast all their cares and burdens upon Him – never to worry as others do.

> *"Seek the Kingdom of God above all else, and live righteously, and he will give you everything you need."*
>
> *(Matthew 6:33 NLT)*

Jesus Teaches About Wisdom

Jesus teaches that being wise means to listen to all His teachings and follow after them diligently. He compares the wise one to a person who has equipped himself with God's word and becomes ready in advance of all the certain to come trials and tribulations that the children of God must face in the world.

> *"Fear of the Lord is the foundation of wisdom. Knowledge of the Holy One results in good judgment."*
>
> *(Proverbs 9:10 NLT)*

A wise person does not embrace hypocrisy. Jesus requires all that choose to come after Him not to judge others. He would want us to focus on our lives to avoid those things that displease God than to look to point out the fault in others. Instead of finding fault with others, Jesus prescribes the show of love by doing unto others as we would want them to do to us. This, according to Him, is the essence of the Christian life and is non-negotiable to all His followers. The lifestyle of His followers must be one of faith – in Him. Jesus admonishes us to be resolute in prayer – always persistent in asking, seeking and knocking until we receive answers to our prayers. He warns that the journey of life still presents with basically two options. One takes the traveller to God's kingdom through the Narrow Gate, while the other leading to hell is a broad highway with a wide entrance. The import of the Jesus counsel here is for His followers to "shine" their eyes. Many, according to Him, will not find the Narrow Way to life; they will instead travel on the broad highway leading to eternal condemnation. He warns that we must watch out for false prophets who take people in the wrong direction – He calls them wolves in sheep's clothing. They will deceive many, but we must not be one of these. Jesus calls us to a life of obedience to His will if we must overcome the deceit of the false prophets.

> *"'Therefore, everyone who hears these words of mine and puts them into practice is like a wise man who built his house on the rock. The rain came down, the streams rose, and the winds blew and beat against that house, yet it did not fall, because it had its foundation on the rock. But everyone who hears these words of mine and does not put them into practice is like a foolish man who built his house on sand. The rain came down, the streams rose, and the winds blew and beat against that house, and it fell with a great crash.'"*

(Matthew 7: 24 – 27 NLT)

Jesus Prescribes That We Must Preach the Good News

In the course of training to be a teacher, a student goes on an assessment programme for an agreed period known as teaching practice. The student-teacher puts to use his or her skills under the supervision of an experienced teacher. The disciples of Jesus also went on a similar practice session after spending some time learning at His feet. Jesus gave His disciples a send forth charge, which is still relevant to His followers today. Jesus charges us today to go and announce to the world that the Kingdom of Heaven is near – it is closer today than when Jesus gave the first charge. It is an essential assignment given to all His followers. In announcing His message, Jesus expects us to impact the lives of the people with the benefits of His resurrection power. He charged His followers to bring succour to the people by attending to all their physical needs – EXPECTING NOTHING IN RETURN (Luke 6:35). Since we cannot give what we don't have, we must ask for help to bear testimony to His power by doing as He did while in the world. Jesus talked about healing the sick, raising the dead, casting out demons; how can we do this if our standing in Christ is shaky? Jesus teaches that we must be open to supporting His other messengers because if according to His counsel, they travel light then who will help meet their needs? The Bible talks about some having entertained angels without knowing it – to their benefit (Hebrews 13:2). As Jesus' followers, we know that the assignment is not for the faint-hearted – only that we are sure of His backing us up to the end.

> *"Jesus came and told his disciples, "I have been given all authority in heaven and on earth. Therefore, go and make disciples of all the nations, baptising them in the name of the Father and the*

Son and the Holy Spirit. Teach these new disciples to obey all the commands I have given you. And be sure of this: I am with you always, even to the end of the age."'

(Matthew 28: 18 – 20 NLT)

Jesus Prescribes a Life of Courage and Sacrifice

Many followers of Christ stand trials today, are hated, persecuted, arrested, betrayed and even killed. Still, Jesus says we must use every opportunity we have to spread the message notwithstanding our situation. It means that those of us living in a comfort zone have no excuse whatsoever – we must cover a lot of ground for the kingdom assignment. He says we must be courageous at all times and fear only God who is the One who has the power to destroy the soul and the body in Hell. Jesus wants all His followers to love Him more than anyone or anything in their lives. That way He assures us that He too will not forget us before His Father in Heaven.

'"But don't be afraid of those who threaten you. For the time is coming when everything that is covered will be revealed, and all that is secret will be made known to all. What I tell you now in the darkness, shout abroad when daybreak comes. What I whisper in your ear, shout from the housetops for all to hear! "Don't be afraid of those who want to kill your body; they cannot touch your soul. Fear only God, who can destroy both soul and body in hell."

(Matthew 10: 26 – 28 NLT)

'"If you love your father or mother more than you love me, you are not worthy of being mine; or if

you love your son or daughter more than me, you are not worthy of being mine. If you refuse to take up your cross and follow me, you are not worthy of being mine. If you cling to your life, you will lose it; but if you give up your life for me, you will find it."

(Matthew 10: 37 – 39 NLT)

Jesus invested a lot in guiding His followers. He was desperate to see to it that nothing stands between them and eternal life. He knew that He alone is the Way, the Truth and the Life, so He did all within His power to ensure that all who care for their eternity were equipped with enough armour for the journey ahead. Jesus made it clear that to follow Him, though very rewarding was not cheap. He warned that those who choose to follow Him must be willing to sacrifice a lot like Him. For the people to understand His message and become His followers, Jesus realised that He needed to teach them using real ordinary life stories known as parables. Jesus told at least 40 parables during His time on earth. These parables guide us in the way we should go in our relationship with our Saviour.

The Sower and the Seeds

The seeds of God's Word must be planted if they will have any chance to grow. This Jesus never hid from His followers as it represents an integral part of the Christian life. A Christian without a strong focus on spreading the message of Salvation is like a human being who does not eat. Christ demands that His followers must focus an integral part of their lives to sharing the Good News, and this is not negotiable. It is a generic commandment that all must obey. In the story that Jesus told, He had encouraged His followers to seek a deep understanding of the Word of God so that it can take root to have meaning in their lives for the full impact of the words to be felt. He warned that those who seek to follow after Him must be wary of the adverse effects of life's problems and persecution in drawing us away from Him. Jesus highlighted the worries of life and the lure of wealth as two frontal Salvation thieves that all His followers must avoid. He warned that to bear fruits, we must guard against these thieves.

> *"'Now listen to the explanation of the parable about the farmer planting seeds: The seed that fell on the footpath represents those who hear the message about the Kingdom and don't understand it. Then the evil one comes and snatches away the seed that was planted in their hearts. The seed on the rocky soil represents those who hear the message and immediately receive it with joy. But since they don't have deep roots, they don't last long. They fall away as soon as they have problems or are persecuted for believing God's word. The seed that fell among the thorns represents those who hear God's word, but all too quickly the message is crowded out by the worries of this life and the lure of wealth, so no fruit is produced. The seed that fell on good soil represents those who truly hear and understand God's word and produce a harvest of thirty, sixty, or even a hundred times as much as had been planted!'"*
>
> *(Matthew 13:18 -23 NLT)*

The Wheat and the Weeds

One of the biggest enemies of a farmer is the weeds that invade his farm. They are unwanted because they compete with the crops for the nutrient in the soil. To have a good harvest, a farmer must bring down to the barest minimum the weed population on his farm. This is usually very challenging, depending on individual situations. The Jesus story here mirrors the end time scenario for all mortals.

In the same way that God later revealed to John in the Island of Patmos, Jesus wanted all His followers to know that the everyday life scenario of good against evil will not stand forever. Time according to Him was coming when all would have to give an account of their stewardship with different consequences. From the story, it is clear that the time to make a choice which camp to belong to is now and not later. Jesus warned His followers that the day of harvest in His story could be likened to the Day of Judgment when God will reward everyone according to the work he or she has done in this life. The choice to make is to join with the righteous so that you "will shine like the sun in your Father's kingdom"(Matthew 13:43). He concluded His story by warning all to heed the lessons therein.

> *"Let the one who is doing harm continue to do harm; let the one who is vile continue to be vile; let the one who is righteous continue to live righteously; let the one who is holy continue to be holy." "Look, I am coming soon, bringing my reward with me to repay all people according to their deeds."*
>
> *(Revelation 22:11 – 12 NLT)*

The Hidden Treasure and the Pearl

These two in one story are one of the shortest told by Jesus to explain the mysteries of the Word of God. The symbolism of the two words – Treasure and Pearl always catches my attention. A treasure can be likened to an item of immense value say for example crude oil deposits or even gold or diamonds found on a piece of land. I recall that the country's abundant diamond resources fueled the ten-year civil war in Sierra Leone. The commitment of the warlords was so intense that all efforts to curtail the war failed to materialise. It was a war that brought child soldiers to the fore, out of the players' desperation, with war crimes of varying dimensions reported. The term blood diamonds came to be as a result of the carnage recorded at that time. Today one of the main protagonists of this mayhem is cooling his heels in a UK prison after receiving a 50-year sentence. The message that Jesus sent to His followers is how they should regard matters of the kingdom of God. He counsels that they should give it the utmost seriousness that it deserves. Nothing, according to Jesus, must His followers find too expensive to sacrifice for a heavenly objective. In both cases, Jesus says we must be ready to give up everything for the cause of God's kingdom.

> *"The Kingdom of Heaven is like a treasure that a man discovered hidden in a field. In his excitement, he hid it again and sold everything he owned to get enough money to buy the field. "Again, the Kingdom of Heaven is like a merchant on the lookout for choice pearls. 46 When he discovered a pearl of great value, he sold everything he owned and bought it!"*

> *(Matthew 13: 44 – 45 NLT)*

The Fishing Nets

Jesus' purpose of coming was to offer His life as a ransom so that anyone who believes in His name and lives as He has prescribed will gain eternal life. It is therefore not surprising that He gave another parable warning of the consequence of living a compromised life. In this instance, Jesus presented a practical situation which much of His audience could easily relate with – some of them being fishermen. Jesus reminded them that just like they do after a big fish haul, separating the good fish from the bad ones, God will do likewise on the Day of Judgment – the good fish being those who have led godly lives and the bad fish being those who have gone in the opposite direction. The fact that Jesus concluded with the remark "Do you understand all these things?" shows His desperation for all His followers to take the matter very seriously. The question is whether we want to take a cue from the story of Jesus, or we choose just to ignore Him and continue to live our lives as if we own it. The fact that all the people answered in the affirmative means that there would not be any excuse for ignorance on the last day.

> *"'Again, the Kingdom of Heaven is like a fishing net that was thrown into the water and caught fish of every kind. When the net was full, they dragged it up onto the shore, sat down, and sorted the good fish into crates, but threw the bad ones away. That is the way it will be at the end of the world. The angels will come and separate the wicked people from the righteous, throwing the wicked into the fiery furnace, where there will*

> *be weeping and gnashing of teeth. Do you under-*
> *stand all these things?" "Yes," they said, "we do."'*
>
> *(Matthew 13: 47 – 51 NLT)*

The Unforgiving Servant

Sometimes Jesus spoke a parable as a follow up to a question to achieve exceptional clarity. Many times people came to provoke Him by asking mischievous questions. In all instances, Jesus being the Word of God, explained the truth in God's Word to provide insight to the queries of all who came to Him. Peter, in this instance, was intent on receiving God's directive on a common but sometimes thorny issue in the relationship between men – that of forgiveness (Matthew 18:21). Jesus teaches His followers that no matter what wrong our fellow humans do to us, it is nothing compared to the wrong we have done to our Creator. If we have already received forgiveness from Him, we have no reason whatsoever to decline mercy to our fellow humans. The Bible also says that while we were yet sinners, God gave Jesus as a ransom for our sins (Romans 5:8). This ransom was paid because God was willing to forgive all our sins and so expects that we too must do likewise. A warning Jesus gave His followers in this parable was that if we fail to emulate God's forgiveness example, then we run the risk of not receiving future forgiveness. Because we can never directly repay God for His gift of Christ Jesus, the cheaper and available alternative in this context is to replicate at our lower level what God has done for us. Little wonder Jesus taught His followers in the Lord's Prayer that we should ask God to forgive us AS WE FORGIVE OTHERS.

'"When some of the other servants saw this, they were very upset. They went to the king and told him everything that had happened. Then the king called in the man he had forgiven and said, 'You evil servant! I forgave you that tremendous debt because you pleaded with me. Shouldn't you have mercy on your fellow servant, just as I had mercy on you?' Then the angry king sent the man to prison to be tortured until he had paid his entire debt. "That's what my heavenly Father will do to you if you refuse to forgive your brothers and sisters from your heart."'

(Matthew 18: 31 – 35 NLT)

The Rich Man

Not to be mistaken for the parable of the rich fool, this was a real-life occurrence that Jesus used to reinforce His teaching with regards to how His followers should handle their wealth. At the beginning of His ministry, Jesus knew it was necessary to address this vital subject. He observed that even in His days, the importance placed on material things was not in line with God's expectation. In His case, Jesus set a perfect example when He declined the fake offer of all the wealth of the world given by the impostor Satan. At that encounter, He made us realise that wealth and material things are tools and vessels that are for God's purpose. Jesus counselled His audience that it was better to seek after the kingdom of God, which is a precursor of all other things, including wealth. Fortunately for His disciples, they witnessed an encounter where Jesus had an opportunity to drive home this message. The young man who came to Jesus was full of himself having according to him been faithful to all the commandments of God. Jesus made all who were around to appreciate that love which can be expressed through giving is more important than mere obedience to the commandments. This is because the purpose of all the commandments is to teach us to love God and our fellow humans. Again Jesus used the opportunity of the encounter to drive home one of the pillars of His Salvation message which is that nothing should be too much to give up for the sake of our entry into God's eternal kingdom. The rich man like many today was desirous of making heaven but not at the expense of letting go of his possessions.

> "He said, "I came naked from my mother's womb, and I will be naked when I leave. The LORD gave me what I had, and the LORD has taken it away. Praise the name of the LORD!"'
>
> (Job 1:21 NLT)

> "And what do you benefit if you gain the whole world but lose your own soul?"
>
> (Mark 8:36 NLT)

The Wedding Feast

Although Jesus told this story to challenge the Jews to take advantage of the gift of God offered to them first before others, many of us who profess to follow Jesus can learn a lot from the parable. In the story, we can see that though God is merciful and willing to wait a long while for His creation to return to Him, this open door of divine mercy is not left ajar forever. The story also teaches us that for every action, there is a consequence. Those who refused to take up the opportunity given to them to attend the wedding feast had the invitation withdrawn and passed on to others. Jesus teaches that His banquet feast is open to all provided they are "well dressed" to attend – the banquet being His heavenly home and to be well dressed is to live a life of holiness. Although the message of Salvation which is the Good News is for all, not all who hear it will enter into God's kingdom. To qualify, you must ensure that your life is not stained with sin so that you do not become disqualified from gaining eternal life.

> *"Then one of the twenty-four elders asked me, Who are these who are clothed in white? Where did they come from?" And I said to him, "Sir, you are the one who knows." Then he said to me, "These are the ones who died in the great tribulation. They have washed their robes in the blood of the Lamb and made them white."*
>
> *(Revelation 7:13 – 14 NLT)*

The Ten Bridesmaids

This story is arguably one of the most popular stories told by Jesus to His followers. It is simple, easy to relate with and logical. Jesus told this story late in His ministry when trying to remind His followers of His return. He dedicated a considerable amount of time to His return message to make sure that His followers do not lose their reward. In Matthew's account, Jesus gave as much importance to this message as He did to the major thrusts of His early teachings. A significant thing to note here is that all the bridesmaids were virgins. They were carefully chosen and had met the criteria that qualified them to go in to meet the bridegroom. Unfortunately, as the story concluded, only 50% of them were successful. It is very frustrating and harrowing for anyone to fail in his or her life's endeavour.

However, the reality is that this is a daily occurrence. The challenge is how to be one of the successful ones. Jesus, in the parable, reminded His followers about the day of reckoning for all who come into this world. This is typified by the arrival of the bridegroom in this parable. This story teaches that better is the end of a matter than the beginning (Ecclesiastes 7:8). It reminds us that as followers of Christ, we must be ready to persevere to the end and be prepared for any eventuality. It reinforces the theme message of Jesus' return which is going to be sudden as no one knows the time or hour.

Most importantly, it warns of the finality nature of His return when no amends can be made. The story did not end without warning of the consequences of not going with the bridegroom. I pray that all who follow Jesus will not meet with this experience.

> *"But while they were gone to buy oil, the bridegroom came. Then those who were ready went in with him to the marriage feast, and the door was locked. Later, when the other five bridesmaids returned, they stood outside, calling, 'Lord! Lord! Open the door for us!' "But he called back, 'Believe me, I don't know you!' "So you, too, must keep watch! For you do not know the day or hour of my return."*
>
> (Matthew 25: 10 – 13 NLT)

The Three Servants

Jesus wanted to emphasise the warning that the story of the virgins threw up. Being a critical subject matter very dear to Him, He went ahead to illustrate His return using another parable. In this story, Jesus talked about three servants entrusted with money each in proportion to his abilities. I see in these servants, three siblings who came to the world and who God allowed to live for varying degree of years and with different measure of opportunities and resources. While two took advantage of their opportunities and resources, the third did nothing about his own. One of the most important talents that God gave us is our lives – the years we spend on this planet before we pass on to eternity. It is to be used to bear fruits for God and not wasted on mundane and earthly things. Once I did an audit of my life, and I discovered that in the things of God, I was nowhere compared with earthy achievements. This is very disappointing and displeasing to God. Jesus reminded His followers that they would give an account one day for all the talents given to them. These talents are given for profitable use and not to be idled away. He warned that when the Giver of the talent returns He will judge us based on fair expectations and duly reward or apply sanctions.

> *"A faithful, sensible servant is one to whom the master can give the responsibility of managing his other household servants and feeding them. If the master returns and finds that the servant has done a good job, there will be a reward. I tell*

you the truth; the master will put that servant in charge of all he owns. But what if the servant is evil and thinks, 'My master won't be back for a while,' and he begins beating the other servants, partying, and getting drunk? The master will return unannounced and unexpected, and he will cut the servant to pieces and assign him a place with the hypocrites. In that place, there will be weeping and gnashing of teeth."

(Matthew 24: 45 – 51 NLT)

The Good Samaritan

It was Apostle John who told us the truth about God that He is love, and anyone who does not love cannot say he knows God (1 John 4:8). Jesus taught His followers about the importance of love. He encouraged them to love one another and gave the best expression of love by laying down His life for us; this example, He expects us to follow. This story too was told by Jesus in response to the very often attempt to test Him and hope that He stumbles or fails. The Word of God failing a test about Himself! What folly of man! The story was told in answer to a similar question asked by a wealthy man. In this instance, the question was from a religious expert. Jesus gave different approaches to the same issue to mirror the life of the questioner to reveal other truths about God's Word. Jesus reminded His audience that love is the centrepiece of God's commandments no wonder the Good News is about the quantum of God's love for humanity leading Him to give us His only begotten Son.

The Samaritans were a racially mixed society with Jewish and pagan ancestry. Although they worshipped Yahweh as did the Jews, their religion was not mainstream Judaism. They accepted only the first five books of the Bible as canonical, and their temple was on Mount Gerizim instead of on Mount Zion in Jerusalem.[1] The hatred between Jews and Samaritans was fierce and longstanding. The religious enmity between the Jews and the Samaritans dated from the return of the former from the Babylonian captivity when the Samaritans worked to prevent the rebuilding of Jerusalem. Later they offended the Jews by extending generous assistance to the armies of Alexander. In return for their friendship, Alexander permitted the Samaritans to build a temple on Mount Gerizim, where they worshipped Yahweh and their tribal gods and offered sacrifices much after the order of the temple services at Jerusalem.[2]

Jesus defined to His listeners that God's version of love prescribed for all His followers should be unaffected by the relationship between the giver and the receiver. He wanted us to know that no matter the subsisting situation or circumstance, we must always express love to others. The Samaritan showing love to a Jew was an unlikely occurrence in Jesus' days, and this probably is the reason why Jesus used this extreme to teach about God's love. The commitment shown by the despised Samaritan is unparalleled as both his time and material resources were deployed to show love to a Jew – his supposed mortal enemy. He understood the Jesus meaning of neighbour to be anyone to whom you can offer help, and so he did not hold back anything. Jesus used another extreme – the Priest and the Temple worker to show that what matters to Him was our being obedient to His words and not the toga we wear around our necks as titles. Little wonder He said that we are His friends ONLY when we obey His commandments. The priest and the temple worker disappointed God and failed woefully while the Samaritan did right in the sight of God. He saw his kindness to the end by offering to pay for any additional care expenses spent on the wounded Jew. Jesus concludes by saying all His followers must do likewise when found in a similar situation.

> *'"Now which of these three would you say was a neighbour to the man who was attacked by bandits?" Jesus asked. The man replied, "The one who showed him mercy." Then Jesus said, "Yes, now go and do the same."'*
>
> *(Luke 10: 36 – 37 NLT)*

The Rich Fool

On another occasion, Jesus was confronted with the subject of inheritance; a very touchy and sensitive issue in the world right from time immemorial. Many families have been destroyed by it and lives lost as a consequence. An unwise parent is one who fails to put his house in order before his departure to the great beyond. Jesus found Himself in many instances where the people sought counsel from Him to guide them. Today the Word of God provides for Jesus' followers the same measure of counsel if only we are prepared to heed all contained therein. In response to the question from the crowd, Jesus told another story but not before telling His followers that greed which is the driving force behind the issue at hand must not be found in their lives. Life, according to Jesus for His followers must never be about acquisition. The rich fool in this parable was focused only and entirely on his wealth. He felt that life was just about this and saw himself as lord and master over his life. He took a position of complete indifference to his Creator, having found for himself what he saw as the only thing that matters - his wealth. He forgot that in life our very existence by God's mercies is the platform on which everything is built, so we must defer to the One who sustains life and not the materials that we acquire as a result of being alive. In our story, God intervened to put the man in his place as he was called back home the same day to his Creator. Little wonder he is commonly referred to as the rich fool having attempted to relegate his Creator.

> *'"But God said to him, 'You fool! You will die this very night. Then who will get everything you worked for?' "Yes, a person is a fool to store up earthly wealth but not have a rich relationship with God."'*
>
> *(Luke 12 20 – 21 NLT)*

The Loving Father

Although this story is more commonly described as the parable of the prodigal son, I have decided to use a more original description - the loving father. This description draws from the setting that Jesus found Himself when He told the story to His followers. The Pharisees and religious teachers had observed that Jesus found home with sinful people and thought this was a misnomer. Consequently, in showing them the mind of God concerning sinners, Jesus told them three parables, one of which is the story of the loving father. Although the most important message that Jesus wanted to pass across was the unsurpassed love of the father to a repentant son, this parable brings to the fore, several lessons in life on how not to behave as followers of Christ. The young man in question demonstrated an extreme desire for wealth which, simply put, is greed. He was not satisfied with the life of controlled comfort under his father's roof and so sought for independence to do his own thing. Unfortunately, he had not leant the attribute of discipline and self-control. Being independent of his father was not in itself wrong, but immediately he gained his freedom, he went on, according to the story, to squander his share of his father's money on wild living. The symbolic meaning of a distant land to which he travelled and the famine he faced, represents man's separation from God and the consequence of it. He had left God's presence which his home represented, and so missed out on the fullness of joy. The struggle he had when he left God's presence mirrors the life of Adam and Eve, who were both thrown out of the safety and comfort of the Garden of Eden.

While they fed fat in the garden, outside, they had to struggle. The reason for Adam and Eve's problems was the severed link between both parties and God their

Creator. The young man's status was so low that upon being employed to look after pigs, "even the pods he was feeding the pigs looked good to him"(Luke 15:16). This low-status experience is the direct consequence of sin. Sin takes us from God's presence to a place of suffering and shame. Fortunately for the young man, he came to his senses! The truth is that leaving the presence of God and living an ungodly life is senseless. The good news is that God is ready to take us back and restore all we have lost when we realise our folly, ask for His forgiveness and return to Him. God is indeed a loving Father. The difference between the faithful followers of Christ and unbelievers is such that only the unwise will choose the way of the world over the direction of God.

> *'"So he returned home to his father. And while he was still a long way off, his father saw him coming. Filled with love and compassion, he ran to his son, embraced him, and kissed him. His son said to him, 'Father, I have sinned against both heaven and you, and I am no longer worthy of being called your son.' "But his father said to the servants, 'Quick! Bring the finest robe in the house and put it on him. Get a ring for his finger and sandals for his feet. And kill the calf we have been fattening. We must celebrate with a feast, for this son of mine was dead and has now returned to life. He was lost, but now he is found.' So the party began."*
>
> (Luke 15:20 – 24 NLT)

> *"For his unfailing love toward those who fear him is as great as the height of the heavens above the earth."*
>
> (Psalm 103:11 NLT)

The Rich Man and Lazarus

There are many lessons that this story provides for Jesus' followers. It is a reminder to the discerning that all things in this world will come to an end someday. Jesus used two extreme lifestyles to show His followers the consequences of their actions while on this planet. Death is inevitable, and after it comes judgment. The regrettable end of the rich man is proof that he lived his life for himself. Little wonder he begged that extraordinary efforts be made to reach his relations who were travelling on a similar path. It is evident in the story that the outcome we receive at the end of our life is dependent on how we live it and is also irreversible. Life in this mortal body is very short, and if we unwisely invest in the things of the world, we face eternal condemnation. The poor earthly Lazarus became the rich, heavenly man because though his difficult human situation could have made him turn his back to God, he remained steadfast to the end even throughout his circumstances. Many today look for evil ways to circumvent their challenges, not minding that they will sell their souls to the devil. May God forbid that we gain the whole world and lose our soul. The truth is that the wealth of the rich man did not condemn him, and neither did the poverty of Lazarus vindicate him. For both of them, it is the way they lived their lives in their situation that gave them the outcome they received. Though difficult, a rich man can enter the kingdom of God, and similarly, poverty is not a passport to heaven.

"'The rich man shouted, 'Father Abraham, have some pity! Send Lazarus over here to dip the tip of his finger in water and cool my tongue. I am in anguish in these flames.' "But Abraham said to him, 'Son, remember that during your lifetime you had everything you wanted, and Lazarus had nothing. So now he is here being comforted, and you are in anguish. And besides, there is a great chasm separating us. No one can cross over to you from here, and no one can cross over to us from there.' "Then the rich man said, 'Please, Father Abraham, at least send him to my father's home. For I have five brothers, and I want him to warn them, so they don't end up in this place of torment.' "But Abraham said, 'Moses and the prophets have warned them. Your brothers can read what they wrote."

(Luke 16: 24 – 29 NLT)

Inner Purity & Discipleship

Jesus faced a lot of challenges in His effort to teach His followers the way they should go. Agelong traditions and hypocrisy were two of the contending issues that He had to deal with as He taught His followers. Jesus found in His time that emphasis was so high on religiosity, which is very much so today. Many still hold on to several worship customs which have no place in the teachings of Jesus. Jesus talked about a people whose hearts were far from God, who only talk about being committed to God without backing it up with actions. He called them hypocrites! He told His followers who want to be His disciples that they must be wholly committed to the way He has prescribed for them. According to Him, they must turn entirely from their selfish ways.

"Blessed are the pure in heart, for they shall see God."
(*Matthew 5:8 NLT*)

The Cost of Being a Disciple

God knew that the effort of man could not qualify him to gain merit for eternal life. He watched as man continually fell short of His expectations. He saw that the efforts of the prophets produced only a level of righteousness that was as filthy rags in His presence. Because of His inexplicable love for man, He decided to send His best to rescue us. God's best, who is Jesus Christ, was adequate to bridge the gap between man and God. Jesus offered the Grace platform that allowed a man to gain Salvation and come on board to a life of holiness prescribed by God. As you read through and have reached this page, I must warn you that though it is desirable and profitable to follow Jesus, it is not a tea party. Jesus Himself warned that we would face many challenges.

"I have told you all this so that you may have peace in me. Here on earth, you will have many trials and sorrows. But take heart, because I have overcome the world."'
(*John 16:33 NLT*)

Jesus also advised that all who seek to follow Him should count the costs before embarking on the journey. Though He desires that all should answer Him, but being mindful of the nature of the walk, He counsels that all

His intending followers must count the costs in advance. Jesus, as Alpha and Omega knows that to follow Him is all about making choices. In many instances the decisions will be difficult, painful and unpopular; however, we have the assurance that when we make the right decision to follow after Him, we will receive power to complete the race – provided we do not look back.

> *"Therefore, since we are surrounded by such a huge crowd of witnesses to the life of faith, let us strip off every weight that slows us down, especially the sin that so easily trips us up. And let us run with endurance the race God has set before us. We do this by keeping our eyes on Jesus, the champion who initiates and perfects our faith."*

> (Hebrews 12: 1 – 2a NLT)

The goal of the race is to reign with Christ. We must follow Jesus not for fun but to reign with Him. Every other thing is inconsequential. We must focus to the end, never looking back or sideways. Jesus was clear to warn that there will be opposition to our running the race. He invested considerable time to prepare His followers for this inevitable eventuality.

In some cases, it may even lead to danger to our lives and even physical death. Jesus also prophesied most of the Christian persecutions of today. However, we are encouraged that we are more than conquerors in Him provided we persevere to the end.

> *"I have told you these things so that you won't abandon your faith. For you will be expelled from*

the synagogues, and the time is coming when those who kill you will think they are doing a holy service for God."

(John 16: 1 – 2 NLT)

In conclusion, let me share a small story with you. I once travelled along with my wife and younger daughter to the United Kingdom. During an inner country south west train shuttle from London to Exeter, Devon, England, I had the opportunity of chatting with a 55-year-old Briton who was travelling in the same direction after visiting his widow mother in London. His father, a minister of God, had previously gone to meet his Creator. Upon presenting him with a copy of a gospel tract, he politely declined to accept it, claiming that he did not believe that God existed. Although I proceeded to discuss further with him on the subject, it was a no-go area for him as he was not inclined to continue with the matter. The thing of note in this encounter was that my younger daughter, who had kept mute all through our discussion, as an African child should, shared something with me upon arrival at Exeter. It is something I later sent to my British friend and which is worth sharing here too. It was posted to my daughter by someone. It reads;

If I am wrong about God, I have wasted my life……, but if you are wrong about God, you have wasted your eternity.

Some people unwittingly choose to play poker with their lives by investing everything here on earth and throwing away their eternity. The truth is that Jesus is the ONLY way to eternal life.

> *"And this world is fading away, along with everything that people crave. But anyone who does what pleases God will live forever."*

(1 John 2:17 NLT)

I pray that the truth of God in these words be made known to you and that you shall not regret your decisions on the last day.

The Narrow Way

"If you think you are standing strong, be careful not to fall."

(1 Corinthians 10:12. NLT)

Paul spoke the above words to the people of Corinth. Old Corinth was conquered and destroyed by the Romans in 146 BC. It was rebuilt a century later as a Roman colony and populated in large part by former Roman slaves. It later became a cosmopolitan city with Romans, Greeks, Jews and other ethnic groups from all over the Mediterranean, as well as international visitors passing through the city. Corinth had a reputation as an important city full of vice linked to its geography. It gained notoriety of a port city and was widely known for prostitution and other vices.[1] To drive home his message of a disciplined life; Paul took them through the history of the people of Israel who in many instances, were not careful to avoid disobeying God's Word. The Israelites led a life of spiritual adultery, and God dealt severely with them.

I know a man who has spent close to ten years in a close walk with God. He was very vibrant and committed to drawing others to Christ. Because he once led a life of disregard for God's commandments and its consequences, he, therefore, appreciated the new experience he had in Christ. He was as a ladies' man, but after giving his life to Christ, he received power through the Holy Spirit to see women in a different light never again falling prey to them. His newfound strength in the Lord continued for a while, and so he started to feel very confident. He gradually began to forget that the power he had in him was from God. He took things for granted such that when the devil struck, he found himself "flat on the ground" not able to help himself. It was a knockdown punch though thankfully not a knockout blow. He had reconnected with an old female friend from young adulthood, and before long, he found himself flirting dangerously with her. He got into a strange situation where all the things he had forsaken began to find a way back into his life. Everything was on the table as the woman made spirited attempts to drag him to his spiritual death. Though he fell into the sin of lust and flirtatious interaction, God fought for him through a constant feeling of guilt and betrayal. The Spirit never left him for a moment as he began to come back to his senses. He remembered his Father's counsel, and God helped him to turn back into safety.

> *"My son, pay attention to my wisdom; listen carefully to my wise counsel. Then you will show discernment, and your lips will express what you've learned. For the lips of an immoral woman are as sweet as honey, and her mouth is smoother than oil. But in the end, she is as bitter as poison, as dangerous as a double-edged sword. Her feet go down to death; her steps lead straight to the grave. For she cares nothing about the path to life. She staggers down a crooked trail and doesn't realise it. So now, my sons listen to me. Never*

stray from what I am about to say: Stay away from her! Don't go near the door of her house! If you do, you will lose your honour and will lose to merciless people all you have achieved. Strangers will consume your wealth, and someone else will enjoy the fruit of your labour. In the end, you will groan in anguish when disease consumes your body. You will say, "How I hated discipline! If only I had not ignored all the warnings! Oh, why didn't I listen to my teachers? Why didn't I pay attention to my instructors? I have come to the brink of utter ruin, and now I must face public disgrace."'

(Proverbs 5: 1 – 14. NLT)

Jesus of Nazareth was first to broach the concept of the Narrow Way. He spoke about the Narrow Gate in the concluding parts of His sermon on the mount. The idea represented the summary position of all the lessons He gave His disciples in what it takes to be His follower. In it, Jesus described discipleship in the metaphor of a road; He likened it to a highway. Jesus described two distinct highways in His message; one with a Narrow Gate and the other with a wide one. He explained with clarity that both roads do not lead in the same direction and neither do they end in the same destination. One lane was rough and bumpy while the other was smooth and level. The Narrow Way led to life eternal, while the broadway led to death and destruction. Jesus recommended the rough road to His followers; He advised them to avoid the broad and smooth way at all cost. He warned that many would not find access to the narrow and profitable way.

"'You can enter God's Kingdom only through the Narrow Gate. The highway to hell is broad, and its gate is wide for the many who choose that way. But the gateway to life is very narrow, and the road is difficult, and only a few ever find it."

(Matthew 7: 13 – 14. NLT)

The call to decide by Jesus deserves our utmost attention and action. It reminds me of my school days when my parents usually gave their final charge to us on the day of our return to school. Jesus used this opportunity to send His final charge to all the listeners of the day to guide them in order not to suffer loss and failure. The decision to opt for the Narrow Way as recommended by Jesus is a definite and consequential decision which calls for deep resolve and consistency. All who choose this route require the Armour of God to succeed on the journey. They receive help from the Spirit of God, and so demonstrate the presence of specific fruits which distinguishes their lives from that of others. They are sensitive to the wiles of the devil designed to take them back to the broadway and so do all to ensure complete rejection of his counsel. They have assurance and believe God's promise that the end justifies the means, so they fix their gaze on Jesus never looking back at all.

"Therefore, since we are surrounded by such a huge crowd of witnesses to the life of faith, let us strip off every weight that slows us down, especially the sin that so easily trips us up. And let us run with endurance the race God has set before us. We do this by keeping our eyes on Jesus, the champion who initiates and perfects our faith."

(Hebrews 12: 1 – 2. NLT)

It is essential to take along all that is necessary for a journey to ensure successful travel to our desired destination—the same way with the drive through the narrow road to the kingdom of God. The trip Jesus talked about refers to the way we live here on earth. To be able to achieve God's expectation in the way we live, the Spirit of God must have complete control of our lives. It is this same Spirit that creates the transition into a new being through the transformation that takes place when a man accepts Jesus into his life.

"God the Father knew you and chose you long ago, and his Spirit has made you holy."

(1 Peter 1:2. NLT)

This Spirit is holy and dwells only in sacred places. He hates sin and takes His flight away from sinful lives. He bears fruits of His kind in the lives of those who allow Him. He is decisive but does not compete when He is unwelcomed. He guides those who allow Him to do the will of God. He destroys the work of the flesh to give advantage to the work of the Spirit. He reassures those who allow Him and backs them up to the end. The Spirit of God gives power to all God's children to do exploits and to go through the Narrow Way. The fruit He bears are the attributes of a Christian which he or she needs while passing through the Narrow Way. The Fruit of the Spirit is the change in our character, and it comes about because of the Holy Spirit's work in us. We do not become Christians on our own, and we cannot grow on our own. Philippians 2:13 says that "it is God who is at work in you, both to will and to work for His good pleasure." Every good thing we do is the Fruit of the Spirit's work in our lives.

"But the Holy Spirit produces this kind of fruit in our lives: love, joy, peace, patience, kindness, goodness, faithfulness, gentleness, and self-control. There is no law against these things!"

(Galatians 5: 22 – 23. NLT)

Jesus summarised the greatest commandments as the love of God and the love of one's neighbour. In both instances, love is paramount. Apostle Paul too gave insight into the importance of love when he compared it to faith and hope; he came up with the conclusion that love is the greatest of the three. Jesus showed us the importance of love when He offered Himself for our Salvation on the Cross of Calvary. The genuine love demonstrated by Ruth to Naomi, her mother-in-law is worth emulating. She took a considerable gamble to commit her life to Noami and follow her back to her ancestral home, notwithstanding her young age. God expects His children who have chosen the Narrow Way to be ready to pay any price to sustain a loving relationship with all around them. Status, creed or circumstances must not hinder it. All that should matter is to please God at all cost. Love is not cheap; it is not easy to sustain, but with God, all things are possible. God is love, and anyone who must love will have a good measure of godliness in him or her. The whole idea of love stems from God, who in His infinite mercy sent His only begotten and willing Son to die for us while we are yet sinners.

"Love is patient and kind. Love is not jealous or boastful or proud or rude. It does not demand its own way. It is not irritable, and it keeps no record of being wronged. It does not rejoice

about injustice but rejoices whenever the truth wins out. Love never gives up, never loses faith, is always hopeful, and endures through every circumstance."

(1 Corinthians 13: 4 – 7. NLT)

Travellers on the Narrow Way show love as a way of life never tiring but looking at the example set by Jesus on the way to the Cross. They are identified differently from others in the way they show love to anyone irrespective of status, race, creed or religious persuasion.

Joy is a stronger, less familiar feeling than happiness which is due to happenings or whether things are going well or not.[2] Joy is an emotion that is acquired by the anticipation, acquisition or even the expectation of something great or wonderful.[3] The Bible describes Joy as a gift. It is present irrespective of unfavourable external situations. The most significant driver of Joy is Salvation which is the assurance of eternal life upon our transition from this world. This Joy drives away human wickedness the way light drives out darkness. It makes a man who is exposed to all forms of undesirable things to be able to look into the horizon and smile. Joy is insulated by the promise of God through Christ to deliver a specific and positive outcome to all who follow Jesus. It makes the Christian look "foolish" in this world because the world cannot understand why this Joy exists within the myriad of problems that surround the believer. The fruit of Joy is the awareness that God is one's strength and protector.[4] The presence of this Joy does not mean that a person may not experience sadness on occasions through the death of a loved one, financial trouble, the actions of others, or depression; but underlying the grief is the sure knowledge that God still loves one.

> *"But don't rejoice because evil spirits obey you; rejoice because your names are registered in heaven."'*
>
> (Luke 10:20. NLT)

The presence of Joy is a sure proof that we have not left the Narrow Way. It is God's way of reminding us that we are still His children no matter what we go through or the challenges we face. It is possible to lose our Joy and by extension, veer off the Narrow Way when we allow sin into our lives. In this instance, God's face would have become hidden from us, and we will then lose our Joy. Little wonder King David reached out to God after the visit of Prophet Nathan, who confronted him with his sin. The loss of our Joy when we fall into sin is God's way of calling us back to Himself. Blessed are those who are sensitive to the disappearance of their Joy to make redress to go back to the Narrow Way. Repentance is the tonic for the restoration of Joy.

> *"Purify me from my sins, and I will be clean; wash me, and I will be whiter than snow. Oh, give me back my joy again; you have broken me— now let me rejoice. Don't keep looking at my sins. Remove the stain of my guilt. Create in me a clean heart, O God. Renew a loyal spirit within me. Do not banish me from your presence, and don't take your Holy Spirit from me. Restore to me the joy*

*of your Salvation, and make me willing to obey
you. Then I will teach your ways to rebels, and
they will return to you."*

(Psalm 51:7 – 13.NLT)

The Peace that God offers His children is different
from that available in the world. Jesus Himself made this
obvious distinction when He spoke to His disciples in the
upper room on His way to Jerusalem. It is a Peace that
finds its source in the Prince of Peace. Paul describes this
Peace as one that humans cannot decipher. It is inexplicable because it thrives even amid all kinds of storms. It
derives from a heart that completely trusts in God. This
trust was the missing link on the Sea of Galilee when the
disciples were afraid of perishing. Jesus, on the other hand,
was sleeping because He knew that He could trust in His
Father, who had sent Him not to abandon Him. This Peace
is a lifestyle. It defines everything in the life of one travelling on the Narrow Way – the confidence that he or she
has to remain in the Lord, continue this walk and the way
he or she lives with others. This Peace is interwoven with
Joy as one cannot exist without the other. It is the result of
resting in a relationship with God. Peace is more than an
absence of conflict. It is the tranquil state of a soul fearing
nothing from God and content with its earthly lot, of what
so ever sort that is. It is a kind of equilibrium that comes
from trusting that everything is in the hands of a good and
loving God who wants the best for you.[5]

"'I am leaving you with a gift-peace of mind and heart. And the peace I give is a gift the world cannot give. So don't be troubled or afraid."

(John 14: 27. NLT)

Peace dominates the traveller on the Narrow Way. He or she has calm, inner stability that results in the ability to conduct himself peacefully, even amid circumstances that would typically be very nerve-wracking, traumatic, or upsetting. Rather than allowing the difficulties and pressures of life to break him, a person who is possessed by peace is whole, complete, orderly, stable, and poised for a blessing.[6]

One of Nigeria's very popular musician now an Evangelist once produced a song extolling patience as the key to a successful life. In the lyrics of his song, he compared money, children, longevity and patience and came up with the advice that patience is still the one to seek after. Although some will argue that the patient dog eats no bone, however, the Word of God is clear that to live a fruitful life, one must be patient most steps of the way. The Christian is a pilgrim on the Narrow Way who has accepted the future promise of Jesus that He has gone to prepare a place for him and that He is coming back again. The mere fact that it is a promise means that he or she must follow the Master patiently not looking right or left to stay focussed. In the parable of the talents, Jesus reported that it took a long time before the master of the servants came back to request for an account. Jesus too has taken over 2000 years, but He will surely come back one day as He has promised. Patience includes the concepts of forbearance, long-suffering, and the willingness to bear wrongs patiently. It applies to a man who could avenge himself but did not. It can also be about God and His attitude towards man. Exodus 34:6 describes the Lord as "slow to anger and rich in kindness and fidelity."[7,8] A successful walk on the Narrow Way to life requires all the ingredients of patience. They are necessary to avoid distractions that may lead to the loss of one's Salvation.

"Whoever is patient has great understanding, but one who is quick-tempered displays folly."

(Proverbs 14:29. NLT)

Without patience, it is impossible to overcome trials and persecutions on the Narrow Way. The taking up of the Cross itself requires that we are patient to carry it to the end. Even our faith is interwoven with patience. It is impossible to retain our faith without being patient. Therefore it is impossible to please God without being patient.

In 1985 as I completed my university education, there was a requirement to write a dissertation as a precondition for the award of a Bachelor's degree. To spice up my project, I looked for and found a quotation that transmitted a value I cherish so much, which is kindness. The quote by Sidney Newton Bremer says thus: **kindness costs nothing; we have unlimited storehouses of it, yet some people hold it back as if it is their last dollar.** Jesus encouraged the show of kindness to others when He advised the rich man who came to Him to request the way to eternal life that he should sell all his property and give to the poor. Although the rich man did not take heed of Jesus' advice, this matter was brought up again by Him to drive home His message.

> *'"Then these righteous ones will reply, 'Lord, when did we ever see you hungry and feed you? Or thirsty and give you something to drink? Or a stranger and show you hospitality? Or naked and give you clothing? When did we ever see you sick or in prison and visit you?' "And the King will say, 'I tell you the truth when you did it to one of the least of these my brothers and sisters, you were doing it to me!'"*

> *(Matthew 25: 37 – 40. NLT)*

Kindness is acting for the good of people, regardless of what they do. It is goodness in action, the sweetness of disposition, gentleness in dealing with others, benevolence, affability etc. The word describes the ability to act for the welfare of those taxing your patience. Kindness means to be friendly to others and often depicted rulers, governors, or people who were kind, mild, and benevolent to their subjects. Anyone who demonstrated this quality was considered to be compassionate, considerate, sympathetic, humane, understanding, or gentle. Kindness is doing something and not expecting anything in return. Kindness is respect and helping others without waiting for someone to help one back. It implies kindness, no matter what.[9]

In his reply to the rich man, Jesus linked the show of kindness through giving to attaining perfection. Though in this case, Jesus requested that he sold all his possession;

either way, it is profitable to show kindness as to do this, will help one build treasure in heaven.

"Don't forget to show hospitality to strangers, for some who have done this have entertained angels without realising it!"

(Hebrews 13:2. NLT)

The Narrow Way lifestyle without kindness is a non-starter. The wealthy woman of Shunem in 2 Kings 4 demonstrated unsought after kindness which brought benefits to her. We too must do likewise.

Goodness can be described as the state or quality of being good. Although I would struggle to explain the difference between goodness and kindness, some have tried to separate the two by saying kindness is more about attitude while goodness is more about the things we do for others. Goodness can be described as a kindly feeling, generosity and joy in being good. It is seen as a twin fruit of kindness. They are so closely related that sometimes it is not easy to distinguish between them. A kind person is also a good person; a good person is, by nature, a kind person. Both of these characteristics stem from love. Someone has said that patience is suffering love; kindness is compassionate love, and goodness is ministering love. Whatever the "experts" say about the similarities or differences between these two words matter very little to me. The important thing is to look for an opportunity to demonstrate the goodness of God as we travel along the Narrow Way. Jesus told a story of a man who in normal circumstances, should not interphase with the other. He is a Samaritan and the other a Jew; Samaritans and Jews were sworn enemies though related to each other. The story was an example of the show of good, one to the other as God would want us to do. The travel on the Narrow Way without looking for an opportunity to display the goodness of God is unChrist-like. The fruit of goodness in the life of the early church was responsible for their care for each other. Today many lay claim to be followers of Christ, but one would need a magnifying glass before finding a drop of God's goodness in their lives.

> *"Therefore, whenever we have the opportunity, we should do good to everyone — especially to those in the family of faith."*
>
> *(Galatians 6:10. NLT)*

> *"Do not be overcome by evil, but overcome evil with good."*
>
> *(Romans 12:21. NLT)*

Goodness is righteousness in action. Goodness boldly does what is right, and encourages others to do good as well. Can people say this about you? Can it be said that you are travelling on the Narrow Way?

Faithfulness is an attribute of God. To be faithful therefore means having a quality similar to that of God. Faithfulness is committing oneself to something or someone, for instance, to one's spouse, to a cause, or a religion. Being faithful requires personal resolve not to wander away from commitments or promises. It's not always easy to be faithful, but God has demanded it so we must pursue it. True faith requires trust in God. The writer of the letter to the Hebrews describes it this way: "Let us fix our eyes on Jesus, the author and perfecter of our faith, who for the joy set before Him endured the cross, scorning its shame, and sat down at the right hand of the throne of God".[10] The root of pistis ("faith") is peithô that is to persuade or be persuaded which supplies the core-meaning of faith as being "divine persuasion", received from God, and never generated by man.[11,12,13] Faithfulness has to do with service, diligence and commitment. It is a time-dependent Spirit gift. As with all the Fruits of the Spirit, God Himself is the model we must study for examples of faithfulness to encourage us to trust and emulate Him. The journey through the Narrow Way requires complete trust and faith in God to be faithful to the end. It calls for a way of life that is unwavering and reliant on the power of God to see the Christian through his pilgrim journey. The very essence of Christian living prescribes a follower-ship lifestyle based on faithfulness "looking" neither left nor right. It is this consistency that draws the attention of God and which ultimately brings reward at the end of the race. Although faithfulness in the context of the Fruit of the Spirit is more of trustworthiness or reliability, it does have faith as an integral component. Indeed if you will be faithful to God, you must have faith in Him.

"And the Lord replied, "A faithful, sensible servant is one to whom the master can give the responsibility of managing his other household servants and feeding them. If the master returns and finds that the servant has done a good job, there will be a reward. I tell you the truth; the master will put that servant in charge of all he owns."

(Luke 12: 42 – 44. NLT)

Faithfulness includes trusting God and remaining loyal to Him and His doctrines. How are you demonstrating this in your daily life? Remember, this fruit comes with the assurance of the Master's reward. You cannot travel on the Narrow Way and enter the Narrow Gate without being faithful to the end.

The New Spirit-Filled Life Bible defines Gentleness as "a disposition that is even-tempered, tranquil, balanced in spirit, unpretentious, and that has the passions under control. The word is best translated 'meekness,' not as an indication of weakness, but of power and strength under control. The person who possesses this quality "pardons injury, corrects faults, and rules his spirit well".[14] Gentleness is "a divinely-balanced virtue that can only operate through faith". It involves humility and thankfulness toward God, and polite, restrained behaviour toward others. The opposites of gentleness are anger, a desire for revenge and self-aggrandisement. It takes a strong person to be truly gentle. When filled with the Spirit's fruit of Gentleness, we will correct others with easiness instead of arguing in resentment and anger, knowing that their Salvation is far more important than our pride. We will forgive readily because any offence towards us is nothing compared to our offences against God - offences for which we have received forgiveness. Competition and sectarianism will disappear, as the goal becomes less about us and more about preaching the Gospel. John the Baptist was a fiery preacher, yet he manifested true gentleness when he said, "[Jesus] must become greater; I must become less".

Jesus is the epitome of perfect gentleness. In many instances, He demonstrated extreme gentleness; even to the Cross. The gentleness shown during His arrest at the garden of Gethsemane and His trial by Pilate can best be imagined. On one occasion, Jesus was travelling to Jerusalem via a Samaritan village, and as is customary, He sent people ahead to get things ready for Him. Unfortunately, the people there did not welcome Him, and as a consequence two of His disciples, James and John requested permission to call down fire from heaven to destroy them. Jesus rebuked the disciples and instead went to another village. Gentleness also means giving up the right to judge what is best for us and others. God is not as concerned with our comfort as He is with our spiritual growth, and He knows how to grow us far better than we do. Gentleness means that we accept that the rain falls on the evil and the just and that God may use methods we don't like to reach our hearts and the hearts of others.[15]

"Be completely humble and gentle; be patient, bearing with one another in love".

(Ephesians 4:2. NLT)

"Let your gentle spirit be known to all men. The Lord is near."

(Philippians 4:5. NLT)

Your journey through the Narrow Way will include several attempts to ruffle you up and make you lose your gentleness. Jesus has set an example for you to follow if you want to be His disciple. Do not relent. You must remain on course.

Self-control or temperance is the ability to control one-self. It involves moderation, constraint, and the ability to say "no" to our baser desires and fleshly lusts. One of the proofs of God's working in our lives is the ability to control our thoughts, words, and actions. Believers need self-control because the outside world and internal forces still attack. Self-control naturally leads to perseverance as we value the long-term good instead of the instant gratification of the world. Self-control is a gift that frees us. It frees us to enjoy the benefits of a healthy body. It frees us to rest in the security of good stewardship. It frees us from a guilty conscience. Self-control restricts the indulgence of our foolish desires, and we find the liberty to love and live as we were meant to as Christians.[16]

To arrive at the pearly gates, one must travel the Narrow Way and resist the myriad of temptations that lie in wait for the pilgrim. There is no chance of smooth travel on a Christian journey. One must yield not to temptation with the power of self-control.

> *"Do not love the world or the things in the world. If anyone loves the world, the love of the Father is not in him. For all that is in the world—the lust of the flesh, the lust of the eyes, and the pride of life—is not of the Father but is of the world. And the world is passing away, and the lust of it; but he who does the will of God abides forever."*
>
> *(1 John 2:15-17. NLT)*

Self-control drives all the Fruits of the Spirit. It is involved in our execution of all of them – to show godly love, have holy joy, make peace, to patiently bear, kindly lookout, do good, be faithful and be gentle; all require self-control.

God is very much committed to wanting His children to be on the Narrow Way to eternal life. His efforts right from the fall of man at creation are towards turning us in the right direction. Though the Fruit of the Spirit gives enough assurance of being on the Narrow Way, God provided through His Revelation to Apostle John, an additional guide to our walk with Him which the Narrow Way represents. In His warning to the seven revelation churches, we can see the mind of God concerning how we must carry on our walk with Him to enter the Narrow Gate to eternal life. God was so particular about our taking in His counsel that He stressed at the end of each letter that we must take heed to His charge. It was to Him not a case of you and me having a choice in the matter; He wants us to do as He commands. God promises to reward those who take His counsel seriously; those who continue on the Narrow Way to the end.

> *"Anyone with ears to hear must listen to the Spirit and understand what he is saying to the churches. To everyone who is victorious, I will give fruit from the tree of life in the paradise of God."*
>
> *(Revelation 2:7. NLT)*

To be victorious, one must follow a prescribed life pattern and finish the race. It is not about playing according to our own rules but ONLY according to HIS standards;

God's laws. God took His time to provide clarity to us through His audit of the revelation churches to help those who are intent on travelling on the Narrow Way. One thing that is clear to all is that nothing is hidden from God. All that we do appear to Him as it were as if on a monitor sitting on His table. Like a songwriter once wrote: **you may cover your sins that no one else could know, you can never hide it from God**. God saw through all the churches just as He is seeing through us today. God showed He is sovereign and so calls us to turn our lives over to Him through His only begotten Son Jesus Christ.

> *"'For this is how God loved the world: He gave his one and only Son so that everyone who believes in him will not perish but have eternal life. God sent his Son into the world not to judge the world, but to save the world through him. "There is no judgment against anyone who believes in him. But anyone who does not believe in him has already been judged for not believing in God's one and only Son."*
>
> *(John 3: 16 -18. NLT)*

Ephesus was an ancient Greek city on the coast of Ionia, three kilometres southwest of present-day Selçuk in Ýzmir Province, Turkey.[17,18] It was the principal city of the Roman province of Asia and had the wealthiest banking centre in that part of the world.[19] Though the church received a good commendation, God saw that they had veered off course on the subject of love. He saw through their work and their lives that they no longer loved Him, and neither did they love themselves as they did before. God longed for the time when their love for Him drove all they did and resented the new order where monotony had set into their spiritual lives. He put it to them that motive is more important than the work itself and that when the purpose is not correct all the work is akin to wood, hay and straw which will be destroyed by God's testing fire. Your purpose of working for God or walking with Him determines acceptability or otherwise. How is love today among brethren; can we compare it to the days of old? On the day of the Lord's return, the question will be more of WHY we did something and not WHAT we did for the Lord.

> *'"But I have this complaint against you. You don't love me or each other as you did at first! Look how far you have fallen! Turn back to me and do the works you did at first. If you don't repent, I will come and remove your lampstand from its place among the churches."*
> *(Revelation 2: 4 – 5. NLT)*

If God removes your lampstand as a Christian, it means He no longer recognises you as His own. Examine yourself to see if you have done anything to warrant this type of sanction. If the answer is in the affirmative, you need to make amends today.

Smyrna was an Ancient Greek city located at a central and strategic point on the Aegean coast of Anatolia. This place is known today as **Ýzmir**, Turkey. Due to its advantageous port conditions, its ease of defence and its good inland connections, Smyrna rose to prominence.[20] God's message here is His demand for our faithfulness and the assurance of His reward. God reminded all His children that they will not have a smooth ride on the Narrow Way to eternal life but that they must focus on storing up treasures in heaven if they want to be heavenly rich. He commends their perseverance, and in doing so, reminds His followers that He sometimes allows His faithful children to endure persecution for a useful purpose. Faithfulness to the end is a prerequisite for Narrow Way travellers to enter into the Narrow Gate.

> *"Don't be afraid of what you are about to suffer. The devil will throw some of you into prison to test you. You will suffer for ten days. But if you remain faithful, even when facing death, I will give you the crown of life."*
>
> *(Revelation 2:10. NLT)*

The life of the Smyrna church mirrors the typical Christian experience of suffering and persecution. Be assured that God knows about your situation and feels your pains. He is your God both when you are on the mountain and in the valley. Don't lose faith, for you are never alone.

Pergamon or **Pergamum** was a rich and powerful ancient Greek city in Aeolis. It was the earliest capital of the Roman province of Asia. It contained a famous library, and its citizens developed the use of animal skins as writing materials. The city is located 26 kilometres from the modern coastline of the Aegean Sea on a peninsula on the north side of the river Caicus (modern-day Bakırçay) and northwest of the modern city of Bergama.[21] God's message here is to the contemporary Christian who lives in a world dominated by Satan. He expects us to remain on the Narrow Way irrespective of societal pressures. He is not prepared to lower His standards under any circumstance. He demands that we let our light shine through the darkness all the time, never compromising just like Antipas, who was martyred in Pergamum because of his unyielding commitment to the faith. The life of this church mirrors that of Christians who start well on the Narrow Way, but later backslide to go back to the world. They fell by the wayside after receiving a commendation for being faithful because they "tolerated" teachings that polluted their faith and which ultimately brought them down on their spiritual knees.

> *"'But I have a few complaints against you. You tolerate some among you whose teaching is like that of Balaam, who showed Balak how to trip up the people of Israel. He taught them to sin by eating food offered to idols and by committing sexual sin. In a similar way, you have some Nicolaitans among you who follow the same teaching. Repent of your sin, or I will come to you suddenly and fight against them with the sword of my mouth."*
>
> *(Revelation 2: 14 – 16. NLT)*

What is your Christian testimony? Are you consistent in your walk with God? Have you abandoned the true faith for something else, different from the way of the truth? Have you exchanged God's truth for the world's variant of Christianity called religiosity? Is your life an accurate reflection of Jesus today as against when you started on the Straight and Narrow Way?

Thyateira (also **Thyatira**) was the name of an ancient Greek city in Asia Minor, now the modern Turkish city of Akhisar ("white castle"). The name is probably Lydian. It lies in the far west of Turkey, south of Istanbul and almost due east of Athens. It is about 80 km from the Aegean Sea.[22] It was an outpost city known for its many trade guilds including weavers and dyers.[23] God is sending a cocktail of messages to you and me through His warning to this church. Nothing is hidden from God. His eyes search throughout the world as He neither slumbers nor sleeps. God is waging war against adulterous living and its perpetrators. He wants all His children to be wary of the destructive effect of physical and spiritual adultery.

Sexual sin is so pervasive today that even the pulpit has not been spared. Many are known to claim a relationship with God and yet go on in friendship with the world. The church is so polluted today that there is no clear distinction between those who stand for Jesus and those against Him. Sexual sin is now a "handbag" to many women and a "briefcase" to many men. MANY OF THESE ARE IN THE HOUSEHOLD OF FAITH. Again there is the polluting effect of adulterous teaching in Christendom, which provides a weak foundation to many and helps to derail others. God is not happy with this development and is warning perpetrators every day of severe consequences while encouraging those who are on the Lord's side to remain steadfast to the end.

> *"'But I also have a message for the rest of you in Thyatira who have not followed this false teaching ('deeper truths,' as they call them — depths of Satan, actually). I will ask nothing more of you except that you hold tightly to what you have until I come."*
>
> *(Revelation 2: 24 – 25. NLT)*

Do not give the devil a foothold in your life. Resist him, and he will flee from you. Be consistent with your travel till you reach the Narrow Gate and enter into your rest.

Sardis or **Sardes** was an ancient city at the location of modern Sart (Sartmahmut before 19 October 2005) in Turkey's Manisa Province. Sardis was the capital of the ancient kingdom of Lydia, one of the principal cities of the Persian Empire, the seat of a proconsul under the Roman Empire, and the metropolis of the province Lydia in later Roman and Byzantine times.[24] God addresses here what is arguably the most significant plague in Christian living. Hypocrisy has eaten so deep; many who are wolves with sheep clothing are taking others away from the Narrow Way. Apostle Paul admonished us to have nothing to do with them because they have only a form of godliness but ultimately deny its power (2 Timothy 3:5). Though God is so apparent in His condemnation of these "dead" Christians, yet He leaves a door of divine mercy open to those among them who want to retrace their steps. Today that door is still open to anyone whosoever will come, with a warning that God's judgment will be on those who have a reputation for being alive but are indeed dead. The love of God brings a second opportunity to all of humanity who live a life that does not meet God's requirement, only if they will repent.

> *"'I know all the things you do, and that you have a reputation for being alive—but you are dead. Wake up! Strengthen what little remains, for even what is left is almost dead. I find that your*

actions do not meet the requirements of my God. Go back to what you heard and believed at first; hold to it firmly. Repent and turn to me again. If you don't wake up, I will come to you suddenly, as unexpected as a thief."

(Revelation 3: 1b – 3. NLT)

Hypocrisy will bring you total rejection and abandonment from your Creator. God is ready to accommodate all who have not soiled their clothes with evil. To which camp do you belong?

Alaδehir in Antiquity and the Middle Ages known as Philadelphia is a town and district of Manisa Province in the Aegean region of Turkey. It is situated in the valley of the Kuzuçay (Cogamus in antiquity), at the foot of the Bozdağ Mountain (Mount Tmolus in antiquity). The town is connected to Ýzmir by a 105 km railway.[25] It was the Apostle Paul who reaffirmed the words of Jesus by saying to his spiritual son Timothy that "Gods truth stands like a foundation stone with this inscription: **"The LORD knows those who are His," and "All who belong to the LORD must turn away from evil"(2 Timothy 2:19).** God has again confirmed this position; He knows those who are faithful. He is not mocked! He diligently rewards those who serve Him. God sees into our hearts. He knows what we are about every second of the day, even inside our closets. He appreciates all that we do and also the difficulties that we face. He knows our limitations but wants us to be faithful in our calling. God is committed to His Word which He honours more than His name. He can never abandon His devoted children. The right hand of God is there to protect and preserve them. The way to God's heart is to be faithful always and to the end.

> *"'I know all the things you do, and I have opened a door for you that no one can close. You have little strength, yet you obeyed my word and did not deny me. Look, I will force those who belong to Satan's synagogue—those liars who say they are Jews but are not—to come and bow down at your feet. They will acknowledge that you are the ones I love."*
>
> *(Revelation 3: 8 – 9. NLT)*

Are you faithful to this God? Are you doing all you can to "hold on to what you have so that no one will take away your crown" (Revelation 3:11)? Your name can be removed from the Book of Life if you do not remain faithful to the end. Faithfulness to Him on the Narrow Way is not negotiable. What is your stand today?

Laodicea on the Lycus was an ancient city built on the river Lycus (Çürüksu). It was located in the Hellenistic regions of Caria and Lydia, which later became the Roman Province of Phrygia Pacatiana. It is now situated near the modern city of Denizli.[26] Southeast of Philadelphia; it was an economic and judicial centre of the metropolitan region that included Colosse and Hierapolis. The citizens of Laodicea were very proud of their self-sufficiency. After a severe earthquake in AD 60, Laodicea refused aid from Rome and rebuilt their city themselves, making it very beautiful.[27] The Bible teaches that pride goes before a fall, while our humility attracts God's hand to exalt us. The life of a Christian must follow the Christ-like humility that started from His leaving His heavenly glory, continued in His dwelling among us and ended with letting Himself go to the Cross. The pride of the Laodicean people was exhibited in the church of God, and the Almighty will have none of it. Whatever it was that made them full of themselves had no value in the sight of God. They lived life with so much inconsistency that God threatened to spit them out of His mouth. The things that matter to God did not matter to them. They thought themselves rich, but they were poor. God offered them a redemptive olive branch to cover their spiritual nakedness.

> *"'I know all the things you do, that you are neither hot nor cold. I wish that you were one or the other! But since you are like lukewarm water, neither hot nor cold, I will spit you out of my mouth! You say, 'I am rich. I have everything I want. I don't need a thing!' And you don't realise that you are wretched and miserable and poor and blind and naked. So I advise you to buy gold from me — gold that has been purified by fire. Then you will be rich. Also, buy white garments from me so you will not be shamed by your nakedness, and ointment for your eyes so you will be able to see. I correct and discipline everyone I love. So be diligent and turn from your indifference."*
>
> *(Revelation 3: 15 – 19. NLT)*

Can you, as a proud Christian claim to know Christ? Can you, as an arrogant Christian claim to be travelling on the Narrow Way? Can you even claim to be a Christian when you have not been broken down enough to let go of pride?

God sees through the window dressing lifestyle of many Christians. He is not prepared to compromise His standards no matter whose ox is gored. He has rejected the loveless, worldly, hypocritical, unfaithful and proud Christian lifestyles of camouflage being displayed all over the world. He is calling us again to repentance and warning anyone with ears to listen to Him. It is important to note that our lives as Christian pilgrims on the Narrow Way predispose us to attack by the fiery arrows of the devil. It is an inevitable experience but for which we have more than adequate antidotes if we are ready to apply them. The flaming darts are anything that discourages or distracts us in our walk with God, anything that destroys what we have (including material possessions), or anything that entices us to curse God. The journey we have chosen to embark on requires fortification with the FULL ARMOUR OF GOD. Without this armour, you will be blown to pieces by the evil forces. It is a long drawn battle, and for those intent on succeeding, nothing must be left to chance.

> *"Therefore, put on every piece of God's armour so you will be able to resist the enemy in the time of evil. Then after the battle, you will still be standing firm. Stand your ground, putting on the belt of truth and the body armour of God's righteousness. For shoes, put on the peace that comes from the Good News so that you will be fully prepared. In addition to all of these, hold up the shield of faith to stop the fiery arrows of the devil. Put on Salvation as your helmet, and take the sword of the Spirit, which is the word of God.*

Pray in the Spirit at all times and on every occasion. Stay alert and be persistent in your prayers for all believers everywhere."

(Ephesians 6:13 – 18. NLT)

The choice for us is a clear and distinct one. You may opt for the straight and Narrow Way or continue along its path if you are already on it, making sure that you do not veer off the road under any circumstance. On the contrary, there is an "easy" road that offers access to the wide gate via the broadway, which takes you in the other direction. The Narrow Way leads to eternal life while the broadway leads to eternal condemnation. Jesus has promised that **"all who are victorious will become pillars in the Temple of my God, and they will never have to leave it. And I will write on them the name of my God, and they will be citizens in the city of my God—the New Jerusalem that comes down from heaven from my God. And I will also write on them my new name" (Revelation 3:12).** He will keep His word. All you have to do is to go on the Narrow Way to the end.

"Then I saw a new heaven and a new earth, for the old heaven and the old earth had disappeared. And the sea was also gone. And I saw the holy city, the New Jerusalem, coming down from God out of heaven like a bride beautifully dressed for her husband. I heard a loud shout from the throne, saying, "Look, God's home is now among his people! He will live with them, and they will be his people. God himself will be with them. He

will wipe every tear from their eyes, and there will be no more death or sorrow or crying or pain. All these things are gone forever."'

(Revelation 21: 1 – 4. NLT)

In conclusion, I remember a discussion that took place between my father and one of his younger brothers more than 20 years ago. The brother was visiting our home, and their conversation veered into the topic of Salvation. I sat with them, so I was able to follow their talk. My uncle wondered if millions of non-Christians who also acknowledge the presence of the Supreme Being and who conduct themselves religiously in their chosen faith will miss eternal life. My father's response was swift and unequivocal; he answered in the affirmative. His response took my uncle by surprise as he felt the share number of people in question could not just be destroyed. My father closed his submission with the bible verse below;

"Jesus told him, "I am the way, the truth, and the life. No one can come to the Father except through me."

(John 14:6. NLT)

That is the whole story of the Narrow Way. There is only one of its kind, and only Jesus knows it. Jesus is that Way; there is none other except we want to deceive ourselves.

"For Jesus is the one referred to in the Scriptures, where it says, 'The stone that you builders rejected has now become the cornerstone.' There is Salvation in no one else! God has given no other name under heaven by which we must be saved."'

(Acts 4: 11 – 12. NLT)

My prayer is that if you haven't found Jesus, He will reveal Himself to you and you will follow Him along the Narrow Way all the days of your life.

You Too Can Be Holy

"So prepare your minds for action and exercise self-control. Put all your hope in the gracious Salvation that will come to you when Jesus Christ is revealed to the world. So you must live as God's obedient children. Don't slip back into your old ways of living to satisfy your own desires. You didn't know any better then. But now you must be holy in everything you do, just as God who chose you is holy. For the Scriptures say, "You must be holy because I am holy."'

(1 Peter 1: 13 – 16. NLT)

The subject of holiness has just begun to find importance in my life. Earlier on, I lived to please the flesh, so holiness always took the back seat in every scheme of my life's endeavour. The life I lived did not mirror that of Jesus, though, I was regarded as a Christian and went to church. Also, I was helpful to people, kind-hearted and a bit generous but when it came to the things of the Spirit, I looked the other way preferring to live my life as if it belonged to me. Today I know differently having found Grace to grow the seeds sowed in my life from early childhood. I now press on to a higher calling pleasing my Creator and emulating the lifestyle of His only begotten Son.

"Work at living in peace with everyone, and work at living a holy life, for those who are not holy will not see the Lord."

(Hebrew 12:14. NLT)

Holiness as a way of life started at creation. God laid the first rule of living, right at the beginning when He told Adam and Eve not to eat the fruit of the tree of knowledge of good and evil in the Garden of Eden. As simple as this may sound, this was God's first attempt to model the life of our forebearers in a way that was right and acceptable to Him. It was the unfortunate fall of man into sin that ultimately led to the unacceptable level of ungodly living witnessed at that time. God regretted these turn of events as His desire was for man to live in a holy and godly way. The intervention of God, therefore, became inevitable as His desired goal of holiness was now a mirage.

> *"The Lord observed the extent of human wickedness on the earth, and he saw that everything they thought or imagined was consistently and totally evil. So the Lord was sorry he had ever made them and put them on the earth. It broke his heart. And the Lord said, "I will wipe this human race I have created from the face of the earth. Yes, and I will destroy every living thing—all the people, the large animals, the small animals that scurry along the ground, and even the birds of the sky. I am sorry I ever made them." But Noah found favour with the Lord."*
>
> *(Genesis 6: 5 – 8. NLT)*

The relationship between God and the children of Israel is another proof of the long-held desire of God for holiness to be second nature to His people. Joseph found himself in Egypt due to the envy and wickedness of his brothers. Still, since God's faithfulness is unwavering and lasting from generation to generation, a breakthrough was made possible at the end as God must always keep His promise.

Even though the obstacle to their deliverance was stupendous, God's power to deliver and save His own is unfailing. God's purpose for His intervention was so that He can build a relationship with the Israelites through their sanctification. They were chosen by God so that He can use them to showcase the example of godly living that He intends all His creation to follow.

> *"Then Moses climbed the mountain to appear before God. The Lord called to him from the mountain and said, "Give these instructions to the family of Jacob; announce it to the descendants of Israel: 'You have seen what I did to the Egyptians. You know how I carried you on eagles' wings and brought you to myself. Now if you will obey me and keep my covenant, you will be my own special treasure from among all the peoples on earth; for all the earth belongs to me. And you will be my kingdom of priests, my holy nation.' This is the message you must give to the people of Israel."'*
>
> *(Exodus 19: 3 – 6. NLT)*

> *"The Lord also said to Moses, "Give the following instructions to the entire community of Israel. You must be holy because I, the Lord your God, am holy."*
>
> *(Leviticus 19: 1 – 2. NLT)*

God gave enough spiritual food to His people to mould them into what He desired.

To be Holy means to be set apart or separate from sin or evil. It is a state of being holy in a life of total devotion to God. Holiness, in the highest sense, belongs to God. It belongs to Christians as consecrated to God's service and in so far as they are conformed in all things to the will of God. Personal holiness is a work of gradual development. It is carried on under many hindrances, hence the frequent admonitions to watchfulness, prayer and perseverance.[1] Holiness is unattainable by self-effort alone even though God commands it. Help is required, and this is available in Christ alone.

> *"Therefore if any man be in Christ, he is a new creature: old things are passed away; behold all things are become new."*
>
> *(2 Corinthians 5: 17. NLT)*

Is Jesus able to carry us over the bridge separating ungodliness from holiness? There is a Yoruba proverb that says that if someone offers to get you a tunic, it is advisable you take a look at what he or she is wearing to determine whether you can rely on them to deliver. The testimony of Jesus demonstrated very clearly that He could provide the holiness He has to all who give their lives to Him for rulership. His Holy Spirit conception is a proof of His divine nature and a confirmation of His exalted status.

> *"As he considered this, an angel of the Lord appeared to him in a dream. "Joseph, son of David," the angel said, "do not be afraid to take Mary as your wife. For the child within her was conceived by the Holy Spirit."*
>
> *(Matthew 1:20. NLT)*

The suitability of Jesus for the Calvary sacrifice is because He had no sin in Him. There is no way He could have become adequate if like man He too was with sin. God had to choose a lamb without blemish to achieve His desired once and for all redemption package.

> *"For God made Christ, who never sinned, to be the offering for our sin so that we could be made right with God through Christ."*
>
> *(2 Corinthians 5:21. NLT)*

Jesus lived our ordinary life to encourage us that we too can overcome all temptations and be holy even as He was during His sojourn on earth. All impossibilities are made possible by Him. He gave an assurance that we can surpass all that He did in the flesh if we remain rooted in Him.

> *"This High Priest of ours understands our weaknesses, for he faced all of the same testings we do, yet he did not sin."*
>
> *(Hebrews 4:15. NLT)*

Although you may think that the decision is yours to make either to be holy or not, God's Word on this subject does not allow for discretion as He expects us to obey Him to the letter. It is also possible that you may be in the camp of those who feel that holiness is an unattainable target, and as such, there is no need to pursue it. The truth is that God will not put you through a test that is beyond the scope of your faith; therefore if He says it is possible to stand firm in holiness, it is indeed POSSIBLE!

> *"The temptations in your life are no different from what others experience. And God is faithful. He will not allow the temptation to be more than*

you can stand. When you are tempted, he will show you a way out so that you can endure."

(1 Corinthians 10:13. NLT)

The possibility that you have to live a holy life is dependent on the Spirit of God – the Holy Spirit. He is the power behind all that you can do with your Christian life. If you allow Him to take charge, He will help you to overcome all hindrances towards holy living. You must, however, accommodate Him and give Him space to operate. His residence IS ALWAYS holy. He cannot inhabit a sinful life.

"But to all who believed him and accepted him, he gave the right to become children of God."

(John 1:12. NLT)

"But ye shall receive power, after that the Holy Ghost is come upon you:"

(Acts 1:8a. NLT)

You must accept Jesus and have faith in Him if you are to receive His gift - the Spirit of Truth. Your becoming a child of God is a confirmation of your willingness to conform with His likeness, one of which is His holy nature.

Holiness is no rocket science. It is a simple and peaceful lifestyle which many have adopted following the example of Jesus of Nazareth. Apostle Paul was so faithful to it that he could ask others to emulate him – that was his confidence (1 Corinthians 11:1). Joseph too set an example not typical for his age then and now when he turned his back on an offer many will die to receive. He chose the preservation of his destiny against a fleeting moment of pleasure which many still fall for even today (Genesis 39:8–12). Shiphrah and Puah are two Hebrew midwives who were approached by Pharoah to destroy newborn male Jewish babies in Egypt. They opted to please God and found a good excuse to extricate themselves from the murderous command of an ungodly king (Exodus 1:15-17). Many today will choose to do the bidding of the powers that be for a single morsel of porridge. Zachariah and Elizabeth, on the contrary, gave a good testimony as ministers of God for they were righteous & careful to obey God's commandments and regulations (Luke 1:6). Cornelius was a Roman army officer who chose the part of godly honour and holiness and therefore became a proof to those who think that a sinful life is inevitable when in service of the people (Acts 10:1-2).

> *"God has called us to live holy lives, not impure lives."*
> *(1 Thessalonians 4: 7. NLT)*

The life of Holiness you are invited into is one with enormous benefits if you are careful to follow through with it diligently. You must remember that faithful is the one who has drawn you to this lifestyle. He will not turn His back on you under any circumstance. God promises a type of intimacy that you can only dream of if you remain steadfast in following His footsteps of holy living. David experienced this intimacy and could not but help give assurance to those who are still holding back.

"Who may worship in your sanctuary, Lord? Who may enter your presence on your holy hill? Those who lead blameless lives and do what is right, speaking the truth from sincere hearts. Those who refuse to gossip or harm their neighbours or speak evil of their friends. Those who despise flagrant sinners, and honour the faithful followers of the Lord, and keep their promises even when it hurts. Those who lend money without charging interest, and who cannot be bribed to lie about the innocent. Such people will stand firm forever."

(Psalm 15: 1 – 6. NLT)

Intimacy with God provides so many privileges to those who are wise to it and remains the sine qua non to a successful life. The intimate one receives classified information from God who builds a wall of protection around him or her. God's promise of divine provision, divine health and long life becomes theirs by right while they continue to enjoy peace with all their enemies. Intimacy with God equals intimacy with His Spirit, and this translates into receiving the Fruit of the Spirit viz love, joy, peace, longsuffering, kindness, goodness, faithfulness, gentleness, self-control and also having control over the damaging effects of the works of the flesh. Most importantly, though, intimacy with God drives us on the Narrow Way to eternal life. For those who choose to call God's bluff by determining to make their own rules of living, they face not only eternal condemnation but denial from accessing their earthly possessions.

"Listen! The Lord's arm is not too weak to save you, nor is his ear too deaf to hear you call. It's your sins that have cut you off from God. Because of your sins, he has turned away and will not listen anymore."

(Isaiah 59: 1 – 2. NLT)

You may think that the message of God to you on living a holy life is unprofitable and so undesirable. King David too felt this way at a time in history. But he soon found out that was not the case. He saw and envied what he later found to be the transient uplifting of the wicked. He wondered at a time why God could be so unjust and unfair. He then sat down under the guidance of God to reflect on this very intriguing matter. God revealed to him the end of the wicked as not to be desired by anyone.

"So I tried to understand why the wicked prosper. But what a difficult task it is! Then I went into your sanctuary, O God, and I finally understood the destiny of the wicked. Truly, you put them on a slippery path and send them sliding over the cliff to destruction. In an instant they are destroyed, completely swept away by terrors."

(Psalm 73: 16 – 19. NLT)

Holiness is not a child's play. It must be taken with the utmost seriousness. You either choose to walk the walk to receive gain for doing so or walk away and face the consequences of your decision. Holiness is profitable to your life only if you completely embrace it. Excerpts from a sermon on holiness by J.C. Ryle reveals that holiness is a habit where one takes the mind of God and this we can find described in the Bible. Its a lifestyle of agreement with God's judgment—in everything and every way by using His word as a yardstick for our decisions and actions. A holy man will endeavour to shun every known sin and to keep every known commandment. His goal will be to live as Jesus lived. In doing so, his life will be entirely dependent on Him as he draws his strength and peace from the Master. His ultimate purpose will be to work to have the mind that was in Him, and to be "conformed to His image."

A holy man will follow after patience, gentleness, meekness, longsuffering, good tempers, and government of his tongue. He will bear much, forbear much, overlook much, and be slow to talk of standing on his rights. We see an excellent example of this in the behaviour of David when Shimei cursed him. A holy man will follow after self-denial and temperance. He will labour to mortify the desires of his body—to crucify his flesh with its affections and lusts—to curb his passions—to restrain his carnal inclinations, lest at any time they break loose. A holy man will follow after brotherly kindness and charity. He will endeavour to observe the golden rule of doing as he would have men do to him, and speak to others as he would want them to speak to him. He will be full of affection towards his brethren—towards their bodies, their property, their characters, their feelings, their souls. "He that loveth another," says Paul, "hath fulfilled the law" (Romans 13:8). He will hate all lying, slandering, backbiting, cheating, dishonesty, and unfair dealing, even in the least things. A holy man will follow after a spirit of mercy and kindness towards others. He will not stand all the day idle. A holy man will follow after purity of heart. He will dislike all uncleanness of spirit, filthiness and seek to avoid all things that might draw him into it. Who shall dare to talk of strength when David can fall? A holy man will follow after the fear of God. This does not refer to the fear of a slave, who only works because of fear, and would be idle if there is no risk of discovery. I refer here to the fear of a child, who wishes to live and move as if he was always before his father's face because he loves him. The example of Nehemiah is very apt in this regard. As Governor at Jerusalem, he could have exploited his position to make money from the Jews in exchange for his support. The former Governors had done so. There was none to blame him if he did. But he says, "So did not I, because of the fear of God"(Nehemiah 5:15). A holy man will follow after humility. He will desire, in lowliness of mind, to regard all others better than himself. He will see more evil in his own heart than in any other in the world. He will understand the import of Abraham's state of mind when he says, "I am dust and ashes;" and Jacob's, when he says, "I am less than the least of all Thy mercies;" and Job's, when he says, "I am vile;" and Paul's when he says, "I am chief of sinners." A holy man will follow after faithfulness in all duties and relationships. He will try, not merely to fill his place as others who take no thought for their souls do, but even better because he has higher motives. Those words of Paul should never be forgotten, "Whatever ye do, do it heartily, as unto the Lord," — "Not slothful in business, fervent in spirit, serving the Lord" (Colossians 3:23).

Last but not least, a holy man will follow after spiritual mindedness. He will determine to set a heavenly focus while placing less importance on things on earth. He will not neglect the business of the life that now is, but the first place in his mind and thoughts will be given to the life to come. His life pattern will be like that of a man whose treasure is in heaven and who is passing through this world like a stranger and pilgrim travelling to his home above.[2]

> *"For God's Kingdom is not a matter of eating and drinking, but of the righteousness, peace, and joy which the Holy Spirit gives."*
>
> *(Romans 14:17. NLT)*

In the journey of Holiness, there exists a crucial step that must be taken by all. You cannot travel on a train without a ticket. The ride on the holiness train has a heavenly kingdom as the destination, and unless you have your Salvation ticket, you won't even get into the holiness train station. The call to Salvation was made over 2000 years ago. The good news is that the offer never expires but each one must take advantage of the gift before it becomes too late when the potential recipient is no longer able to access it.

> *"Jesus replied, "I tell you the truth unless you are born again; you cannot see the Kingdom of God."'*
>
> *(John 3:3. NLT)*

As you desire today to join the holiness train, I offer Jesus to you AGAIN! My prayer is that you will seize the opportunity to come on board to enjoy this beautiful experience. Indeed YOU TOO CAN BE HOLY!

Pathway to God's Blessings

"Then the Lord said to Samuel, "I am sorry that I ever made Saul king, for he has not been loyal to me and has refused to obey my command." Samuel was so deeply moved when he heard this that he cried out to the Lord all night. Early the next morning Samuel went to find Saul. Someone told him, "Saul went to the town of Carmel to set up a monument to himself; then he went on to Gilgal." When Samuel finally found him, Saul greeted him cheerfully. "May the Lord bless you," he said. "I have carried out the Lord's command!" "Then what is all the bleating of sheep and goats and the lowing of cattle I hear?" Samuel demanded. "It's true that the army spared the best of the sheep, goats, and cattle," Saul admitted. "But they are going to sacrifice them to the Lord your God. We have destroyed everything else." Then Samuel said to Saul, "Stop! Listen to what the Lord told me last night!" "What did he tell you?" Saul asked. And Samuel told him, "Although you may think little of yourself, are you not the leader of the tribes of Israel? The Lord has anointed you king of Israel. And the Lord sent you on a mission and told you, 'Go and completely destroy the sinners, the Amalekites, until they are all dead.' Why haven't you obeyed the Lord? Why did you rush for the plunder and do what was evil in the Lord's sight?" "But I did obey the Lord," Saul insisted. "I carried out the mission he gave me. I brought back King Agag, but I destroyed everyone else. Then my troops brought in the best

of the sheep, goats, cattle, and plunder to sacrifice to the Lord your God in Gilgal." But Samuel replied, "What is more pleasing to the Lord: your burnt offerings and sacrifices or your obedience to his voice? Listen! Obedience is better than sacrifice, and submission is better than offering the fat of rams. Rebellion is as sinful as witchcraft, and stubbornness as bad as worshipping idols. So because you have rejected the command of the Lord, he has rejected you as king."'

(1 Samuel 15: 10 – 23 NLT)

The simple meaning of holiness is complete obedience to God. In Luke 6:64, Jesus said, "Why do you call Me Lord when you don't do those things that I command you?" The evidence that Jesus is Lord to you in spirit and truth is doing whatever He commands you. Holiness is obedience: not just half obedience but total obedience.[1]

The truism that without obedience, no one can please God is exemplified by the fall of King Saul from Grace to grass. God chose Saul and so must have wanted him to succeed at his assignment, but alas it was not to be because what is most important to God was not that important to Saul. The rest they say is history as Saul lost not only his crown but ultimately his life. God is known to have no qualms about putting His foot down when it comes to the issue of obedience. Jesus describes only those who obey God's commands as His friends further confirming how highly He regards obedience in the lives of all humans.

"You are my friends if you do what I command."

(John 15:14 NLT)

The Children of Israel were God's chosen people. God loved them so much that He did not hide from them. In doing so, He made every effort to bring them up the way that will be pleasing to Him and profitable to them. God's way is simply about Holiness, nothing more and nothing less. Holiness is like second nature to God such that if He had skin, it would be made of holiness. God created man for the sole reason of fellowship, and there is no way fellowship can be initiated with God without one signing up to His holiness mantra. There is no holiness without obedience, and once obedience is missing, holiness will take flight and God becomes immediately displeased. Man will be separated from God once obedience leading to holiness disappears.

God makes His friendship only with those who love and live in holiness. It is to them alone that He enjoys intimacy and provides His abundant blessings. The best way to win His heart is through obedience. God's "weak" points are the "holiness receptors" in His body, and it is through these that we have a chance to gain His attention. God makes no apologies and takes no prisoners about His unequivocal love for holiness. His best friends are those who eat, drink and sleep holiness and He listens to them whenever they seek Him. He never disappoints them and always rises to their help when they call on Him.

At creation, God set the holiness agenda in the Garden of Eden. He gave Adam a single rule for his compliance to maintain fellowship with Him. Unfortunately, Adam found pleasing God a very tall order to achieve. Though he was quick to transfer blame to Eve and the Almighty when asked to give account, God was not fooled as He expected Adam to take responsibility and he did not. God was naturally unable to condone this unholy act and so began the development of a gulf between man and God.

As a consequence of this misdemeanour, God then had to wield the big stick with Adam paying the price for his action. As is always the case with Him, God rejects all excuses because what He wants from us is our total obedience. Although God sanctioned Adam and asked him to go away from His presence, he still did not learn his lessons. All the way to when Noah was born, man did not come to accept that the only way to make his Creator pleased with him is if he was found worthy in the way he lived his life. It finally came to a point when God regretted the existence of man expressing deep sadness that He chose to create him.

> *"The LORD observed the extent of human wickedness on the earth, and he saw that everything they thought or imagined was consistently and totally evil. So the LORD was sorry he had ever made them and put them on the earth. It broke his heart. And the LORD said, "I will wipe this human race I have created from the face of the earth. Yes, and I will destroy every living thing— all the people, the large animals, the small animals that scurry along the ground, and even the birds of the sky. I am sorry I ever made them." But Noah found favour with the LORD."*
>
> *(Genesis 6: 5 – 8 NLT)*

Although God went on to do what He purposed for the world, He was able to find Noah, which means that even today we can safely conclude that God's expectation from us is not an impossibility. Noah found favour with God to be spared because "Noah was a righteous man, blameless in his time; Noah walked with God"(Genesis 6:9). And so God began His pursuit of holiness with Noah anew. Unfortunately by the time the people came to building the Tower of Babel, it was clear that man had not learnt obedience; that what is best for him is to remain subjugated to God and to defer to Him in all situations and circumstances. And so God had to start again! He never gives up on us. Our living in holiness does not add to or subtract from God; it is only to us that benefits of holiness accrue. Nevertheless, God continues to invest His wisdom and energy to find a way to draw us to Himself – something that can only happen when we embrace holiness. This second beginning started with Abram!

"The LORD had said to Abram, "Leave your native country, your relatives, and your father's family, and go to the land that I will show you. I will make you into a great nation. I will bless you and make you famous, and you will be a blessing to others. I will bless those who bless you and curse those who treat you with contempt. All the families on earth will be blessed through you." So Abram departed as the LORD had instructed, and Lot went with him. Abram was seventy-five years old when he left Haran. He took his wife, Sarai, his nephew Lot, and all his wealth—his livestock and all the people he had taken into his

household at Haran—and headed for the land of Canaan. When they arrived in Canaan, Abram travelled through the land as far as Shechem. There he set up camp beside the oak of Moreh. At that time, the area was inhabited by Canaanites."

(Genesis 12: 1 – 6 NLT)

God saw something special in Abram. He saw a willingness to obey Him, which is why He had promised to bless him, make him a great nation and make him a blessing itself. God planned to carve out a unique nation from Abram, which will hopefully be like their progenitor. God kept His promise to Abram. He gave him a new name Abraham and did bless him with numerous descendants. His mandate to Abram was that he should be perfect. God, after that, entered into a special covenant with Abraham.

"When Abram was ninety-nine years old, the LORD appeared to him and said, "I am El-Shaddai— 'God Almighty.' Serve me faithfully and live a blameless life. I will make a covenant with you, by which I will guarantee to give you countless descendants."'

(Genesis 17: 1 – 2 NLT)

"Then Abraham bowed down to the ground, but he laughed to himself in disbelief. "How could I become a father at the age of 100?" he thought. "And how can Sarah have a baby when she is ninety years old?" So Abraham said to God, "May Ishmael live under your special blessing!" But God replied, "No—Sarah, your wife, will give birth to a son for you. You will name him Isaac, and I will confirm my covenant with him and his descendants as an everlasting covenant.

> *As for Ishmael, I will bless him also, just as you have asked. I will make him extremely fruitful and multiply his descendants. He will become the father of twelve princes, and I will make him a great nation. But my covenant will be confirmed with Isaac, who will be born to you and Sarah about this time next year." When God had finished speaking, he left Abraham."*
>
> *(Genesis 17: 17 – 22 NLT)*

Abraham's relationship with God was built on his total commitment and obedience to his Creator. There is no greater proof of this than at mount Moriah when Abraham was prepared to sacrifice his only son just because God asked him to do so. God gave Abraham the descendants He had promised through Isaac. His promised covenant was therefore activated once Isaac was born, and it was to Jacob and then the nation of Israel that this promise was later transferred. However, the promises of God contained in His covenant can only come to pass when man plays his part in obedience to God's word. This continued obedience is summed up in holiness. Since God desires that His children receive the benefits of His covenant with them, He, therefore, proceeded to teach the Israelites to know His laws so that they will know His mind in all things.

Isaac was born to the 90-year-old Sarah as God broke all barriers for His friend Abraham. Then came Jacob after God in His wisdom chose the younger in preference to the older Esau. Much later, several thousand Jews found themselves in ancient Egypt when first Joseph was sold into slavery by his brothers and then Jacob had to send his children to look for food in Egypt to prevent the family from starving to death during a famine. The family on finding the forgiving and now prominent Joseph stayed back in Goshen, Egypt. The years went by, and after Joseph's death, the tide began to turn against the previously successful and free Israelites under a new king in Egypt. But God never forgets His covenant. He had a plan to bring His chosen children of Abraham back to the Promised Land and to teach them the way He wants them to go to show forth His glory.

After over 400 years of oppression and repression, God's plan was placed on the front burner through His mighty hand placed on the shoulders of Moses. God personally took charge of the situation and removed His elect from the hands of their oppressors. The children of Israel as descendants of Abraham were divinely connected to God's covenant. Still, since the fulfilment of this covenant is contingent on obedience, it was essential for them to know the mind of God to please Him in all their ways. God invested so much in teaching them to be holy so that none of the accruing covenant blessings will elude them. God does not toy with the subject of obedience. It is the easiest way to win His heart, and its converse, which is disobedience is the best way to make Him turn His back. Moses was one of God's greatest generals. The bible described him as "a very humble man, more humble than anyone on the face of the earth"(Numbers 12:3). However, because of disobedience, one single act of disobedience in Kadesh at the desert of Zin; only because he struck the rock instead of speaking to it as directed by God, he lost arguably his biggest earthly reward which was the entry to the Promised Land. And although he pleaded with God for pardon to enter "the good land beyond Jordan - that fine hill country and Lebanon"(Deuteronomy 3:25), God in His wisdom declined to give him the opportunity.

> *'"But the LORD was angry with me because of you, and he would not listen to me. 'That's enough!' he declared. 'Speak of it no more. But go up to Pisgah Peak, and look over the land in every direction. Take a good look, but you may not cross the Jordan River."*
>
> *(Deuteronomy 3: 26 – 27 NLT)*
>
> *"Don't be fooled by those who try to excuse these sins, for the anger of God will fall on all who disobey him."*
>
> *(Ephesians 5: 6 NLT)*

Obedience is the precursor of holiness, which God seeks from all His children. Obedience to God guarantees our physical and spiritual Salvation and ensures we end up in heaven. Disobedience, on the other hand, takes you in the opposite direction and occurs when we do what God forbids, refuse to do what He commands, add to or take away from His word and substitute something He has commanded with what is pleasing to us. One of the things God forbids is idolatry. Idolatry challenges God's position and by extension His authority over us so He is very much against it. Our God is very jealous, and nothing we do must relegate Him. We must be ready to let go of all things for the sake of this God, who is a Consuming Fire.

Many of us do not make graven images to idolize. Still, we have become more "sophisticated" in our idol worship such that we regard many things in higher priority to God. This is covetousness and is the modern-day idolatry.

> *"Don't be greedy, for a greedy person is an idolater, worshipping the things of this world."*
>
> *(Colossians 3:5b NLT)*

> *"'But be very careful! You did not see the LORD's form on the day he spoke to you from the heart of the fire at Mount Sinai. So do not corrupt yourselves by making an idol in any form—whether of a man or a woman, an animal on the ground, a bird in the sky, a small animal that scurries along the ground, or a fish in the deepest sea."*
>
> *(Deuteronomy 4: 15 – 18 NLT)*

God must be the priority person in your life. Your Alpha and Omega, He must direct all your affairs, and in every way, you must defer to Him. Your will must be subsumed into His, and just like Jesus, you must continue to honour Him alone. It is impossible to attain the holiness status that God has demanded from us if we do not first and foremost see and take Him as Almighty in our lives. No one can and must compete with Him. He must be the centrepiece of all that surrounds us, and everything that pleases Him must please us and everything that displeases Him must also displease us. This way, we retain our status as the apple of His eyes and no weapon fashioned against us shall prosper. He then continues to watch over us without sleeping nor slumbering.

God wants us to reverence Him so that He will occupy first place in our lives. In turn, He assures us of safety and blessings for our children and us. He wants everything we do and every way we conduct our lives to show that we love Him and also love our brothers and sisters. No part of our living should conflict with this position. God is explicit in this dictum, and He is unwavering in His demand that we follow them.

> *'"Listen, O Israel! The LORD is our God, the LORD alone. And you must love the LORD your God with all your heart, all your soul, and all your strength. And you must commit yourselves wholeheartedly to these commands that I am giving you today. Repeat them again and again to your children. Talk about them when you are at home and when you are on the road, when you are going to bed and when you are getting up. Tie them to your hands and wear them on your forehead as reminders. Write them on the doorposts of your house and on your gates."*
>
> *(Deuteronomy 6: 4 – 9 NLT)*

Holiness in God's dictionary mandates our relationship with Him to continue for the rest of our lives. We must never forget Him or put Him aside in our lives, even for a single minute. It was Peter who took his eyes away from Jesus when walking towards the Lord on the Sea of Galilee, and immediately he began to sink. Every day we must remember all His faithful deeds so that we can have the strength to hold on till the end. We must understand that forgetting God means turning our backs in another direction and going our separate ways, which translates into backsliding. God wants us to be fully committed. He does not want us to be faint-hearted. The reference to "all your heart, all your soul and all your strength" is a quality of total commitment. Compromise of any sort makes His heart to bleed and takes us away from the holiness path. Holiness requires us to be wholeheartedly committed to all His commands. This is when we are said not to have forgotten Him! In asking us never to forget Him and His commandments, God puts on our table immeasurable blessings which are available to us today and to generations yet unborn to us.

> *"Understand, therefore, that the LORD your God is indeed God. He is the faithful God who keeps his covenant for a thousand generations and lavishes his unfailing love on those who love him and obey his commands. But he does not hesitate to punish and destroy those who reject him. Therefore, you must obey all these commands, decrees, and regulations I am giving you today. "If you listen to these regulations and faithfully obey them, the LORD your God will keep his covenant of unfailing love with you, as he promised with an oath to your ancestors. He will love you and bless you, and he will give you many children. He will give fertility to your land and your animals. When you arrive in the land he swore to give your ancestors, you will have large harvests of grain, new wine, and olive oil, and great herds of cattle, sheep, and goats. You will be blessed above all the nations of the earth. None of your men or women will be childless, and all your livestock will bear young. And the LORD will protect you from all sickness. He will not let you suffer from*

the terrible diseases you knew in Egypt, but he
will inflict them on all your enemies!"

(Deuteronomy 7: 9 – 15 NLT)

God's holiness does not exploit in any way. They are good seeds that we are wise to sow and to which God assures a rich harvest. Do not be found on the unprofitable road to destruction. The devil offered Jesus that route in the wilderness, but the Son of God saw through his deceit and made the better choice. The rules to obey are not burdensome as they will only help us to find peace in the Lord. They also serve as a gateway to many things we can only dream about which only God can provide. These blessings are permanent provided we are careful to obey Him always.

> *"'Look, today I am giving you the choice between*
> *a blessing and a curse! You will be blessed if you*
> *obey the commands of the LORD your God that*
> *I am giving you today. But you will be cursed if*
> *you reject the commands of the LORD your God*
> *and turn away from him and worship gods you*
> *have not known before."*

(Deuteronomy 11: 26 – 28 NLT)

One of the purposes of tithing is to test our truthfulness and faithfulness. Although God also wants us to put Him to test to see if we trust Him, the fact that God owns the whole universe and all that is in it proves that He needs nothing from us. Why would someone who has given you life and power to make wealth, who owns and knows everything about you ask for only a tenth of your income? Why would someone who holds your total being ask for only a tenth of your salary? The critical question will be that if you cannot give a token of your material possession to God, would you be willing to give your whole life to Him in holiness? The type of faith which you are expected to embrace must honour God with your substance and is also expected to extend hands of generosity to the less privileged. Holiness without the love of giving or sharing is dead!

> *"'You must set aside a tithe of your crops — one-tenth of all the crops you harvest each year."*
>
> *(Deuteronomy 14: 22 NLT)*

> *"'But if there are any poor Israelites in your towns when you arrive in the land, the LORD, your God, is giving you, do not be hard-hearted or tightfisted toward them. Instead, be generous and lend them whatever they need."*
>
> *(Deuteronomy 15: 7 – 8 NLT)*

Holiness, as a lifestyle, touches every area of our lives. God values His creation, and no one knows better than Him what has gone into making man to transit from mere dust to a living being. This means that He is more than anyone else committed to life's preservation until He calls us back to Himself. Cain was the first one to shed innocent blood when he killed his brother Abel. God was very angry then and is still so today with anyone who tows the line of Cain. The life of all His children is of utmost importance to God, and anyone who wants to follow God's holiness lifestyle must value life just like the Creator. The shedding of innocent blood truncates a destiny and prevents the fulfilling of God's purpose. The destruction of innocent life is an attack on God's handiwork, and He cannot be happy with its perpetrators. The destruction of life is, however, not limited to the physical. Many do not care even if they bring the other down spiritually, financially or psychologically. Those who want to live a life of holiness must flee from all these viles.

> *"Do not feel sorry for that murderer! Purge from Israel the guilt of murdering innocent people; then all will go well with you."*
>
> *(Deuteronomy 19: 13 NLT)*

The purpose of living in holiness is to please God and make Him happy with us. This cannot be achieved without faith. Our faith in God means that we depend on Him to deliver us and bring to reality all His promises. This, in turn, makes Him do more as He knows we are not relying on anyone else. Our faith in God, therefore, helps us to please Him because it drives us to do what He asks of us, which leads us to live a life of holiness. Faith and holiness are practically inseparable. It is your faith in God that makes you trust His choice of a holiness lifestyle for you, and it is the same faith that helps you to continue on this path believing that all He has promised you on this journey of holiness will come to pass.

> *"And it is impossible to please God without faith. Anyone who wants to come to him must believe that God exists and that he rewards those who sincerely seek him."*
>
> *(Hebrews 11:6 NLT)*

Faith in God also helps you to overcome all obstacles on the Narrow Way of holiness.

> *'"When you go out to fight your enemies, and you face horses and chariots and an army greater than your own, do not be afraid. The LORD your God, who brought you out of the land of Egypt, is with you!"*
>
> *(Deuteronomy 20:1 NLT)*

The choice to live in holiness means that you have resolved to be uncompromising with sin. God hates sin but loves the sinner who has resolved to forsake his sins. If you decide to continue in sin, then God is likely to transfer His sin hatred to you by turning His back. However, if you come back to your senses and go back to your Father, He will not cast you away. Sin is like cancer to our spiritual body, and anyone who destroys God's temple becomes an enemy of God. God has a zero-tolerance for sin of any kind, and in His book, there is no sin categorization. He is a holy God who is only compatible with a holy you. A life of holiness means every day you must be prepared to fight for your victory. The enemy will come at you with many devices and schemes, but the battle is not beyond you to win if you remain resolute and steadfast. Remember that the One who has enlisted you will not compromise His standards. His rules are unbendable and unchangeable. In them, you will find your peace and route to success.

You cannot travel on this Holiness highway if you are not prepared to honour your parents. Our parents are one of God's authority representatives on earth, and since

God is not an author of confusion, He would expect us to give them their due regard. Jesus Himself in emphasizing this position always deferred to His heavenly Father, and always His will was subsumed into God's will. I am persuaded to believe that God's thinking is that if you cannot honour your earthy parents whom you can see, then it is unlikely you will honour Him. But again if you are hypocritical in honouring God, today He is telling you to put aside your honour for Him; go back and begin to honour your parents after that you can then come back, and He will be happy to receive His honour from you. Again do not let anyone fool you; the recognition God is talking about is not only reserved for your biological parents. They must go to elders and those who are in a position of authority over you – notwithstanding their ages.

> *"Children, obey your parents because you belong to the Lord, for this is the right thing to do. "Honor your father and mother." This is the first commandment with a promise: If you honour your father and mother, "things will go well for you, and you will have a long life on the earth."'*
>
> *(Ephesians 6:1 – 3 NLT)*

Holiness without love is a counterfeit. God's holiness is interwoven with love because God is love. The holiness journey travels with love every single day. It was because God so loved the world that you have received your Salvation which is the ticket with which you started your holiness journey so surely you too must radiate love. In all your ways, let the love found in Christ Jesus, flow out of you to others so that they also will be drawn to the life that you live. This is the best way to share the good news with others who are perishing to rescue them. Always remember that you have been a beneficiary of the most excellent show of love which occurred on a Cross in Calvary and so you too must go forth and show love to others. Be assured that the promise of Jesus that we can do more extraordinary things than He did is no fluke and so all you need is to guard your loins and march forward. He who has called you from the world's darkness will back you up to do these exploits. The Samaritan love shown was by a man like you. Stephen also demonstrated an exceptional love for those who stoned him to death (Acts 7:60). Many of the disciples of Jesus lost their lives because they loved the sinning world and wanted them to hear about Jesus so as not to perish.

> *"Dear friends, let us continue to love one another, for love comes from God. Anyone who loves is a child of God and knows God. But anyone who does not love does not know God, for God is love."*
>
> *(1 John 4: 7 – 8 NLT)*
>
> *"'If you see your neighbour's ox or sheep or goat wandering away, don't ignore your responsibility. Take it back to its owner. If its owner does not live nearby or you don't know who the owner is, take it to your place and keep it until the owner comes looking for it. Then you must return it. Do the same if you find your neighbour's donkey, clothing, or anything else your neighbour loses. Don't ignore your responsibility. "If you see that*

your neighbour's donkey or ox has collapsed on the road, do not look the other way. Go and help your neighbour get it back on its feet!"

(Deuteronomy 22: 1 – 4 NLT)

One of the purposes of living a life of Holiness is so that you can set the right example for the world. As the light and salt of the world, others must see you as God's example in doing all things well. Your appearance must please God at all times, and you must ensure that anything controversial is far from you. Your lifestyle example must be so guided that no one would find any reason to argue against your standpoint or position. You must conduct yourself in a way that will not make others to fall and lose their Salvation. If you know any of your actions can lead others to sin in any way, it is better to err on the side of caution and be safe in pleasing God. It is better to appear foolish and conservative to the world while you make God happy with you. The heart of holiness is a gentle one. Out of it flows the milk of human kindness, which is pleasing to God. You must never set standards for yourself from examples common with those who live by the dictates of the world. This will be displeasing to God and is an antithesis to the life of holiness you are to follow after. See yourself always as a pilgrim in the world living in non-conformity with most inhabitants of the earth. You will have fixed your gaze on Jesus so all these lifestyle modifications will be easy for you.

"Don't copy the behaviour and customs of this world, but let God transform you into a new person by changing the way you think. Then you will learn to know God's will for you, which is good and pleasing and perfect."

(Romans 12:2 NLT)

The holiness that God mandates for you is at loggerheads with the customs and practices of today. The peoples of the world today are celebrating homosexuality and lesbianism. Countries are being blackmailed into making laws to legalize it. The church of God has joined the bandwagon with gay bishops ordained. God is reminding us that He who is Almighty has not sanctioned those sins, and anyone who touches them without repenting will pay with his life in the second death. God is no respecter of persons, and His laws remain immutable till kingdom come. The sin games we play with ourselves are an abomination to Him. We must go back home to Him so that He can save us from this folly. The important matter of virginity for both male and female occupies an essential part of God's holiness.

"'But suppose the man's accusations are true, and he can show that she was not a virgin. The woman must be taken to the door of her father's home, and there the men of the town must stone her to death, for she has committed a disgraceful crime in Israel by being promiscuous while living in her parents' home. In this way, you will purge this evil from among you. "If a man is discovered

committing adultery, both he and the woman must die. In this way, you will purge Israel of such evil."

(Deuteronomy 22: 20 – 22 NLT)

One reason for the choice of Mary was because she was a virgin and so if God finds this requirement so important, you have no choice but to tow the line. The world where many have made their bodies as cheap as the sand of the seashore is perishing. You must endeavour to do the will of God so as not to be destroyed with it. The holy life we speak of makes it mandatory for us "to offer our bodies as a living sacrifice, holy and pleasing to God"(Romans 12:1). Anything else is doomed and goes with the devil into the pit of hellfire.

> *"That is why God abandoned them to their shameful desires. Even the women turned against the natural way to have sex and instead indulged in sex with each other. And the men, instead of having normal sexual relations with women, burned with lust for each other. Men did shameful things with other men, and as a result of this sin, they suffered within themselves the penalty they deserved."*
>
>
>
> *(Romans 1:26 -27 NLT)*
>
>
>
> *"God's will is for you to be holy, so stay away from all sexual sin. Then each of you will control his own body and live in holiness and honour— not in lustful passion like the pagans who do not know God and his ways."*
>
>
>
> *(1 Thessalonians 4: 3 – 5 NLT)*
>
>

God is also very concerned about how we treat those who are under us. He wants us to show the example of Christ, which encourages regard for people of low status everywhere we find ourselves. God's holiness detests class or status propagation. Christ set this example through His lowly birth and all steps of the way. His message of humility was very prominent. A life of holiness is non-negotiable as it should define everything about us. You cannot identify with God and embrace anything repulsive to Him. The very essence of your life and being matters to Him. You cannot join to do the things that the world finds acceptable and still expect God's friendship. He will spit you out of His mouth so fast you won't believe what hit you. Your work and what you do for a living must align with His holiness. God cannot be bribed as the quality is more important to Him than the quantity. You cannot bridle God with your money. His words will speak to condemn you no matter who you are. Let your brother in faith, enjoy the benefits of your holy life and do not fail to keep your promises to God.

> *"Let them live among you in any town they choose and do not oppress them."*
>
> *(Deuteronomy 23:16 NLT)*

> *"Since God chose you to be the holy people he loves, you must clothe yourselves with tender-hearted mercy, kindness, humility, gentleness, and patience."*
>
> *(Colossians 3:12 NLT)*

In practice, holy living will entail all the genuine show of leniency, kindness, mercy and goodness that we deliver to others who we meet on our life's journey. Christ is still the best example of holiness, and He ensured that everywhere He went; He was doing good.

> *'"Do to others whatever you would like them to do to you. This is the essence of all that is taught in the law and the prophets."*
>
> *(Matthew 7:12 NLT)*

One of the tests of being in sync with the holiness that God requires takes place in our homes. Marriage is essential to God, and if one must continue in holy living, then those who are married must ensure that the joy of the Lord is present in their union. This joy comes when we live in submission to one another in reverence to God. The foundation of marriage is love, and the driving force of successfully living a holy life is the love of God. The presence of love in a home is the panacea to all challenges that may arise. God is happy when we lead a holy life and is also pleased when our home is in a blissful state. He hates separation and divorce, so those who want to follow after Him must endeavour to do His bidding in their marriages.

> *"Didn't the LORD make you one with your wife? In body and spirit, you are his.[And what does he want? Godly children from your union. So guard your heart; remain loyal to the wife of your youth. "For I hate divorce! "Says the LORD, the God of Israel. "To divorce your wife is to overwhelm her with cruelty," says the LORD of*

Heaven's Armies. "So guard your heart; do not be unfaithful to your wife."'

(Malachi 2: 15 – 16 NLT)

"Always be humble and gentle. Be patient with each other, making allowance for each other's faults because of your love. Make every effort to keep yourselves united in the Spirit, binding yourselves together with peace."

(Ephesians 4: 2 – 3 NLT)

Holiness is not an academic exercise. It deals with our practical lives and what we do daily with those who are around us. A life of holiness that is laden with the knowledge of God's words without the accompanying goodness is undesirable. Jesus taught us this message in His sheep and goats parable of the final judgment so that we can appreciate that kindness and show of mercy is integral to the lifestyle of holiness which He has asked us to emulate. If you are still unable to show this in your everyday life, something big is missing, and you must find it.

Dishonesty of any kind is wickedness and an abomination to God. Any enterprise that is modelled to exploit and take advantage of the other is ungodly and must never be found amongst God's children. Your life of holiness must be a shining light for God, even in a capitalist world where profit is king.

"Return the cloak to its owner by sunset so he can stay warm through the night and bless you, and the LORD, your God, will count you as righteous. "Never take advantage of poor and destitute labourers, whether they are fellow Israelites or

foreigners living in your towns. You must pay them their wages each day before sunset because they are poor and are counting on it. If you don't, they might cry out to the LORD against you, and it would be counted against you as sin."

(*Deuteronomy 24: 13 – 15 NLT*)

A life of holiness in itself is programmed to build treasures in heaven, so the style of the world takes a back seat in its schemes. Profit in heaven then matters more to it than the benefits on earth. This life is set up not to have your cake and eat it but is one where any gain that can be made by bending God's rules is not pursued at all. It's a life of godliness and contentment which is the greatest gain of all.

"'You must use accurate scales when you weigh out merchandise, and you must use full and honest measures. Yes, always use honest weights and measures, so that you may enjoy a long life in the land the LORD your God is giving you. All who cheat with dishonest weights and measures are detestable to the LORD your God."

(*Deuteronomy 25: 13 – 16 NLT*)

Although He has the power to compel you to do anything, the nature of God and what is pleasing to Him is that whosoever will should come. God has shown Himself dependable, reliable and Almighty right from creation, and this is clear for all to see. God is faithful, loving and trustworthy. You cannot fail if you pitch your tent with Him. He was in the beginning, is now and forever will be God. Some may wonder if it will be worthwhile for them if they follow His holiness guidelines preferring instead to continue to rule over their own lives. This God is the One who made the heavens and earth, and on the sixth day, He created you. He single-handedly rescued the children of Israel from the then world power. He did this through the extraordinary intervention at the red sea. He fought all battles for them on the way to giving them a brand new land filled with milk and honey. He sent His Son to die for you just because of His greater love. He brought Lazarus from the grave after four days to set him free from the power of death. He raised Jesus from the tomb after three days to give you Salvation. He is Almighty God from beginning to the end, and there is no place for any argument. Why then can't you trust Him with your life and follow Him in holiness? All that He has promised to do He will surely do them!

> *"Moses summoned all the Israelites and said to them, "You have seen with your own eyes everything the LORD did in the land of Egypt to Pharaoh and to all his servants and to his whole country— all the great tests of strength, the miraculous signs, and the amazing wonders. But to this day, the LORD has not given you minds that understand, nor eyes that see, nor ears that hear! For forty years, I led you through the wilderness, yet your clothes and sandals did not wear out. You ate no bread and drank no wine or other alcoholic drink, but he provided for you so you would know that he is the LORD your God. "When we came here, King Sihon of Heshbon and King Og of Bashan came out to fight against us, but we defeated them. We took their land and gave it to the tribes of Reuben and Gad and to the half-tribe of Manasseh as their grant of land.*

"Therefore, obey the terms of this covenant so that you will prosper in everything you do."

(Deuteronomy 29: 2 – 9 NLT)

"Forever since the world was created, people have seen the earth and sky. Through everything God made, they can clearly see his invisible qualities—his eternal power and divine nature. So they have no excuse for not knowing God."

(Romans 1:20 NLT)

Living a life of holiness purifies you, but sin, on the other hand, poisons your spirit, soul and body. You must guard against any sin with all your might. Sin, with its destructive venom, must be purged away from your life. Never allow it to take hold no matter how small for it is the seed of destruction which will come upon you through the anger of God. Sin festers, and so in just a little while will grow into an "oak tree" and then it is all doom and gloom. It drives away the presence of God wherefore help is no longer available to you. Remember the journey of life is tough with many unwinding bends of challenges and difficulties; life is a mystery so if you must master it, you need help from above, but this God only comes to the aid of His friends. And His friends are those who obey His commandments. If you choose to ignore God and live your life the way that is pleasing to you, you may even gain something worthwhile out of this world, but in heaven when it matters most, God is going to reject you and ask His angels to throw you into the lake of fire. Which do you prefer? To gain the whole world and lose your soul or to gain eternity with Jesus Christ?

> *"Don't be fooled by those who try to excuse these sins, for the anger of God will fall on all who disobey him."*
>
> *(Ephesians 5:6 NLT)*

The desire of God is for you to prosper both physically and spiritually. Although He is stern and uncompromising with His standards, what is uppermost in His heart is to give you rest from all your troubles. He has an open door which is always available where you can gain access to Him by turning away from your wicked ways. He is ready to restore all you have lost provided your repentance is sincere and genuine. This is what He loves to do and for which heaven rejoices whenever a sinner comes to repentance.

> *"If at that time you and your children return to the LORD your God, and if you obey with all your heart and all your soul all the commands I have given you today, then the LORD your God will restore your fortunes. He will have mercy on you and gather you back from all the nations where he has scattered you."*
>
> *(Deuteronomy 30: 2 – 3 NLT)*

God's help is available to the returnee. His love is immeasurable and will be manifested in the new care you will receive when you come back home to Him. He will dress you in a new robe proving your reinstatement to all and sundry. All that you have lost will be given back to you. The Lord will begin again with you, and your life will never be the same. God's ways remain His ways, but it is not an impossibility for you to follow after them. He will help you to stay steadfast provided you hand over the reins of your life to Him. He can never fail! Make a wise choice to follow Him in the holiness of His ways; it will lead you to gain treasures untold. Your life depends on the wise choice you make.

The Holiness walk is one that requires you to be strong and courageous. You are going in the opposite direction to many in the world. Never look back, for ahead of you is your example – Jesus Christ. Many who travel with you on the same way will turn back and leave you but do not be discouraged as this is to be expected. They will earn their reward, but you must go forward to escape the wrath of God's judgement, which will come upon the deserters. You may even lose your life in the battle for your soul but be not dismayed, for nothing should be too expensive for you to give in exchange for your soul. God will be very much pleased with your decision to follow Him. He will reward you and all who are faithful to His words and His ways. Joseph followed after God's holiness, and he had no cause to regret it. You too must not relent in following the godly path. There lies your pathway to God's blessings.

> *"Moses said this about the tribes of Joseph: "May their land be blessed by the LORD with the precious gift of dew from the heavens and water from beneath the earth; with the rich fruit that grows in the sun, and the rich harvest produced each month; with the finest crops of the ancient*

mountains, and the abundance from the ever-lasting hills; with the best gifts of the earth and its bounty, and the favour of the one who appeared in the burning bush. May these blessings rest on Joseph's head, crowning the brow of the prince among his brothers. Joseph has the majesty of a young bull; he has the horns of a wild ox. He will gore distant nations, even to the ends of the earth. This is my blessing for the multitudes of Ephraim and the thousands of Manasseh."'

(Deuteronomy 33: 13 – 17 NLT)

My sincere prayer for you is that at the end of your race on earth, you too will be able to say:

"As for me, my life has already been poured out as an offering to God. The time of my death is near. I have fought the good fight, I have finished the race, and I have remained faithful. And now the prize awaits me—the crown of righteousness, which the Lord, the righteous Judge, will give me on the day of his return. And the prize is not just for me but for all who eagerly look forward to his appearing."

(2 Timothy 4: 6 – 8 NLT)

If Saul, who later became Paul could do it, you too can!

The Destination City

"Then I saw a new heaven and a new earth, for the old heaven and the old earth had disappeared. And the sea was also gone. And I saw the holy city, the New Jerusalem, coming down from God out of heaven like a bride beautifully dressed for her husband. I heard a loud shout from the throne, saying, "Look, God's home is now among his people! He will live with them, and they will be his people. God himself will be with them. He will wipe every tear from their eyes, and there will be no more death or sorrow or crying or pain. All these things are gone forever."'

(Revelation 21:1 – 4. NLT)

Some time ago, I found myself having to spend quality time in the presence of God seeking His face over a matter of vital importance. I wanted Him to give me specific instructions on how I should go in respect to something that was weighing heavily on my mind – and I asked Him to provide me with a reply overnight. Instead of giving me an answer to my request, I woke up the next morning, with a completely different message. God chose to reveal to me the title of the next volume of my Christian literature, which I had reflected upon some time ago. The title God gave me is The Destination City. God went on to answer my prayers on the substantive request at His appointed time. I proceed to share with you what God laid upon my mind under this topic.

"'My thoughts are nothing like your thoughts,"
says the Lord. "And my ways are far beyond any-
thing you could imagine."

(Isaiah 55:8. NLT)

God's redemptive plan for His children is anchored on the offer of Jesus His only begotten Son to all who believe to gain eternal life. Everything Jesus did when He came in the flesh was to guide all who follow Him to His father's house. The message of the Destination City is, therefore first and foremost attributed to Jesus. He made it clear that the end objective of life after death must be to receive commendation and reward for a life well spent. This city is a creation of God and consists of many room houses which Jesus has promised to go and prepare for His friends. The certainty of its existence is confirmed by Jesus putting His reputation on the line for coming back someday to take His disciples home.

"'Don't let your hearts be troubled. Trust in God,
and trust also in me. There is more than enough
room in my Father's home. If this were not so,
would I have told you that I am going to prepare
a place for you? When everything is ready, I will
come and get you, so that you will always be
with me where I am."

(John 14: 1 – 3. NLT)

Apostle Paul spent his whole life with only one singular purpose, which was to show many the way to eternal life in the Destination City. He put all his resources to this good cause and in many instances, put his life at risk. Paul received a divine confirmation when he found favour in

God's sight to see a vision of this great and beautiful city. God probably wanted to give assurance to encourage him in his marketing efforts for the Destination City.

> *"This boasting will do no good, but I must go on. I will reluctantly tell about visions and revelations from the Lord. I was caught up to the third heaven fourteen years ago. Whether I was in my body or out of my body, I don't know — only God knows. Yes, only God knows whether I was in my body or outside my body. But I do know that I was caught up to paradise and heard things so astounding that they cannot be expressed in words, things no human is allowed to tell."*
>
> *(2 Corinthians 12: 1 – 4. NLT)*

There cannot be a Destination City without the death and resurrection of Jesus. Christ died for our sins on the Cross of Calvary and was buried, but on the third day, He arose! His resurrection is proof of the claim He made on the Cross that it is finished before giving up His spirit. Jesus has therefore provided you with the gate pass to the Destination City through His work of Salvation. The access to this city is, therefore only possible for a life that has gained resurrection having ended believing in Christ. This is the assurance that we have – that just as Christ rose, we too will experience resurrection someday. This means that just like Christ was raised, everyone who belongs to Him will be given a new life. This resurrection will occur at the return of Jesus.

> *"It is the same way with the resurrection of the dead. Our earthly bodies are planted in the*

ground when we die, but they will be raised to live forever. Our bodies are buried in brokenness, but they will be raised in glory. They are buried in weakness, but they will be raised in strength. They are buried as natural human bodies, but they will be raised as spiritual bodies. For just as there are natural bodies, there are also spiritual bodies."

(1 Corinthians 15: 42 – 44. NLT)

The importance of reaching the Destination City was also impressed upon the people of Philippi. Paul made it clear that they must invest in a lifestyle that qualifies them to enter therein. He was torn between continuing to share the message of the good news and arriving at the pearly gates. Paul was able to confirm the existence of this city and also his urgent preference to relocate there. To the people of Corinth, he likened this arrival as akin to reaching the finishing line in a race. He encouraged them to show the required commitment and zeal needed to hit the tape and win the race. He reminded them that not everyone will get the prize of reaching the Destination City and that to be one of the few, will take more than just a wish or prayer. It will take discipline, training and purpose.

"Above all, you must live as citizens of heaven, conducting yourselves in a manner worthy of the Good News about Christ. Then, whether I come and see you again or only hear about you, I will know that you are standing together with one spirit and one purpose, fighting together for the faith, which is the Good News."

(Philippians 1: 27. NLT)

The alternative to the Destination City is the world that we live in today and all that it entails. God gave unique wisdom to King Solomon to help him decipher much about this planet. Solomon received a better understanding, and through his counsel, we can choose the best way to live our lives. He exposited so many aspects of life such that we can gain insights that will help us lead a better life and also help us to appreciate the need to focus on reaching the Destination City.

> *"Getting wisdom is the wisest thing you can do! And whatever else you do, develop good judgment. If you prize wisdom, she will make you great. Embrace her, and she will honour you. She will place a lovely wreath on your head; she will present you with a beautiful crown."'*

> *(Proverbs 4:7 -9. NLT)*

Solomon made all his inferences based on his experiences. His knowledge and conclusions were based on what he had found to be true with the world that we live. He remarkably started his message with what should be the conclusion. In summarising everything about the world as meaningless, Solomon was inevitably directing our attention to something better and more significant. The king did not draw his conclusions overnight. He invested his time and energy on searching out with wisdom, understanding, knowledge and even madness; he still came to the same end. The Hebrews calls it "Hebel" which means vapour; their way of describing what the world and everything about it represent to them.

"I observed everything going on under the sun, and really, it is all meaningless — like chasing the wind."

(Ecclesiastes 1: 14. NLT)

"So I set out to learn everything from wisdom to madness and folly. But I learned firsthand that pursuing all this is like chasing the wind."

(Ecclesiastes 1: 17. NLT)

One of the reasons why man trades off his eternity is because of the pleasures of the present. Unlike Jesus, who was offered these same things by the devil and yet rejected them, most people opt for the pleasures of this world in exchange for the greater glory of spending eternity with God. Solomon took the pains of indulging himself in all the comforts available to man on earth. He tasted them all to find out whether suitable or not as adequate alternatives for what is on offer in God's kingdom. Perhaps he wanted to determine whether in having access to these pleasures, man will no longer lack anything good and by extension not need to accept God's offer of His better place. Solomon did a thorough job like the wise king that he was, not leaving out any pleasure he could lay his hands on – property, money, women and many other things, yet he remained insatiable.

"Anything I wanted, I would take. I denied myself no pleasure. I even found great pleasure in hard work, a reward for all my labours. But as I looked at everything I had worked so hard to accomplish, it was all so meaningless — like chasing the wind. There was nothing really worthwhile anywhere."

(Ecclesiastes 2: 10 - 11. NLT)

Relationships represent another area where man establishes dominance over his fellow human. Many judge themselves to be wiser or better than others just because of education, exposure or social interactions. Forgetting that the wisdom of this world is foolishness in the sight of God, they proceed to create social classes based on these classifications all to set themselves above others. Solomon was able to establish that all these mean nothing as well. It does not matter whether you see yourself as wise and others foolish, all of us will end up the same way someday, levelling up all so-called differences and making all that we count as something become meaningless.

> *"For the wise can see where they are going, but fools walk in the dark." Yet I saw that the wise and the foolish share the same fate. Both will die. So I said to myself, "Since I will end up the same as the fool, what's the value of all my wisdom? This is all so meaningless!"'*
>
> *(Ecclesiastes 2: 14 – 15. NLT)*

A renown Nigerian playwright once said "the struggles of man begins at birth" while according to the Bible it is only in the grave that work ceases which means that man must continue to work till he dies. There is so much struggle in life as man does all he can to outwit his neighbour to gain more for himself and his family. Although the Bible teaches that he who does not work must not eat, however, we must pray for the wisdom required to balance our work lives in order not to leave out the more essential things. A life that is focused entirely on work will undoubtedly be meaningless and inevitably miss out on the Destination City. Solomon realised this too.

> *"So what do people get in this life for all their hard work and anxiety? Their days of labour are filled with pain and grief; even at night, their minds cannot rest. It is all meaningless."*
>
> *(Ecclesiastes 2: 22 – 23. NLT)*

Life is straightforward and yet complicated. It is merely made of a myriad of seasons all sandwiched between the time we enter the stage that the world represents and when we exit it. Man inevitably has to contend with different occurrences in life at God's appointed time. He cannot change the plan of God. He must live and manage through it just like others before and after him. The lesson is to take things easy and depend on God, who is Almighty to guide him through. Life is a passing phase, and so we must not dwell too much on it but instead look at the bigger picture of where the experience is leading us. No matter who we are, life will throw at us a mixture of good and evil, positive and negative, favourable and unfavourable, gain and loss; for this is the world that God has created. The world is no ideal place to love and want to stay forever.

> *"For everything, there is a season, a time for every activity under heaven."*
>
> *(Ecclesiastes 3: 1.NLT)*

> *"What is happening now has happened before, and what will happen in the future has happened before, because God makes the same things happen over and over again."*
>
> *(Ecclesiastes 3: 15. NLT)*

This world is not a desirable place to spend eternity which is why there existed the need for the Destination City. There is so much evil, wickedness and injustice on this earth. The world is full of oppression. Man continues to use all his power to take advantage of his brother; something that is against the will of God. There is so much envy, and brotherly love has gone into extinction. Solomon even concluded that being in the world is unenviable and that lucky are those yet to be born. He observed that many people struggle for material possession only to do an appraisal and find that not all that glitters is gold. In this world, the rich virtually put their foot down on the poor while those in authority continue to take advantage of the system. Again while many see the opportunity in the world to amass wealth and grow rich, there is no certainty of sustained wealth, and even when wealth is attained, it can easily be lost. Nothing in this world is definite, for, when life comes to an end; everything is left behind.

> *"Don't be surprised if you see a poor person being oppressed by the powerful, and if justice is being miscarried throughout the land. For every official is under orders from higher up, and matters of justice get lost in red tape and bureaucracy. Even the king milks the land for his own profit!"*

> *(Ecclesiastes 5: 8 – 9. NLT)*

> *"There is another serious problem I have seen under the sun. Hoarding riches harms the saver. Money is put into risky investments that turn sour, and everything is lost. In the end, there is nothing left to pass on to one's children. We all come to the end of our lives as naked and empty-handed as on the day we were born. We*

can't take our riches with us. And this, too, is a very serious problem. People leave this world no better off than when they came. All their hard work is for nothing—like working for the wind. Throughout their lives, they live under a cloud—frustrated, discouraged, and angry."

(Ecclesiastes 5: 13 – 17. NLT)

Man will not get all he wants while in the world. He must accept what he receives and make the best use of it; after all, it's a transit camp. Life itself is temporary, so it is expected, no matter one's situation, to come to terms with it if there is nothing we can do about it. Outstanding success can be made out of life if one is appropriately guided. Guidance comes from God's words, and success is defined by the level of our compliance with it, which in turn determines whether we make it to the Destination City or not. Solomon talked about the importance of our reputation, comparing it with costly perfume and judging that the former is more important than the latter. He counselled that anything that will help us think about life after death is profitable for us. Thoughts of funerals and death for him should occupy the front burner of our lives to help us keep in our horizon the fact that we must focus beyond this life.

"Better to spend your time at funerals than at parties. After all, everyone dies—So the living should take this to heart. Sorrow is better than laughter, for sadness has a refining influence on us. A wise person thinks a lot about death, while a fool thinks only about having a good time."

(Ecclesiastes 7:2 – 4 NLT)

God's desire is for a man to live a virtuous life, but then we continue to disappoint Him. Instead of a life that turns its back to sin, many embrace it like second nature and destroy their chance of gaining entrance to the Destination City. Solomon, who should know better, has warned all to flee the seductive woman. He describes her as a "trap more bitter than death". She provides the shortest course to the loss of one's destiny if we do not flee from her and what better future than to gain eternal life with Christ in His father's kingdom. Life is a mystery, and you need the wisdom in God's words to navigate it so that you can end with a good testimony. Do all you can to please God and do not follow your desires.

> *"I discovered that a seductive woman is a trap more bitter than death. Her passion is a snare, and her soft hands are chains. Those who are pleasing to God will escape her, but sinners will be caught in her snare. "This is my conclusion," says the Teacher. "I discovered this after looking at the matter from every possible angle. Though I have searched repeatedly, I have not found what I was looking for. Only one out of a thousand men is virtuous, but not one woman! But I did find this: God created people to be virtuous, but they have each turned to follow their own downward path."'*
>
> (Ecclesiastes 7: 26 – 29. NLT)

We must remember that we are mortals. We cannot live forever, and when death comes, we must let go of our spirit to its final destination. The story was once told of a man who was visited by the angel of death, and to avoid losing his life; the man arranged an excellent meal with assorted drinks to bribe his august visitor. The angel of death accepted the offer, had a good time and after that slept off. While he was asleep, the man reversed the death list and put his name at the bottom. When the angel woke up, he decided to compensate his host by taking the life of the last person on the list. It was the name of his host. This is the reality of death. When it comes, no one can stop it. The best remedy is to be prepared for its eventual and inevitable arrival so that we can get a home in the Destination City. Death indeed comes to all!

"None of us can hold back our spirit from departing. None of us has the power to prevent the day of our death. There is no escaping that obligation, that dark battle. And in the face of death, wickedness will certainly not rescue the wicked."

(Ecclesiastes 8:8. NLT)

Everything is meaningless, utterly meaningless, so the best way to go about life is to fear God and obey His commandments. Our life does not belong to us. It is like an asset we have leased from someone and which we have to give an account of someday. Life confirms to us that the older ones were once young while the young ones will be old eventually. Everyone will arrive at a point one day at the gate of the Destination City. While you are still young, stay in the lane that your Creator has set for you. Do not waver and get out of line. Look to the older ones not with disrespect as you too will get there. Remember that when you reach the gate of the Destination City in death, you cannot go back to the world to make amends. The time you have now is the only asset you can exploit. Tomorrow you won't have access to it. Take advantage of this opportunity and buy a house in the Destination City.

> *"Yes, remember your Creator now while you are young, before the silver cord of life snaps and the golden bowl is broken. Don't wait until the water jar is smashed at the spring and the pulley is broken at the well. For then, the dust will return to the earth, and the spirit will return to God who gave it."*
>
> *(Ecclesiastes 12: 6 – 7.NLT)*

Bible scholars have interpreted the vision God gave Apostle John as describing the "plight of Christians, God's judgments on their persecutors and the eternal hope and promise for God's faithful people."[1] The offer of residence at the Destination City is THE GREATEST HOPE AND PROMISE FOR GOD'S FAITHFUL PEOPLE.

> *"And if our hope in Christ is only for this life, we are more to be pitied than anyone in the world."*
>
> *(1 Corinthians 15:19. NLT)*

The trial of John on the Island of Patmos is not a pleasant experience for a disciple. However, when we see what God made out of it through His revelations to the human race, one cannot but appreciate God as Almighty. The is proof that He is alive and has gone to provide a place for you and I. John confirms that the revelation he got was from Jesus Himself.

"When I saw him, I fell at his feet as if I were dead. But he laid his right hand on me and said, "Don't be afraid! I am the First and the Last. I am the living one. I died, but look—I am alive forever and ever! And I hold the keys of death and the grave."

(Revelation 1: 17 – 18. NLT)

Jesus spent three years telling all who cared the way to reach the Destination City. His commitment to the eternal life project is reflected in His love for you and me as epitomised by the warning letters He mandated John to deliver to the seven churches in Asia. The warnings were to guide us away from death and destruction. All our actions are known to Him. We cannot hide it from Him. He sees through us and knows the thoughts we keep away from others. Jesus saw through all the seven churches and told them that His love does not hold back His justice and judgment.

"Look! I stand at the door and knock. If you hear my voice and open the door, I will come in, and we will share a meal together as friends. Those who are victorious will sit with me on my throne, just as I was victorious and sat with my Father on his throne. "Anyone with ears to hear must listen to the Spirit and understand what he is saying to the churches."'

(Revelation 3: 20 – 22. NLT)

Reaching the Destination City will not be a piece of cake. The battle for the soul of the traveller will be immense. The evil forces will lay siege all the way and choices will have to be made by all. Perseverance and focus on the long-term will play a vital role in the outcome. Those who are ready to endure will have an excellent story to tell at the end.

> *"Then a third angel followed them, shouting, "Anyone who worships the beast and his statue or who accepts his mark on the forehead or on the hand must drink the wine of God's anger. It has been poured full strength into God's cup of wrath. And they will be tormented with fire and burning sulfur in the presence of the holy angels and the Lamb. The smoke of their torment will rise forever and ever, and they will have no relief day or night, for they have worshipped the beast and his statue and have accepted the mark of his name." This means that God's holy people must endure persecution patiently, obeying his commands and maintaining their faith in Jesus. And I heard a voice from heaven saying, "Write this down: Blessed are those who die in the Lord from now on. Yes, says the Spirit, they are blessed indeed, for they will rest from their hard work; for their good deeds follow them!"'*

> *(Revelation 14: 9 – 13. NLT)*

Those who pitch their tent with God Almighty are assured of His inevitable victory. This victory will be confirmed by the fall of the world empire of false religion represented by Babylon the Great. There is indeed no other outcome for them in the contest. Their failure is assured! He will help you overcome in any area you want help from Him. All you need to do is TRUST HIM.

> *"After this, I heard what sounded like a vast crowd in heaven, shouting, "Praise the Lord!*

Salvation and glory and power belong to our God. His judgments are true and just. He has punished the great prostitute who corrupted the earth with her immorality. He has avenged the murder of his servants."'

(Revelation 19: 1 – 2. NLT)

"Then I saw heaven opened, and a white horse was standing there. Its rider was named Faithful and True, for he judges fairly and wages a righteous war. His eyes were like flames of fire, and on his head were many crowns. A name was written on him that no one understood except himself. He wore a robe dipped in blood, and his title was the Word of God. The armies of heaven, dressed in the finest of pure white linen, followed him on white horses. From his mouth came a sharp sword to strike down the nations. He will rule them with an iron rod. He will release the fierce wrath of God, the Almighty, like juice flowing from a winepress. On his robe at his thigh was written this title: King of all kings and Lord of all lords. Then I saw an angel standing in the sun, shouting to the vultures flying high in the sky: "Come! Gather together for the great banquet God has prepared. 18 Come and eat the flesh of kings, generals, and strong warriors; of horses and their riders; and of all humanity, both free and slave, small and great." Then I saw the beast and the kings of the world and their armies gathered together to fight against the one sitting on the horse and his army. And the beast was captured and with him the false prophet who did mighty miracles on behalf of the beast—miracles that deceived all who had accepted the mark of the beast and who worshipped his statue. Both the beast and his false prophet were thrown alive into the fiery lake of

burning sulfur. Their entire army was killed by the sharp sword that came from the mouth of the one riding the white horse. And the vultures all gorged themselves on the dead bodies."

(Revelation 19: 11 – 21. NLT)

The defeat of Satan is a foregone conclusion. You have no business following in his footsteps. His end is terrible and disastrous. No one in his right senses should see an adverse outcome and embrace it. God has made the best possible gift available to you at the Destination City. All you need to do is to travel on the Narrow Way leading to it. The option from the failed loser – the devil, is not an option for you to consider. Everybody loves a winner, and JESUS IS A WINNER MAN. Take your matter to Him, and He will crown all your efforts with a victory. The victory He has won over the devil is for you too.

"Then I saw an angel coming down from heaven with the key to the bottomless pit and a heavy chain in his hand. He seized the dragon—that old serpent, who is the devil, Satan—and bound him in chains for a thousand years. The angel threw him into the bottomless pit, which he then shut and locked so Satan could not deceive the nations anymore until the thousand years were finished. Afterwards, he must be released for a little while."

(Revelation 20: 1 – 3. NLT)

"When the thousand years come to an end, Satan will be let out of his prison. He will go out to deceive the nations—called Gog and Magog—in every corner of the earth. He will gather them together for battle—a mighty army, as number-less as sand along the seashore. And I saw them

as they went up on the broad plain of the earth and surrounded God's people and the beloved city. But fire from heaven came down on the attacking armies and consumed them. Then the devil, who had deceived them, was thrown into the fiery lake of burning sulfur, joining the beast and the false prophet. There they will be tormented day and night forever and ever."

(Revelation 20: 7 – 10. NLT)

The Destination City is indescribable. God confirmed the truth of its existence by allowing Apostle John to have a glimpse of it. It is a city created by God in fulfilment of the promise Jesus made to His friends. It is a city that all who are wise must seek to find a home for themselves. It is a city that you must not allow anything to hinder you from reaching. It is a city that you should be prepared to lose the whole world to enter. It is a city that you must not view from the other side, which is hellfire. It is a city that you must be ready to sacrifice even your eyes to get there. It is a city where there will be no more death or sorrow or crying or pain. It is a city where you MUST spend eternity.

"Then one of the seven angels who held the seven bowls containing the seven last plagues came and said to me, "Come with me! I will show you the bride, the wife of the Lamb." So he took me in the Spirit to a great, high mountain, and he showed me the holy city, Jerusalem, descending out of heaven from God. It shone with the glory of God and sparkled like a precious stone — like Jasper as clear as crystal."

(Revelation 21: 9 – 11. NLT)

"The wall was made of Jasper, and the city was pure gold, as clear as glass. The wall of the city was built on foundation stones inlaid with twelve precious stones: the first was jasper, the second sapphire, the third agate, the fourth emerald, the fifth onyx, the sixth carnelian, the seventh chrysolite, the eighth beryl, the ninth topaz, the tenth chrysoprase, the eleventh jacinth, the twelfth amethyst. The twelve gates were made of pearls— each gate from a single pearl! And the main street was pure gold, as clear as glass. I saw no temple in the city, for the Lord God Almighty and the Lamb are its temple. And the city has no need of sun or moon, for the glory of God illuminates the city, and the Lamb is its light. The nations will walk in its light, and the kings of the world will enter the city in all their glory. Its gates will never be closed at the end of day because there is no night there. And all the nations will bring their glory and honour into the city. Nothing evil will be allowed to enter, nor anyone who practices shameful idolatry and dishonesty— but only those whose names are written in the Lamb's Book of Life."

(Revelation 21: 18 – 27. NLT)

To get into the Destination City, everyone must attend the final judgment. It is upon success at this judgment that we will receive our pass into the city. There is no other entry process. Unfortunately, there is another place of abode other than this city. It is a place where God does not want any of us to end up. It is a place you should only read about but never discover. God has a good plan for you, and this plan is that you will not perish but come to the saving knowledge of the truth.

"And I saw a great white throne and the one sitting on it. The earth and sky fled from his presence, but they found no place to hide. I saw the dead, both great and small, standing before God's throne. And the books were opened, including the Book of Life. And the dead were judged according to what they had done, as recorded in the books. The sea gave up its dead, and death and the grave gave up their dead. And all were judged according to their deeds. Then death and the grave were thrown into the lake of fire. This lake of fire is the second death. And anyone whose name was not found recorded in the Book of Life was thrown into the lake of fire."

(Revelation 20: 11 – 15. NLT)

Take the step today to invite Jesus into your life. Confess your sins and turn COMPLETELY away from them. Begin a new life in Christ, and you are on your way to the Destination City.

End Word

A few years ago, I had the privilege of sharing with a group of friends the message of the Cross; Christ offering Himself as a ransom for the sins of the world. I told my friends that I once lived like the foolish man that Mathew spoke about in his account of the Gospel of Jesus Christ.

> *"'Anyone who listens to my teaching and follows it is wise, like a person who builds a house on solid rock. Though the rain comes in torrents and the floodwaters rise, and the winds beat against that house, it won't collapse because it is built on bedrock. But anyone who hears my teaching and doesn't obey it is foolish, like a person who builds a house on sand. When the rains and floods come, and the winds beat against that house, it will collapse with a mighty crash."'*

(Mathew 7:24 – 27 NLT)

At that time, I was building my life on a faulty foundation. I told all who cared to listen that God gave me a second chance by extending His Grace for me to have an opportunity at aligning my life with His. All the friends who knew the life I used to live, made a mockery of my offer, preferring to "enjoy life" the way I had done before giving my life to Christ. How foolish! I told them about the Grace I had, which may not be available to them - the fact that while I had a second chance, they may not have one.

We all know that God does not order the sequence of death based on our ages. Some die young, and others live long depending on how it pleases God. How then should a wise man act? The happenings around us every day call us to ponder and to think seriously about our life, to choose wisely either to follow Jesus to eternal life or foolishly follow the devil to eternal condemnation. God reminds us that after death comes judgment:

> *"'And as it is appointed for men to die once, but after this the judgment'".*
>
> *(Hebrews 9:27 NLT)*

He is interested in your affairs and mine too. He does not want any of us to gain the whole world and lose his soul. He is waiting for you to open the door of your heart for Him to come in.

> *"'Look! I stand at the door and knock. If you hear my voice and open the door, I will come in, and we will share a meal together as friends'"*
>
> *(Revelation 3:20 NLT)*

The offer of Jesus is always on the table. Some take it while others reject or ignore it. The truth is, we may reject the Jesus offer of Salvation, but we cannot dismiss His judgment when it comes – and it will surely come.

> *"Let the one who is doing harm continue to do harm; let the one who is vile continue to be vile; let the one who is righteous continue to live righteously; let the one who is holy continue to be holy. Look I am coming soon, bringing reward with me to repay all the people according to their deeds. I am the Alpha and Omega, the First and*

the Last, the Beginning and the End. Blessed are those who wash their robes. They will be permitted to enter through the gates of the city and eat the fruit from the tree of life. Outside the city are the dogs – the sorcerers, the sexually immoral, the murderers, the idol worshipers and all who love to live a lie."

(Revelation 22:11 – 15 NLT)

My dear friends, it is not enough to know about Jesus and His free offer of Salvation by Grace through faith. The critical issue is, what are you doing with this gift? The question – what if I die today is very real as death can come at any time.

Frances J Crosby reminded us of the importance of death in her song – Will Jesus find us watching? It will be a time of reward which will happen unexpectedly. She reminded us that the assessment would be on an individual basis; with the desire of all being to receive commendation - though not all will get it. Jesus will want to know if we have been faithful to the trust He left us and if we did our best with all He commended to our hands. The songwriter assures that those the Lord will find watching will be the blessed few; they will share in His glory.

The critical question you must ask yourself is this - If Jesus comes at dawn or midnight, Will He find you watching and waiting? What are you doing with the opportunity that Jesus offers you now?

Julia Harriette Johnston brought the subject of Grace to the fore in her hymn entitled "Grace greater than our sins." The song, written in 1910, talks about God's Grace which exceeds all our sins and our guilt, made possible by Jesus' blood shed on Calvary's tree. It is available to all who accept Jesus at no cost whatsoever. No wonder Apostle Paul in his letter to the people of Ephesus, said; "God saved you by His Grace when you believed. And you can't take credit for this; it is a gift from God. Salvation is not a reward for the good things we have done, so none of us can boast about it"(Ephesians 2:8-9). As much as this Grace comes freely, only those who access it can receive the Salvation that comes through it.

Although Ms Johnston had the Grace of living for 70 years; many of us may not have this quantum of Grace. What are you, therefore, doing with the Grace time that you have? How old are you today and what percentage of 70 years have you lived already? How many more years do you have to live if God is gracious enough to allow you live to 70 years? What happens if God calls you home much earlier? What happens if you die today?

The question you must ask yourself is this: When Jesus comes to reward his servants, will He find you waiting and watching? I pray that you will be prepared and ready for the Master's return. The time is now. Tomorrow, as they say, maybe too late.

The Grace you have is to be utilised – today and not tomorrow. Take it and do not wait a minute longer.

Notes

Room at the Cross

1. College of Open Bible

The Ultimate Prize

1. Mason, Charles Peter (1870). "Agrippa, Herodes II". In Smith, William (ed.). *Dictionary of Greek and Roman Biography and Mythology*. **1**. p. 78.

2. Chisholm, Hugh, ed. (1911). "Felix, Antonius". Encyclopædia Britannica. **10** (11th ed.). *Cambridge University Press*. p. 239.

The Solid Rock

1. Price, Milburn, "Edward Mote," in Handbook to the Baptist Hymnal (*Nashville: Convention Press*, 1992), 411.

2. Terry, Lindsay L., "The Day the Cabinet Shop was Closed" in Stories Behind Popular Songs and Hymns (Grand Rapids: Baker Book House, 1990), 178.

3. Keith W. Ward (Spring 1998). "A Hymn of Grace – "The Solid Rock". *Journal of the Grace Evangelical Society*. Retrieved 9 March 2012.

4. Hymn Stories Christian Articles and Sermons: The Solid Rock

Divine Mercy

1. A Second Chance, Daily Encourager 22nd August 2014

2. Subversive Influence. HoMY 77: Jesus Paid it All by brother Maynard, November 2, 2008. Hymns

3. "Crimson". Oxford English Dictionary (3rd ed.). *Oxford University Press*. September 2005.

4. Naturenet article with images and description of *Kermes vermilio* and its foodplant.

5. Kershner, Isabel (6 August 2007). "Abbas hosts meeting with Olmert in West Bank city of Jericho". *New York Times*. United States. Retrieved 16 November 2016.

6. Schreiber, 2003, p. 141.

7. Ring et al., 1994, p. 367–370.

8. Bromiley, 1995, p. 1136.

9. "The Creation Account in Genesis 1:1–3" (PDF). *Bibliotheca Sacra* 132: 327–42. 1975.

10. Smith, William, Dr. "Entry for 'Bartimaeus'". "Smith's Bible Dictionary". 1901

He is Coming Soon

1. Wholesome Words: Fanny Crosby — Biographies and Information

He is Able

1. Blue Letter Bible: Hymns/Music – Must I go, and empty-handed?

2. Sankey, Ira David: My Life and the Story of the Gospel Hymns. New York: Harper & Brothers, 1906.

3. New College Latin Dictionary

4. Bible History Online: Roman Centurion

I will follow Him

1. Holy Wisdom Monastery: Mary Gordon's Homily, March 19, 2017: Woman at the Well.

2. The Truth Book: Why the Jews hated the Samaritans?

The Narrow Way

1. Muncherian.com: Notes on 1 Corinthians.

2. The Rev Dr Christopher Benek, October 7 2014: God can be found in difference between happiness and Joy.

3. Jack Wellman, May 21 2015: What is the Biblical definition of Joy? How does the bible define Joy?

4. Diana Leagh Matthews, October 12, 2017: Fruits of the Spirit: Joy.

5. Penny Haynes, January 8, 2017: Self-Control as the culmination of the Fruit of the Spirit (Ministry House).

6. Darren Wilson,2015. Got Fruits?: Understanding Spiritual Growth and Fruit Bearing.

7. Pope, Charles. "A Brief Treatise on the Fruits of the Holy Spirit", Archdiocese of Washington, January 27, 2013.

8. Thayer's Greek Lexicon - STRONGS NT 3115: μακροθυμία

9. Strong's Greek Concordance 5544. Chréstotés. Romans 11:22, 2 Cor 6: 6 - 7

10. St Joseph's Catholic Church, Ohio Lesson 20 - The Holy Spirit's Gift of Faithfulness.

11. Strong's Greek Concordance 4102. Pistis

12. Strong's Greek Concordance 3982. Peithó

13. Strong's Greek lexicon (KJV) G4103. Pistos

14. Diana Leagh Matthews, November 24, 2017: Fruits of the Spirit: Gentleness.

15. Got Questions Ministries: The fruit of the Holy Spirit – What is Gentleness?

16. Got Questions Ministries: The fruit of the Holy Spirit – What is Self Control?

17. Hawkins, J. David (2009). "The Arzawa letters in recent perspective". *British Museum Studies in Ancient Egypt and Sudan* (14): 73–83.

18. Sharon R. Steadman; Gregory McMahon; John Gregory McMahon (15 September 2011). The Oxford Handbook of Ancient Anatolia: (10,000–323 BCE). *Oxford University Press.* p. 366, and 608.

19. NLT Study Bible, Second edition 2008, Tyndale House Publishers Inc

20. Fant, Clyde E. (2003). A Guide to Biblical Sites in Greece and Turkey. *Oxford University Press.* Retrieved 5 February 2020.

21. The Pergamon Altar, P. v Zaubern, Staatliche Museen zu Berlin, 1991

22. Stephanus of Byzantium, Ethnica, Th319.1

23. NLT Study Bible, Second edition 2008, Tyndale House Publishers Inc

24. Rhodes, P.J. A History of the Classical Greek World 478-323 BC. 2nd edition. Chichester: Wiley-Blackwell, 2010, p. 6.

25. Chisholm, Hugh. (1911). "Ala-Shehr". Encyclopædia Britannica. 1(11th ed.). *Cambridge University Press*. p. 472

26. "Archaeological site of Laodikeia". UNESCO World Heritage Centre. Retrieved 19 June 2018

27. NLT Study Bible, Second edition 2008, Tyndale House Publishers Inc

You Too Can Be Holy
1. Easton's Bible Dictionary Online – Holiness

2. J.C. Ryle: Holiness

Pathway to God's Blessings
1. Enoch Adeboye: Open Heavens 10th March 2018

The Destination City
1. NLT Study Bible, Second edition 2008, Tyndale House Publishers Inc

Author's Contact Information

@ oyewo611@yahoo.co.uk
souls4christ@hodm.com.ng

f adeoye oyewo

@ @adeoyeoyewo

🐦 @adeoyeoyewo

📞 +2348034022617